Contents

Writing Resistance in the Workplace

Claiming an Identity

In Memory of Constance Coiner:
A "Foremother" of Contemporary Working-Class Studies

Resources

Editorial

The Current State of Working-Class Studies

In her introduction to "A Woman Is Talking to Death," Judy Grahn writes that one characteristic of "working-class writing is that we often pile up many events within a small space rather than detailing the many implications of one or two events. This means both that our lives are chock full of action and also bursting with stories" (112). This special issue of *Women's Studies Quarterly, Working-Class Lives and Cultures,* tells the stories of working-class lives through an unusual infusion of poetry and autobiography, as well as critical essays that draw upon cultural theory, literary criticism, history, sociology, and psychology.

Interest in working-class issues—as distinguished from proletarian literature and labor history—has grown in recent years. New approaches, including but not limited to traditional Marxist approaches, are being developed in literary studies, history, sociology, psychology, and a new interdisciplinary field, working-class studies. Working-class studies is thriving, as can be seen by, among other indicators, the formation of the Youngstown Center for Working Class Studies. Since the center was formed in the fall of 1995, its members have been committed to integrating scholarship with service to the surrounding working-class community.

Research, pedagogy, and workplace education are the center's linchpins and provide a model for ways to connect work done in the academy with that done in the workplace. One of our editors, Linda Strom, has taught in a program bringing college classes to steelworkers in the workplace. Such classes are one of the ways in which academics are seeking both to offer instruction to and to learn from working-class people outside the academy. The Youngstown Center's web site can be found at http://as.ysu.edu/as/cwcs.

Another way in which we see the growth of working-class studies is in the formation of a number of Internet discussion groups focusing on class as a theoretical issue and/or the experiences of working-class academics. Another sign of the growing importance of working-class studies is its increasing recognition as an integral part of multicultural studies. Indeed, the Association of American Colleges and Universities'

"American Commitments: Diversity, Democracy, and Liberal Learning" now calls for including working-class studies in its multicultural curriculum.

In addition, more publications are dealing with working-class topics, with several scholarly studies of working-class literature, the representation of the working class in popular culture and film, and the history, formation, attitudes, and sociology of the U.S. working class published in the past few years (see Bibliography). In addition to scholarly studies, several anthologies have recently been compiled on the experiences of working-class writers: Janet Zandy's *Calling Home: Working-Class Women's Writings: An Anthology* (1990) and *Liberating Memory: Our Work and Our Working-Class Consciousness* (1995), Michelle Tokarczyk and Elizabeth Fay's *Working-Class Women in the Academy: Laborers in the Knowledge Factory* (1993), Barney Dews and Carolyn Law's *This Fine Place So Far from Home: Voices of Academics from the Working Class* (1995), and Julia Penelope's *Out of the Class Closet: Lesbians Speak* (1994). Academic journals, too, have responded to the burgeoning interest in the field. Issues of *Women's Studies Quarterly* 23, nos. 1 and 2, and *Radical Teacher* 46 were devoted to working-class studies. A new journal, *Race, Gender & Class,* also concentrates on working-class studies.

A growing number of courses on working-class studies are now offered at universities around the country, including Youngstown State University; California State University, Stanislaus; and Metropolitan State University. Participants at the Youngstown biannual conference shared syllabi, and more online forums are dedicated to class issues.

In addition to academic work, much is happening in the arts. More works of fiction and poetry by working-class writers are being published as working-class literature, partially because of the commercial success of the works of writers such as Dorothy Allison and Carolyn Chute. Publishers such as The Feminist Press and the ILR Press have marketed books specifically as working-class literature. Working-class filmmakers such as John Sayles (*Lone Star*), John Turturro (*Mac*), Victor Nuñez (*Ruby in Paradise*), Allison Anders (*Gas Food Lodging*), and Kevin Smith (*Clerks*) have brought American working-class characters to the screen. Photographers such as Milton Rogovin, Margaret Evans, Sandy Thacker, and Martin J. Desht (in his recent show *Faces from an American Dream*) are documenting deindustrialization and other aspects of contemporary working-class life. Bruce Springsteen's 1996 album *The Ghost of Tom Joad* combines the rhythms of folk and rock in a series of songs that present the lives of working-class characters from steelworkers to migrant farm laborers.

It is our hope that this issue of *Women's Studies Quarterly* also will contribute to the emerging field of working-class studies.

This Issue of *Women's Studies Quarterly*

This issue was put together by an editorial collective composed of Renny Christopher (California State University, Stanislaus), Lisa Orr (Utica College of Syracuse University) and Linda Strom (Youngstown State University). As is clear from our affiliations, our geographic locations span the breadth of the continent, and much of our editorial work was done via e-mail, a wonderful boon to present and future scholarship. All three of us came from working-class backgrounds into the academic world, and we all make class a central part of our scholarly work.

In assembling this issue, we found we had significant differences, with the subject of "theory" proving to be divisive. The three of us attended a working-class studies conference where one speaker suggested that a working-class scholar doing literary theory may be thought similar to Samuel Johnson's dancing dog—remarkable not because of the quality of its performance but because it can dance at all. This statement, with its suggestion that "high theory" is beyond working-class scholars, all three of us found disturbing. The comment also implies that the most salient quality of high theory is the difficulty of its language, dependent on a jargon known only to an elite. But as Renny noted—and we all agree—this need not be the case for working-class literary theory—clear, plain language can convey very complicated ideas.

On the more fundamental question of the usefulness of theoretical concepts, no matter how clearly expressed, the three of us did disagree, however, mainly about questions of "identity politics" and "difference." None of us wishes to use these terms unselfconsciously, or to create a niche for working-class studies by profiting from a fashion for multiculturalism. We each find a different degree of usefulness in these terms. For Renny, codifying the notion of difference is tacitly agreeing with the assertion of power that is the norm, from which all else deviates. For her, the idea of "difference" is a form of liberal multiculturalism, with which she cannot agree because it embraces the values of tolerance rather than those of resistance. In addition, to her, "difference" is not an appropriate term to apply to class, which is a category different from race and gender. Although it may be possible to fight (and even legislate) against discrimination based on gender or race, it makes no sense to say "no person shall be discriminated against on the basis of class," because the very existence of class is built on discrimination. For this reason, Renny's work remains sharply focused: "Everything I write about class is aimed at showing the necessary injuries of class, with the aim of raising class consciousness in order to overthrow capitalism."

Lisa would never deny that oppression is damaging, but she resists the suggestion that working-class people are solely the sum of their injuries. This is where she finds the idea of difference useful. Unique working-class cultures have developed in response to imposed differences that have little basis in fact—just as has been the case with race, gender, and sexual orientation. The fact that these differences are imposed does not negate the value of what is generated in creative response to oppression—as demonstrated, for instance, in the "cheap amusements" that factory girls in turn-of-the-century New York devised (as rediscovered by historian Kathy Peiss). Lisa builds on recent theory when she argues that race and gender constructs are no more natural, and no less imposed by outside forces, than class constructs are.

Linda negotiates between these two positions in her notion that working-class theory has become the site for analyzing the intersections of class, race, gender, and sexual orientation. For example, in works such as Agnes Smedley's *Daughter of Earth*, class and gender discrimination work together to oppress Marie Rogers. Finding a theoretical language and framework for articulating the cumulative effect of oppression is part of Linda's teaching and work.

However, as Renny notes—and Lisa and Linda agree—focusing on differences can lead to cultural relativism, an approach unsuited to addressing inequities. John Russo and Sherry Linkon, two members of the Center for Working-Class Studies at Youngstown State University, address the drawbacks of identity politics:

> In academic circles, attention to individualism surfaced in the form of ideas about subjectivity. While subjectivity questions the existence of the unified individual subject and highlights the influence of membership in various cultural groups on individual consciousness, it nonetheless suggests that each person attempts to negotiate his/her identity individually, not as a member of a class.
>
> Likewise, contemporary discussions of multiculturalism and identity politics defined cultural groups and/or political groups in largely separate terms such as race, gender, ethnicity, sexuality, environmentalism, pro-life, et al. While apparently focusing on collective identities, the emphasis on individuality is retained by emphasizing

that each individual negotiates multiple membership in cultural and political groups. In this context, celebrating diversity can mean just the opposite—celebrating individual identity. (Mullen et al.)

This argument deserves more of an answer than we have space for here, but it highlights the difficulties we, as editors, faced. We were in effect celebrating diversity by calling for contributions from authors from various backgrounds. Does this challenge the very idea of collective action? Perhaps, as Linda hoped, the fact that we included the works of scholars and activists who collaborated with unions and community groups was enough to resolve this dilemma.

Given our conflicting feelings on these subjects, our "call for papers" for this issue was a compromise:

> This new issue seeks to build on and expand the contribution to the field of working-class studies begun in the spring/summer 1995 issue of *WSQ* by emphasizing the intersecting points of gender, race, ethnicity, sexual preference, and class. . . . One of the main goals of this issue will be to continue to develop a vocabulary and appropriate "theoretical" framework for teachers, scholars, and activists. By "theory" we do not mean so-called High Theory with its exclusionary discursive practices, but rather, we mean creating an intellectual framework for discussing working-class culture, artistic production, and the material conditions of working-class people.

Luckily, our call elicited excellent work to include in this volume: even while we differ in our approaches to working-class studies, we agree without compromise on the quality of our selections, which address a number of important areas of working-class studies.

Part 1, "Family: Supporting, Resisting, Shaping," presents poems by Carolyn Whitson, Patty See, and John Gilgun. All of these works represent the strengths of working-class family ties, along with the divisions of working-class life and the pain of loss. Also in this part, Kathlene McDonald examines the nonstereotypical representation of working-class characters in Dorothy Allison's novel about working-class family relationships, *Bastard out of Carolina.*

Several of the essays in part 2, "Learning and Unlearning: Class Lessons in and out of the Classroom," address issues of education. Maureen Dyer uses her own life experience as a working-class British student to critique contemporary sociological theory. Carolyn Whitson uses the unusual subject of how a "classical" education can empower, rather than marginalize, working-class students. Terry Easton analyzes the ideological transformation of the *Silent Worker* (a publication for, by, and about the deaf) into the *Deaf American* by representing the deaf as workers and persons. Deb Busman challenges the class bias of traditional definitions of "intelligence," and Eileen Bresnahan presents her experiences as a working-class, Catholic, lesbian Southerner who entered the academic world.

Part 3, "Writing Resistance in the Workplace," documents in theory and practice the struggles of workers through the past two centuries. Julia Stein's "Tangled Threads" links the legacy of worker activism represented in the proletarian fiction of the 1930s with Maureen Brady's *Folly* and Nancy Zaroulis's *Call the Darkness Light*, two contemporary novels about textile factories. Through Carol Tarlen's personal essay, we witness the everyday struggles of working-class women, in this case a secretary. A recognition of the importance of activism also underscores Tim Libretti's theorizing about the intersection of sexuality, race, and gender in Katya and Bert Gilden's 1971 novel *Between the Hills and the Sea*. Karen Kovacik looks at the way contemporary working-class poets have used the history of the 1911 Triangle fire, which killed 146 workers, as subject matter for their poetry. Will Watson discusses the latent class biases in Rebecca Harding Davis's *Life in the Iron Mills*. These pieces of working-class literary criticism represent an important new trend in the field, a developing perspective that brings together working-class critics and working-class texts, producing insights that we hope will revitalize literary theory. Singer Pat Wynne offers lively suggestions for teaching the heritage of labor history through labor songs, and she has created new songs based on old tunes to address current labor problems. Finally, Joan Jobe Smith's poetry details the struggles of women—go-go dancers—who work on the fringes of the sex trade.

In part 4, "Claiming an Identity," Merrihelen Ponce and Jane Greer focus on the centrality of language to forming a sense of self. For Ponce, who grew up speaking "Spanglish," English is her language as a writer and of economic opportunity but also of "Americanization." For Greer, the "privileged," authoritative writing of managers can undermine working-class women's own written voices, but it can also be rejected in favor of a class-affirming style based on workers' experiences outside work. Barbara Jensen discusses how class position shapes consciousness and calls for psychological theories appropriate to the life experiences of working-class people. Janet Zandy's "Traveling Working Class" speaks of "carrying our knowledge of working-class life into the world," for which it is necessary to maintain or, in class-phobic America, "decloak" a working-class identity. In each of these works, a sense of identity is necessary to "speak" about class, but "identity or class" need not be mutually exclusive loyalties.

Dedication

This issue is dedicated to Constance Coiner, who was killed, along with her daughter Ana, in the July 17, 1996, crash of TWA flight 800. Constance was a guiding force in working-class studies, and both directly and indirectly, this issue owes its existence to her.

As many people writing in our special memorial section note, one of the things Constance did best was bring people together. She gave new meaning to networking, as she pursued it for social good, not personal advancement. She deliberately made herself a human bridge, connecting people she felt would work well together, especially to produce some greater good. She introduced Renny and Lisa to each other and told us several times afterward that all her life she would be proud of having done so. She sat between us at the conference where Florence Howe suggested this second issue on working-class studies and immediately straightened in her seat and said, "That would be great for you two!" Anyone who knew her can guess what happened next—within moments she introduced us to Linda, presented us all to Florence, and buzzed with the excitement of how we could represent the "new generation" of working-class scholars. Constance in the full flush of a new idea was not a force to be restrained.

So many people loved Constance that it was difficult to limit the contributions to this part, and inevitably some who should have been included were left out. What has been included is a representative sampling of the people who knew her in her different roles, as sister, student, teacher, and comrade. Virginia Coiner Classick uses her personal pain as a reminder of the preventable suffering of others and of the need for preventing violence everywhere. Liz Rosenberg writes about Constance as an enthusiastic and generous sister teacher at the State University of New York at Binghamton; Karen Rowe remembers her as an overworked but still exuberant student/mother/teacher at the University of California, Los Angeles. Diana Hume George discusses their work together editing a book about combining family life and academic life, *The Family Track: Keeping Your Faculties While You Mentor, Nurture, Teach, and Serve.* Janet Zandy's dedication of the 1997 Youngstown Working Class Studies conference to the memory of Constance talks about Constance's contribution to that conference and to the field of working-class studies. All the pieces also speak of Ana, Constance's daughter, who carried so much of her parents' promise. And finally, Constance's partner, Steve Duarte, contributed the lovely photo of Constance holding a sunflower up to the light.

For those who wish to make their own contributions to maintaining Constance's memory and to support working-class students and scholarship, two separate funds are accepting donations: The Constance Coiner Lecture Series Endowment Fund at Binghamton University, where she taught (Binghamton University Foundation, P.O. Box 6005, Binghamton, NY 13902-6005), and The Constance Coiner Endowment Fund to support undergraduate prizes and a graduate fellowship at the University of California, Los Angeles, where she completed her doctorate (The UCLA Foundation, P.O. Box 24209, Los Angeles, CA 90099-4214).

Bibliography

Appy, Christian. *Working Class War: American Combat Soldiers & Viet Nam.* Chapel Hill: University of North Carolina Press, 1993.

Brommell, Nicholas K. *By the Sweat of the Brow: Literature and Labor in Antebellum America.* Chicago: University of Chicago Press, 1993.

Burke, Martin J. *The Conundrum of Class: Public Discourse on the Social Order in America.* Chicago: University of Chicago Press, 1995.

Coiner, Constance. *Better Red: The Writing and Resistance of Tillie Olsen and Meridel Le Sueur.* New York: Oxford University Press, 1995.

Cornford, Daniel, ed. *Working People of California.* Berkeley and Los Angeles: University of California Press, 1995.

Dews, C. L. Barney, and Carolyn Leste Law, eds. *This Fine Place So Far from Home: Voices of Academics from the Working Class.* Philadelphia: Temple University Press, 1995.

Dimock, Wai Chee, and Michael T. Gilmore, eds. *Rethinking Class: Literary Studies and Social Formations.* New York: Columbia University Press, 1994.

Foley, Barbara. *Radical Representations: Politics and Form in U.S. Proletarian Fiction, 1929–1941.* Durham, NC: Duke University Press, 1993.

Grahn, Judy. *The Work of a Common Woman: The Collected Poetry of Judy Grahn, 1964–1977.* Trumansburg, NY: Crossing Press, 1978.

Hapke, Laura. *Daughters of the Great Depression: Women, Work, and Fiction in the American 1930s.* Athens: University of Georgia Press, 1995.

Lott, Eric. *Love & Theft: Blackface: Minstrelsy and the American Working Class.* New York: Oxford University Press, 1993.

Mullen, Bill, and Sherry Linkon, eds. *Radical Revisions: Rereading 1930s Culture.* Urbana: University of Illinois Press, 1996.

Mullen, Bill, Sherry Linkon, John Russo, Susan Russo, and Linda Strom. "Working-Class Studies: Where It's Been and Where It's Going." In *U.S. Labor in the 20th Century: Studies in Working-Class Fragmentations and Insurgency,* edited by John Hinshaw and Paul LeBlanc. Atlantic Highlands, NJ: Humanities Press, forthcoming.

Orr, Lisa. "On Doing Working-Class Theory: Or, Am I the Dancing Dog?" In *Working Class/Academics,* edited by Thomas Bredehoft and Janie Hinds, forthcoming.

Penelope, Julia, ed. *Out of the Class Closet: Lesbians Speak.* Freedom, CA: Crossing Press, 1994.

Tokarczyk, Michelle M., and Elizabeth A. Fay, eds. *Working-Class Women in the Academy: Laborers in the Knowledge Factory.* Amherst: University of Massachusetts Press, 1993.

Wray, Matt, and Annalee Newitz, eds. *White Trash.* New York: Routledge, 1997.

Zandy, Janet, ed. *Calling Home: Working-Class Women's Writings: An Anthology.* New Brunswick, NJ: Rutgers University Press, 1990.

———, ed. *Liberating Memory: Our Work and Our Working-Class Consciousness.* New Brunswick, NJ: Rutgers University Press, 1995.

Zaniello, Tom. *Working Stiffs, Union Maids, Reds, and Riffraff: An Organized Guide to Films About Labor.* Ithaca, NY: ILR Press, 1996.

Renny Christopher teaches in the English department at California State University, Stanislaus. Her book The Viet Nam War/The American War: Images and Representations in Euro-American and Vietnamese Exile Narratives *was published by the University of Massachusetts Press in 1995.*

Lisa Orr earned a doctorate at the University of California, Los Angeles, where she specialized in twentieth-century American literature, working-class literature, and feminist theory. She is a visiting assistant professor of English and the acting director of the Writing Center at Utica College of Syracuse University.

Linda Strom is an associate professor at Youngstown State University. She is currently writing a book with a colleague tentatively entitled Resisting Boundaries: Teaching Writing to Working Adults.

Use the Broken Things

for James W., 1931–1988

When I moved in with my father,
he went to a garage sale to get more plates:
old, stiff, coated plastic,
painted with turquoise and lime green leaves.
Some were cracked, and a few had faded,
but I liked the one that had crayon marks
on the underside—
a child's stick drawing of her daddy.
That never washed off for some reason.

Of course I didn't like the used plates at first.
Not after being raised by my mother,
for whom everything had to look rich and spotless,
or be old and costly.

I was ashamed of Dad's Salvation Army shoes,
and the plaid polyester pants
he'd gotten for a dollar.

He gave me money to buy books and dresses new,
but cooked for us in pots that were dented,
and dined with me on a Goodwill sofa.

Once, while removing the cracked clear covering
of a clock radio, he told me:
"Angel, you've got to learn to use the broken things."

It took me years to realize he wasn't cheap,
nor his pension too small;
he just couldn't stand to see good things discarded.

After he died, his lesson endured
in the worn fragments left of our life together;
his words mending me
even in my grief.

—*Carolyn E. Whitson*

Carolyn E. Whitson *is an assistant professor in literature, women's studies, and humanities at Metropolitan State University. She writes a feminist book review column for* La Gazette, *a central California women's newspaper, and has published poetry in* Matrix *and* Porter Gulch Review. *She is currently working on a book on critical approaches to working-class literature.*

Talking Trash, Talking Back: Resistance to Stereotypes in Dorothy Allison's *Bastard out of Carolina*

Kathlene McDonald

They were of a kind not safely to be described in an account claiming to be unimaginative or untrustworthy, for they had too much and too outlandish beauty not to be legendary. Since, however, they existed quite irrelevant to myth, it will be necessary to tell a little of them.

—James Agee, referring in his *Let Us Now Praise Famous Men* to poor-white, southern tenant farmers during the Depression

I read Dorothy Allison's *Bastard out of Carolina* for the first time while living in the South, working with young children at a day care center, and volunteering at the local rape crisis center, where I was working with both adult survivors of child sexual abuse and currently abused children. The novel's character of Bone felt very real to me then; her experience seemed painfully, strikingly believable. Allison takes up the issue of believability in "A Question of Class," an essay in her collection *Skin,* in which she discusses the politics of the "we" (those in power) and the "they" (all others, the disempowered, the working class), and the necessity of exploring those categories from the inside.

By presenting an insider's view of white-trash experiences in *Bastard,* Allison helps those on the outside understand the reality and diversity of those experiences. She says, "The need to make my world believable to people who have never experienced it is part of why I write fiction" (*Skin* 14). In this essay, I look at some of the ways in which Allison constructs her subjects in order to make the white-trash world more believable. I begin by looking at depictions of white trash in literature and culture as a means of establishing the stereotypes. Then I explore the ways in which Allison constructs a white-trash subject that defies these stereotypes. I conclude by discussing some of the ways in which *Bastard* can be used in a working-class studies course.

The characters that Allison constructs represent part of a long and paradoxical literary history. Whether as lubber, cracker, po buckra,

redneck, hillbilly, or white trash, the southern poor-white character
has been a popular literary figure at least as far back as the eighteenth
century. In 1728, William Byrd II headed an expedition of commis-
sioners from Virginia and North Carolina to survey the disputed
boundary line between the two colonies. Byrd, a wealthy Virginian,
wrote about his encounters with the inhabitants of the North Carolina
backwoods, or "Lubbers," as he referred to them, in *The History of the
Dividing Line*. He characterized these "Wretches" as lazy, dirty, vulgar,
ignorant, promiscuous, and deceitful, thereby setting a precedent for
future fictional stereotypes.

Byrd's lubbers also helped establish precedents for two conflicting
and enduring ethical positions that have attempted to explain the so-
called immorality and depravity of the southern poor white. One theory blames environmental conditions such as diet, climate, and
disease. The other theory, what David Reynolds refers to as the "blood-
line theory," argues that poor whites are "biologically inferior" and
thus "genetically predisposed to be white trash" (359–60). This second
theory continues to be used today as a means of perpetuating the myth
of America as a classless society. In this way, Reynolds argues, America
cannot be blamed if white trash are biologically depraved, and belief
in "the land of opportunity, where prosperity is possible for all" can
thus be maintained (360).

While journalists and sociologists have continued to use these positions to theorize the supposed inferiority of poor whites, fiction writers in the eighteenth and nineteenth centuries had more interest in
using the white-trash character to generate responses of "laughter, pity,
discomfort, indignation, revulsion" (Cook 4–5). The moral, emotional,
and intellectual behavior of the poor white became a focus of
Southern literature, with little attention paid to social, economic, or
historic conditions. The southern poor white became an established
literary figure during the nineteenth century, appealing to audiences
as either comic or contemptible, while the material concerns of poor
whites remained invisible.

Ignorance of and indifference to the shame and suffering caused
by economic violence prevailed for many years, emerging as a subject
for national concern during the Great Depression. Southern poverty
gained a "fashionable prominence" (Cook 144) in the 1930s through
magazine articles and newspaper reports, artistic experiments, and
government investigations. But in spite of this raised national consciousness, American audiences remained fascinated with humorous
portrayals of white-trash culture in the novels and plays of the 1930s.
For example, the theatrical adaptation of Erskine Caldwell's *Tobacco*

Road became one of Broadway's longest-running productions, attracting huge audiences with the comedy of its stereotypical white-trash characters. Reynolds writes that the play's "animalistic sex was surely at least partially responsible for the record attendance" (361). Although Caldwell intended to use *Tobacco Road* to express his outrage against an economic system that kept its victims impoverished, the sexual titillation and the absurd caricatures merely reinforced the prevailing stereotypes.

Today, the American culture industry perpetuates the fascination with white trash. As in the past, the harsh realities of poverty do not interest most consumers of culture, but white-trash experiences continue to appeal to a wide audience. The popular television situation comedy *Roseanne* spent years on top of the Nielsen ratings, entertaining millions of viewers with its humorous portrayals of a working-class family. Although *Roseanne* addressed material conditions and dealt with real concerns, often in a serious and thoughtful manner, much of the humor derived from mocking white-trash culture. In one episode, Roseanne and her husband, Dan, discuss the upcoming marriage of their pregnant teenage daughter to a boy they consider a son. After remarking that their grandchild will be the same age as their youngest child, Roseanne comments that these circumstances make them "just about the white-trashiest family in America." The two exchange high fives and then clap their hands to activate "the Clapper," turning off the lights. By continually making fun of Roseanne's and Dan's white-trash status, the show's writers call attention to the characteristics on which many of the stereotypes are based. Although in many ways the show does accurately portray the realities of working-class life, it ultimately reinforces white trash as humorous, allowing viewers to witness, without guilt, the social and economic conditions that create that reality.

Another popular show, *Grace Under Fire,* also draws much of its comedic value from white-trash experiences. The main character, Grace, repeatedly refers to her dysfunctional family, her alcoholic father, her slutty adolescence, and her southern roots. She makes no connections between her family's economic situation and their lived realities; rather, her family becomes merely a source of humor for her anecdotes, perpetuating standard characterizations of white trash. In both shows, the effort to portray working-class experiences is reduced to their entertainment value. The sitcom format allows viewers to consume passively only one dimension of white-trash culture, without needing to question the material conditions out of which these comic "situations" arise.

Allison's characters in *Bastard* reflect stereotypical white-trash images in many ways. Bone is the illegitimate child of fifteen-year-old Anney. Most of the adults drink heavily, chain-smoke, drive jacked-up cars, talk dirty, display frightening tempers, work in mills and diners, and frequently spend time in jail. In an interview with Amber Hollibaugh, Allison discussed writing about her family, the basis for many of the characters in *Bastard*:

> I show you my aunts in their drunken rages, my uncles in their meanness. And that's exactly who we're supposed to be. That's what white trash is all about. . . . Some of that stuff is true. But to write about it I had to find a way to . . . show you those people as larger than that contemptible myth. (16)

Allison incorporates many of the "true" elements of dominant stereotypes into her characters so that they simultaneously reinforce and resist standard images of white trash. By refusing the one dimensionality of traditional cultural stereotypes, Allison allows her characters to move beyond them.

Like most judgments made from the outside, generally accepted stereotypes ignore the material conditions that make them true, focusing instead on the humorous or pitiable aspects of white-trash culture. Exploring the role of poverty in shaping identity provides a means of examining these conditions from the inside. The one-dimensional nature of most cultural representations of white trash allows consumers to overlook the painful aspects of poverty. But Allison makes this pain difficult to avoid by refusing to keep the reality invisible. In showing the hunger, the despair, the limited choices, and the shame of contempt and class hatred, Allison forces her readers to confront the everyday realities of her characters, to see them as larger than their stereotypes.

In writing *Bastard,* Allison purposefully chose to use the language of poor and working-class white southerners, a voice traditionally mocked in literature, television shows, and movies. In an interview with Minnie Bruce Pratt, Allison described the stereotypical ways of writing this voice "as if it is in the back pages of men's magazines with the letters cut off and a whole lot of extra letters thrown on. It's barely intelligible and has an aura of stupid about it" (31). Rather than covering up this voice or accepting conventional ways of writing this speech that make it sound stupid, Allison tries instead to capture the rhythms of country music, gospel music, and the church that influence this dialect. In refusing to correct the grammar in the statement "The law never done us no good. Might as well get on without it" (5) and to rewrite "An't nobody says nothing to my little sister, an't nobody can touch that girl or what's hers" (14) to conform to the conventional spelling of *ain't,* Allison allows for an acceptance of her characters' dialect and thus its respect.

The male figures in *Bastard* provide a useful point of entry for discussing Allison's construction of white-trash identities. Fully understanding the women in the book necessitates an equal understanding of the men in the story. Lyle Parsons, Anney Boatwright's first husband, frequently reeks of beer, spends much of his time at stock-car races, and defines his masculinity by "providing well for his family." He proves himself a man by getting Anney pregnant "almost immediately" and doesn't "want her to go out to work at all" (6). Economic necessity forces Anney to go back to work, but she has already become accustomed to relying on a man. She continues to work throughout the novel but holds to the belief that she needs a man to take care of her.

The Boatwright brothers, Earle, Beau, and Nevil, have no respect for any situation that "could not be handled with a shotgun or a two-by-four" (10). The county both respects and fears their legendary tempers, and they are known for their drunken binges and rumored affairs. They love their wives, but they cannot (or will not) "stay away from other women" (24). Even though the uncles embody stereotypical white-trash characteristics in many ways, they are "invariably gentle and affectionate" toward their sisters, nieces, and nephews (22). They maintain a fierce loyalty to the Boatwright clan, often assuming the role of the protector. At the same time, they allow themselves to be taken care of by their sisters, who treat them "like overgrown boys" (23).

The Boatwright men represent everything that Glen Waddell, Anney's second husband, "had ever wanted to be" (12). Scorned and laughed at by the men in his own family for "his hot temper, bad memory, and general uselessness" (12), Glen aspires to be like Earle Boatwright, embracing a white-trash identity in order to anger his respectable, middle-class family. After his marriage to Anney, his family's respect again becomes important to him. But his family continues to look down on him, for both marrying "trash" and having a wife who works. "In Daddy Glen's family the women stayed at home" (98). He alternates between "complaining of how badly they treated him" and desperately trying to win their respect (99). Unable to feel like a man in his family's eyes, Glen resorts to either childlike behavior or violent rage.

Femininity in the novel is defined largely through these constructions of masculinity. In many ways the women depend on their men for protection, economic survival, and love. "Being pregnant" proves that their men love them, and a man's love proves that they are "worth something" (230–31). They do not value love from other women, such as their sisters, in the same way. In an interview with Carolyn E. Megan, Allison described the women's role as caught up "in the things they were supposed to do . . . keep the kids safe, find a good man, save him, and hang on for dear life" (76–77). Thus Anney falls in love with Glen's need for attention and mothering yet maintains that she needs him to take care of her.

Anney provides the main financial support for Glen and her children. Glen's inability to hold down a job and frequent periods of unemployment make him more a liability than a source of support. But even though Anney does not depend on Glen financially, she believes she needs a man to survive. She cannot leave him, despite his intensifying violence toward Bone and his failure to put food on the table more often than not. Her final decision to remain with Glen thus has less to do with her love for him than her fear of being without a man. Anney clearly loves Bone very deeply, but she chooses Glen, even though doing so means losing Bone.

The Boatwright women seem unable to recognize the support they derive from the strong community of women in the novel. In her interview with Megan, Allison pointed out, "They knew it was important but didn't think it was nearly as important as what a man and woman made together" (77). The aunts' "nasty and strong" support network provides an alternative world to that of the "spitting, growling, overbearing males" (91). Together, the Boatwright sisters can draw support from one another rather than devoting all their energy to caring for their men. The aunts nurture and sustain one another, give one another power and strength, and help one another survive, but ultimately they believe they need to rely on their men.

Bone, her sister Reese, and their cousins attempt to imitate the Boatwright aunts and uncles while simultaneously finding ways to resist their predetermined roles. Bone idolizes her uncles. She begs to wear their cast-off clothes and follows them around, mimicking their actions. At the same time, she values the strength of her aunts; she likes "being one of the women" (91). This embracing of contradictions allows Bone to draw on the positive characteristics of both her aunts and her uncles. After Daddy Glen's terrifying rape and assault, Bone learns that she needs both her uncles' violent rage and quest for vengeance and her aunts' support and strength in order to survive the ordeal.

The Boatwrights maintain fierce pride and loyalty toward their family, but they also suffer deep feelings of shame and hopelessness.

Taught by experience that nothing ever changes, they refuse to believe that they will ever escape from poverty. After Lyle Parsons's death, Aunt Ruth tells Anney that she looks "like a Boatwright" now and that she will look that way until she dies. Both Ruth and Anney resign themselves to their lot in life. For Anney, "it didn't matter to her anymore what she looked like" (8).

Much of this shame and self-hatred of poverty derives from the contempt of those in the middle and upper classes. The cruel judgments rendered by other people deeply wound the Boatwrights. Bone repeatedly hears the labels of "*No-good, lazy, shiftless*" (3) and can see the disdain in the eyes of others when they look at her family. "How am I supposed to know anything at all?" she wonders, when "I'm just another ignorant Boatwright. . . . Another piece of trash barely knows enough to wipe her ass or spit away from the wind" (258). Yet she and Reese are better behaved than the middle-class Waddell children. Well aware of the low expectations that others have of her family, Anney strives to raise her children respectably. And although Bone longs for the middle-class acceptance that Anney tries to cultivate, she sometimes wishes she "could complain for no reason but the pleasure of bitching and act like the trash we were supposed to be" (66). She knows she will forever be judged by those on the outside, no matter how she behaves.

Raylene is perhaps the strongest, most fulfilled character in the book—the only one "completely satisfied with her own company" and the only one able to disregard the scorn of the upper classes. She smokes and talks rough, wears her hair short, and dresses in "trousers as often as skirts" (179). While the other Boatwrights move from house to house, never staying in one place for too long, Raylene stays put, creating a secure environment for herself that serves as a refuge for various family members in need. Living alone, away from anyone else, she can be her own person. "Out here where no one can mess with it," she jokes, "trash rises" (180). By isolating herself from a world in which the Boatwrights are judged as trash and from her family, whose roles for men and women are strictly defined, Raylene is able to transcend other people's ideas of her. Her sexuality remains ambiguous until the end of the novel, when she confesses to Bone that she once loved, and failed, another woman. She thus represents an alternative to both the gender roles of her family and the expectations of the upper and middle classes.

Although Allison does not deal with race as explicitly as she does gender or class, the silences and absences in *Bastard* concerning race require examination. The chances of surviving and escaping the conditions of poverty are greater for the Boatwrights than for the African American members of the community. This relative privilege of whiteness remains unspoken, but its presence cannot be ignored if we are to understand white-trash identity. The few African Americans that appear in the text are "niggers" or "peckerwoods," and the Boatwrights scorn them, feeling no shame about being racist. Understanding this racial hatred requires understanding its economic and historical context. Howard Zinn claims that racism became "practical" during the colonial era as a means of preventing black slaves and white indentured servants from joining forces against the wealthy white landowners. Racism was not something "'natural' to the black-white difference, but something coming out of class scorn, a realistic device for control" (56).

In her interview with Pratt, Allison explained that much of the hatred and contempt that poor whites in the South feel toward African Americans derives from "being hated and held in contempt" themselves (33), and they can pass on that hatred to African Americans. The Boatwrights believe the lies about African Americans, just as the upper and middle classes believe the lies about them. At moments, Bone recognizes the connections between racial and class oppression. For example, when her friend Shannon tells her, "My daddy don't handle niggers," the word _nigger_ tears at her, for Shannon's tone sounds "exactly like the echoing sound of Aunt Madeline sneering 'trash' when she thought I wasn't close enough to hear" (170). But because _Bastard_ takes place in Greenville, South Carolina, in the 1950s, Bone has little contact with other African Americans and remains unable to find out the truth (or lack of truth) about racial stereotypes.

The deeply ingrained gender, race, and class roles of the Boatwright family help support and shape their identities while at the same time limiting and containing them. The characters find ways of resisting their appointed roles even as they submit to them, demonstrating "audacity within confinement," a phrase of Thomas Mann's that Constance Coiner was particularly fond of quoting in both her graduate seminar discussions and her own writing. Rather than presenting a falsely unified definition of white-trash experiences, Allison acknowledges conflicting meanings. Her refusal to synthesize the contradictions of her characters permits a dialectical understanding of the reality and diversity of their lives. Her characters contradict preconceived stereotypes and commodified images, thereby creating space for a historical understanding of white-trash identities.

In interviews and her own writing, Allison frequently expresses her frustrations with feminist theories that either ignore class altogether or do not consider it to be as significant as gender or sexual identity. She writes, "My sexual identity is intimately constructed by my class and regional background . . . however much people, feminists in particular, like to pretend this is not a factor" (*Skin* 23). In an essay in *Out of the Class Closet: Lesbians Speak,* Elliott, a self-identified redneck, discusses similar feelings of anger toward middle- and upper-class lesbian feminists who don't "get the tie between privilege, ignorance, and stereotypes" (281). Understanding constructions of gender or sexual identity, she argues, necessitates understanding class and racial backgrounds. Likewise, the power of Allison's book lies not only in its resistance to the myths, lies, and stereotypes about white trash. In offering a more complex portrayal of white-trash experiences, *Bastard* also provides a better understanding of the effects of class on identity that is not limited to or by gender and sexual identity.

In the introduction to *Calling Home: Working-Class Women's Writings: An Anthology,* Janet Zandy explains the ways in which working-class writing can "show the connections between individual identity and collective sensibility" (10). White-trash identity is only one facet of this larger working-class sensibility. So by portraying the reality of white-trash lives, Allison demonstrates the diversity of working-class identities, thereby subverting a unified definition of identity. Rather than theorizing differences as a means to critique the power structure that exploits and oppresses differences, identity politics has become an end in itself. This approach to multiculturalism commodifies individual identities, obscuring the larger relations of structures of oppression that create these identities. Without a systematic ideological critique of these relations, any sort of collective vision for social change remains impossible. For those teaching working-class studies, *Bastard out of Carolina* provides a useful approach to understanding working-class experiences that illustrates an alternative to the commodification of identities. Rather than celebrating individual groups or identities, *Bastard* looks at the reality and diversity of working-class experiences as part of a larger system of exploitation. Teachers can discuss with their students the "intersections and potential alliances" of race, gender, class, and sexual identification (Coiner 262), thereby allowing for multiple perspectives while promoting collective social change.

When they understand the constructions of identity in *Bastard,* students can then consider the choices the book's characters make in regard to these constructions. Rather than debating about whether Anney should have left Glen, students can look at the reasons that she stays with him. Rather than viewing the uncles' drunkenness and violence as characteristic white-trash traits, students can explore these traits as responses to their lived experiences. Rather than reducing *Bastard* to being a book primarily about incest, students can look at the physical violence and emotional abuse in the context of the material conditions and talk about the difficulties that Bone's family has in protecting her from the abuse.

Examining *Bastard out of Carolina* in terms of resistance to white-trash stereotypes can also give students a greater understanding of working-class culture. In presenting the painful aspects of oppression, what is mean and ugly about her characters as well as what is good and beautiful about them, Allison portrays her characters in ways that resist categorization. She says, "I did not want anyone to ever be able to use the words 'white trash' again without thinking about all my characters" (Hollibaugh 16). Allison's constructions of white-trash identity force readers to confront their own preconceptions and to question the material conditions from which these notions arise.

Bibliography

Agee, James, and Walker Evans. *Let Us Now Praise Famous Men*. 1941. Reprint, New York: Ballantine, 1966.

Allison, Dorothy. *Bastard out of Carolina*. New York: Plume-Penguin, 1992.

————. *Skin: Talking About Sex, Class, and Literature*. Ithaca, NY: Firebrand, 1994.

Coiner, Constance. "U.S. Working-Class Women's Fiction: Notes Toward an Overview." *Women's Studies Quarterly* 23, nos. 1 & 2 (1995): 248–67.

Cook, Sylvia Jenkins. *From Tobacco Road to Route 66: The Southern Poor White in Fiction*. Chapel Hill: University of North Carolina Press, 1976.

Elliott. "Whenever I Tell You the Language We Use Is a Class Issue, You Nod Your Head in Agreement—And Then You Open Your Mouth." In *Out of the Class Closet: Lesbians Speak*, edited by Julia Penelope. Freedom, CA: Crossing Press, 1994.

Hollibaugh, Amber. "Telling a Mean Story: Amber Hollibaugh Interviews Dorothy Allison." *Women's Review of Books* 9, nos. 10 & 11 (1992): 16.

Megan, Carolyn E. "Moving Toward Truth: An Interview with Dorothy Allison." *Kenyon Review* 16 (1994): 71–83.

Pratt, Minnie Bruce. "Dorothy Allison." *Progressive* 59, no. 7 (1995): 30–34.

Reynolds, David. "White Trash in Your Face: The Literary Descent of Dorothy Allison." *Appalachian Journal* 20, no. 4 (1993): 356–66.

Zandy, Janet. *Calling Home: Working-Class Women's Writing: An Anthology*. New Brunswick, NJ: Rutgers University Press, 1990.

Zinn, Howard. *A People's History of the United States*. New York: Harper, 1980.

Kathlene McDonald *is a Ph.D. student in English at the University of Maryland at College Park. Her research interests include American working-class literature and culture, leftist writers (1930s to the present), and critical* *theory. Her current project involves looking at texts that challenge or subvert traditional representations of the working class and (from a historical perspective) the ways that labor organizers have excluded or ignored the concerns of those who do not fit a certain image of what it means to be "working class."*

Copyright © 1998 by Kathlene McDonald

Counting Tips

for Janet Zandy

My mother came home from work,
sat down at the kitchen table
and counted her tips, nickel by nickel,
quarter by quarter, dime by dime.
I sat across from her reading Yeats.
No moonlight graced our window
and it wasn't Pre-Raphaelite pallor
that bleached my mother's cheeks.
I've never been able to forget
the moment she said—
interrupting *The Lake Isle of Innisfree*—
"I told him to go to hell."
A Back Bay businessman
had held back the tip, asking,
"How much do you think you're worth?"
And she'd said, "You can go to hell!"
All evening at the Winthrop Room she'd fed
stockbrokers, politicians, mafioso capos.
I was eighteen, a commuter student at BU,
riding the MTA to classes every day
and she was forty-one in her frilly cap,
pink uniform, and white waitress shoes.
"He just laughed but his wife was there
and she complained and the boss fired me."
Later, after a highball, she cried
and asked me not to tell my father
(at least not yet) and Ben Franklin
stared up from his quarter
looking as if he thought she deserved it,
and Roosevelt, from his dime, reminded her
she was twenty years shy of Social Security.
But the buffalo on the nickel, he—
he seemed to understand.

—*John Gilgun*

John Gilgun *is the author of* Everything That Has Been Shall Be Again:
The Reincarnation Fables of John Gilgun, From the Inside Out, The
Dooley Poems, Music I Never Dreamed Of, *and* Your Buddy Misses You.

My Mother, According to Me

My mother kneads dumplings with one hand
cuts up a ten-pound capon with the other
but I wanted a concert pianist, perhaps a soprano
though I'll settle for a bongo woman
some lost female Beat.

My mother never met a person without a kind word
but I wished her quick witted and well read
spewing Dickinson each night
quoting *Ample make this bed*
instead of *Now I lay me down.*

My mother caresses toddlers to sleep
or calms any infant with one coo
cuddles the down off a chick
talks the paint off a barn without bothering a soul
or nurses the spindliest plant back to life.

She pulls bargains off the rack
faster than a zephyr across the plains,
or cranks a one-armed bandit till four A.M.
and doesn't miss a note of "How Great Thou Art"
three hours later at morning mass.

My mother tells me in detail
about the most recently condensed
volume from *Reader's Digest*
the heroes, the horrors.
She calls my poetry my writings

says I use college words she doesn't know
wonders where I get those ideas
and boasts to her friends all the while
wanting nurse or engineer or farmer's wife
something tangible she can spell out over cards.

A lifetime accommodates the breach
between what we are and who we are not
Old West hostages without a clue for escape
one end of the rope fraying, mother,
as I tie myself to you with the other.

—*Patti See*

Patti See *supervises tutoring and mentoring programs at the University of Wisconsin at Eau Claire, where she also teaches developmental education courses. Her work has appeared in* Cincinnati Poets' Collective, Gypsy Cab, Southeast Review, Talking River Review, Upriver: Wisconsin Poetry and Prose, Wisconsin Academy Review, *and other magazines and anthologies.*

Taking A/part

Maureen Dyer

In this essay, as I think and I write, I am trying to make sense of myself—my own experiences, my own history, and the significance of education in all of that. I am interested in exploring the importance of race, class, ethnicity, and the specific historical and geographical contexts in my own and other people's lives. Because I am a sociologist, this essay is also a critique of some of the recent theorizing in the sociology of education. In telling my story, I am aware that I am presenting it with a coherence and clarity that it certainly lacked at the time I experienced it. So I acknowledge and indeed stress the then-and-now reality of a patchwork persona, and in this essay I gather them up from an irretrievable past and attempt to construct a seamless and ultimately illusional identity to be understood as the working-class academic that I am.

I grew up under a Labour government in postwar Britain. At the time, there was a new enthusiasm for using education to produce specific social outcomes, a more equitable society. People believed that the schooling process would be able to uncover talented individuals and then nurture those meritorious few, grooming and preparing them for the climb to privileged positions. This idea downplayed the significance of social class, holding that talent, combined with effective teaching, would win in the end. Although contemporary sociological research did not support this simplistic analysis, the political orthodoxy of the time suggested that with a few changes, the education system alone could achieve the desired outcome. Both the Crowther (1959–1960) and the Robbins (1963) reports called for expanding higher education, arguing that only a greater investment in the system would ensure the elimination of "talent wastage," caused by neglect of the unfulfilled capacities of working- and lower-middle-class children. Onward social justice. But few were achieving success at school, and most continued to be "wasted."

In the 1950s and 1960s, sociological and educational explanations for the lack of academic success enjoyed by "bright" working-class children concentrated on the inadequacies of their families, particularly their mothers. To overcome what was described as deprivations, a compensatory form of education was recommended. Such a policy again suggests a simplistic analysis of complicated factors working on the lives of children from underprivileged backgrounds. When reading about it years later, my response was deeply ambivalent. Working-class life is not just "different"; to cite different priorities and pressures is to obfuscate. Rather, working-class life is a narrow and circumscribed life, rendered thus by the material and social circumstances in which individuals live. Many of the things that enrich and enliven my life now were absent from my childhood, and there is no doubt that I missed a good deal as a result, in opportunity, enjoyment, and intellectual development.

Working-class children lack the "cultural capital" that Bourdieu (1976) theorized is necessary for children's success at school. He argued that success at school is judged more on social-class styles learned at home than on what is taught in school. If you have the right style or "habitus" that fits with the school's, then you have the "cultural capital" for success. The inaccessibility of this capital for working-class children and their having the "wrong" habitus have far-reaching and often crippling effects on young lives, even when the parents of these kids work as hard as they can, doing the best they can, with what they have. Through such mechanisms, Bourdieu contended, the school contributes to the social reproduction of the class system.

My experience taught me, and still tells me, that making access more equal is not sufficient when that to which access is given remains fundamentally unequal. Greater accessibility is a convenient catch phrase but ultimately suffers from being no more than that, ignoring the underlying issues raised for me by the Marxist writings of Raymond Williams (1976).

I was born and raised in Dagenham, then the largest public housing estate of its kind in the United Kingdom—a huge, sprawling, industrial suburb of Greater London, built to house the overspill and relocated populations of the slums. I heard a speaker many years later, when discussing the stratification of cities, note that you can always pick the class of an area from the sky: if it has no green, no open areas, you're probably above a working-class part of town. Certainly, this was true of Dagenham. Characterless and bleak, it contained a building that claimed to be the "Civic Center," which only underscored the lack of one. The failure, or maybe the absence, of urban planning meant there was no center to the suburb, in either geographical or social terms. Just long gray streets, with long gray rows of houses, each identical to the next, thrown up quickly and cheaply for their new occupants. The chemical, car, and asbestos factories on the banks of the Thames provided the livelihoods for most of those in the area and were a dark, constant presence, covering the area with dense, suffocating smoke and foul fumes. The "pea soupers"—thick, dense, suffocating fogs—are vivid memories from my childhood.

In the early 1920s, both sets of my grandparents moved with their young families to Dagenham, in search of a better life. Better housing they found—not a hard task, given that they came from the slums of Deptford, which Margaret Macmillan described when she was opening schools in the area at the turn of the century as "the place of the deep ford. Very deep and steep it is, the soft black yielding mass under the black waters of Poverty. At every step one goes down and down . . . the stained and tumbling walls, the dark and noisy courts, the crowded alleys all hidden behind roaring streets" (Steedman 1990, 115).

A better life? I can't answer that for them, but reading *Family and Kinship in East London* (Willmott and Young 1957) years later, I recognized the story of my grandparents, a story of those who abandoned all that was familiar in order to house young families adequately and, in the process, lost their communities. It seemed to me that their home remained in the east, the "slums," and my youthful Sundays were characterized by awkward journeys on public transport, when my grandparents returned to areas they had sought to leave behind, to visit relatives and friends they could not.

For my parents, the official school-leaving age was fourteen, but my mother, the eldest of nine children, left long before that. Her consequent inability to read and write "properly" was the source of much shame to her throughout her life, and her lack of success at school during her brief tenure there led her to accept and internalize the school's definition of her as stupid. Such definitions are pervasive and enduring, and it was not until much later—almost too late—that I recognized her astuteness and applauded her skill as a needle woman. My father attended the Macmillan sisters' school in Deptford. Like my mother, he was the eldest in his family and thus shouldered financial responsibility for himself early on. Contributions to the upkeep of his younger siblings were also required, and so his early academic promise was never explored. Money to continue his education at the selective school could never have been found, particularly during the Depression. Anyway, staying on at school was just not what working-class children did.

Working-class children went to work in the asbestos factory. And oblivious to the dangers, that is exactly what my mother and my father did.

It was during the years working and choking in the asbestos factory that my father contracted asbestosis. He died relatively young. My mother died of cancer mere months after my father, and although I cannot say that it was exposure to asbestos that caused her untimely death, to suggest it might have been a contributing factor does not seem unreasonable.

Ultimately, life in Dagenham was hard, very hard. Unlike some ex-working-class male sociologists, these memories bring me no joy; I do not and cannot romanticize the past. In the world I remember, there was no great hands-across-the-factories working-class camaraderie, comrades struggling together in the face of great adversity and hardship. My family, like most of our neighbors, lived a very isolated existence and had only limited contact with other people nearby. Outside our immediate family, no one ever set foot in our house, giving rise to limited opportunities for the development of a working-class consciousness. We were just poor. Perhaps I didn't experience the grinding poverty of some, but there was only just enough for the absolute necessities of life, and sometimes not even them.

My parents met in 1937—a workplace romance. They married later that year, and I was born in the 1940s, after the outbreak of World War II—not a baby boomer, just a war baby, making my entrance into the world at a time of great uncertainty and dislocation for all. My father joined the navy, and after his departure for active service, my mother gave up their marital council house (low-rent government-financed house) and moved in with his parents. This supposed temporary sacrifice ultimately dragged on considerably longer than just the duration of the war. Initially because of the housing shortage after the war and then inertia, my parents continued to live with my father's parents until my grandparents' deaths in 1963 and 1979. In keeping with the war spirit and industrial imperatives, Dagenham's industries were turned over to munitions production, which, together with the presence of the dock, transformed it from a boring, little-known bastion of poverty and pollution into a major bombing target. We were bombed out, and I, along with my mother and my grandmother, were evacuated to the English Midlands, leaving my grandfather behind to serve as a fire warden.

In 1942 we returned to our "new" home in Dagenham. This was another council house that had been allocated to my grandparents. I have no real memories of wartime: just fleeting thoughts, random glimpses into the past, provoked perhaps more by what others have told me than by actual recall. I cannot remember any real fear of injury or death. I do remember the ration books that provided us with orange juice, something called Virol—whatever it was, I loved it—and dried egg, which, whatever it really was, I loathed. Ironically, these rations were my passport to a healthy diet, and, courtesy of the war-torn state, made me one of the first generation of working-class kids to enjoy a balanced, nutritious diet. My mother was working part time at this stage, and so I was raised almost exclusively by my grandparents and had virtually no contact with my father until well after the war. Since he had been transferred into the army to assist with the cleanup in Germany, he did not return home until 1947.

In 1946, in the midst of all these changes, I began school. It was very frightening at first, and I cried incessantly for my family and home. Because the teacher's departure from the classroom only brought forth more tears and tantrums, she was reluctant to leave the room at all, and when she did, she took me with her. How long this went on I cannot say, although memory dictates it was a fair stretch of time. From a household of adults, my opportunities for mixing with other children had been extremely limited, so a classroom full of people my own age was alien, confronting, and deeply confusing. Although I gradually adjusted to my new environment, I always remained anxious for affirmation from the sole adult figure, my long-suffering teacher. I began to work hard to please her and so gained a reputation for being clever—intelligence born of insecurity and isolation. My family thought this "nice." I was seen as reliable if "highly strung": I cried if I was criticized. But my early school days were generally very positive, even without a mother who could tutor me in the ways, the rituals, and the etiquette of school, as middle-class mothers have been shown to do, and so give me "cultural capital" (Walkerdine and Lucey 1989). Much later, I learned that my positive experiences were not necessarily typical of talented but struggling working-class youngsters. Perhaps because of the atypical headmistress of the infants school I attended, I had a very broadly based education and acquired a modicum of the "cultural capital" required. The headmistress was later awarded a MBE (Order of the British Empire) for her work with disadvantaged children.

Despite the educational disadvantages suffered by the working class and my own reservations about its efficacy as a means of social mobility, education indisputably did work for me. Despite my working-class background, I was able, because of my successes at school and university and the particular historical moment of my advent into the educational system, to join the ranks of the middle class. My conviction that this was the exception rather than the norm—especially for a girl—remains unswerving and borne out by research.

One of the main tests of a British child's worthiness to join the meritocracy came at the early age of eleven, when he or she sat the "scholarship" exam, or "eleven plus." This examination consisted of literacy and numeracy tests and an intelligence test. Those people concerned that today's public examinations at seventeen or eighteen years of age put too much emphasis on one exam would be horrified: this exam decided definitively which school one would attend, either the academic grammar or the secondary modern. At that time, only the grammar schools gave access to public exams, university, and thus the professions; it was academic make-or-break time before you'd even reached puberty.

It was deemed appropriate that approximately 20 percent of the school population attend grammar school. This was a fairly arbitrary figure, thought to represent the number of students who were of above-average intelligence and able to benefit from academic schooling. The actual numbers and proportions of children varied tremendously, however, from one part of the country to another, and the demographic breakdown of the numbers by class was the cause of much outrage later in my life. Not one student from my primary school class of forty was initially successful. I was granted an "interview"; one other got a "re-sit," which meant that she could sit the examination again. From there, we both were successful. The rest of our young class was consigned to the then dead-end secondary modern school and to the maintenance of their place in the working class.

It is scarcely surprising that later in the 1970s, I found persuasive the theories of schooling emphasizing its tendency to perpetuate the status quo. Researchers such as Bowles and Gintis (1976) showed that the educational system is crucial to reproducing the existing division of labor and thus the prevailing class system, rather than the means of establishing equality of opportunity. No sociologists, we Dagenham students believed—as we were expected to believe—that we had failed the eleven plus because we all lacked the "brains" or innate abilities required for further schooling. We did not know that entire school classes in middle-class England scored 100 percent after intensive, year-long coaching (Jackson and Marsden 1966). We could not have guessed that the measurement of so-called innate intelligence was a construction of educational psychologists, one of whom, Burt, had fudged his results (Kamin 1974) and that in reality, intelligence was dramatically affected by environment and even more by those with the power to decide what should constitute intelligence. So my mother was illiterate and stupid rather than astute, and ignorant of all but the dominant discourse, we never knew how the odds were—and still are—stacked against children of the working class.

But despite all this, I was a winner. I was a member of the first generation to benefit from Labour's education reforms, in particular the Education Act of 1944, which universalized secondary education. I was doing something no one in my family had ever done: I was going to high school.

I went to the school feeling myself to be an alien and an interloper. Securing my entry only after an interview, I was convinced I was a mere pretender to my place at grammar school. This was true, even though my grammar school was in Dagenham. To compensate, I worked harder than ever before, and my subsequent academic success reinforced my status as the ideal girl student: hardworking, helpful, and obedient.

My time in secondary education was punctuated by a number of conflicts between school and home, stemming from little-understood cultural clashes. School uniforms have long been applauded for masking class differences and thus avoiding students' embarrassment. Yet they could not do this completely, and although the alternative may well have been worse, my parents' inability to recognize that a navy blue tunic was not always just a navy blue tunic, regardless of its place of purchase, was a major bone of contention between us. They ridiculed the idea of wearing a hat to school and refused to waste money on another when I had outgrown my first. I never did grow into the regulation coat that was bought too many sizes too big for me! Looking back, I can only agree with their position, although for different reasons; the uniforms and rules relating to girls' behavior were class based, designed to mold us into young ladies. At the time, however, my homemade tunic and lack of headgear were a source of much shame. Another conflict was caused by incomplete homework: the difficulty of finding somewhere to study at home received no consideration—a small three-bedroom place in Dagenham, inadequately heated and housing six people, afforded little space for a girl to do her homework.

Perhaps the rawest aspect of my working-class travails at grammar school was money itself. Teachers appeared to assume that the extra costs of school excursions and outings, cooking ingredients, and special sporting equipment could readily be absorbed by the students' families. The hardship that many of us faced in our attempts to find the money was never even considered, let alone addressed. Most of the middle-class teachers seemed to have no comprehension of the realities of our lives outside school. Indeed, I once was summoned to the office of the deputy headmistress and upbraided for my greed at working on Saturdays rather than representing the school at hockey.

Clearly, she remonstrated, my priorities were awry, I did not have the right attitude for university or college. But working on Saturday mornings instead of going to the hockey field was not a free choice. My parents believed it only right that I should contribute to my upkeep, particularly after my decision to spend unnecessary extra years at school. I was mortified by the deputy's criticisms but felt completely unable to tell her that my family needed the money I earned. Now I am angry at her lack of understanding and her insensitivity to the material constraints limiting the lives of many of her students. I am sad at the shame and awkwardness she engendered in the lives of those she was supposed to help.

Other staff occasionally enraged me even then by offhand comments about "us" or "people like us" being scum, arguing that raising our aspirations was wrong, futile, misplaced. Maybe my fuming indicates that the dominant hegemony was not completely successful and that at times, I was able to resist. Mostly I did not. The rewards of succeeding were too great and too necessary to me; I was more than prepared to swallow my unformed class awareness to get them.

Gender awareness was, at that time, nonexistent. So natural a division was gender that I gave it little if any thought: whether it was for lining up for registration, sports, assembly, or, more significantly, course choices, we split "naturally" along gender lines, just as described by Delamont in *Sex Roles and the School*. The head of the school, the overall boss, was male, and he was assisted by a faithful female, who looked after the girls' affairs. We all knew that those girls who studied science subjects did so only to spend time with the boys and were therefore "fast" and to be avoided. Maintaining our reputations was all-important—certainly more important than pursuing a fleeting, futile interest in physics. Much feminist research has since documented the way that male definitions of females, especially those with sexual innuendoes, control girls in coeducational schools (see, for example, Lees 1987).

It was not only the male students who hindered the girls' pursuit of science subjects; the (male) science teachers did so as well. I became one of three female students to take chemistry at high school in order to fulfill the requirement to take one science course. No budding Marie Curie, I had no drawing skills, so I was reluctant to take biology and be unable to sketch plant life or various reproductive organs with any degree of accuracy. Physics was a complete mystery, so chemistry it was. The chemistry teacher sat the three girls at the front of the lab and got the "dizzy dames," as he liked to call us, to do the experiments first, to demonstrate to the serious (male) students what not to do.

Confronting that pressure, we often conformed to these lowly expectations—expectations voiced "only in fun," of course. Although embarrassed and humiliated, we did not have the framework to contest this treatment as sexist, as harassment. Instead, we bore it bravely, and working in this hostile environment and under these handicaps, we were determined to pass. I did—with 50 percent. I was not in the least surprised to read Pratt's (1985) findings that science teachers are the most conservative of all teachers and that the Girls into Science and Technology project (Kelly 1987) failed to alter this conservatism in any fundamental way. My determination to pass this hated subject, to spite the hated teacher, and to prove that the dizzy dames were not so dizzy, did later, however, cause me to read with some misgivings feminist theories about sex role socialization that see socialization into dominant modes as unproblematic and that constantly consign girls to the victim role. My attitude toward the chemistry curriculum was just an extreme example of my attitude toward the high school curriculum in general. None of it seemed in any way relevant to my life, its usefulness restricted to its ability to allow me to pass the necessary exams. I certainly enjoyed some courses more than others, but never did it register that they should or did have any application to my own life.

And in the end, pass the exams I did. At sixteen I had achieved eight O levels, and my father got me a full-time job in a bank. I, however, dreamed of further study, of A levels and teachers college, and rejected the common working-class wisdom that I should enter the workforce and pay back my parents for allowing me to continue at school longer than strictly necessary. I did not take up the bank job. At that time—the early 1960s—academic success was no guarantee of continuing study even for middle-class girls. For those girls whose families were struggling and scrimping, thoughts of indulging in schooling were heretical. But even in the face of scathing criticism and sly cynicism, stay on at school I did. Sad old clichés about wasting education on a girl echoed constantly around our Dagenham home, and angry voices condemned my selfishness at allowing my parents to continue to support me. Surely I would be destined to leave anyway and become an overeducated wife.

The path from the working class to the middle class is marked "Teachers College, this way," and it would have been my way, had it not been for my history teacher. Himself from the working class, he encouraged me to think of applying for university. But thinking about the application process was easier then than thinking about what university might be or mean. Looking back, it is incredible, and I am incredulous how hazy my knowledge of university actually was. I knew nothing more than that I had to go there if I wanted to fulfill my dreams and escape the poverty and narrowness of working-class life. With the help of scholarships and no small amount of determination and resilience, I went. It was there that I came crashing down to near total disaster. Adrift, reeling, alone, I found my early days of university like nothing I had ever experienced. The culture shock was all-encompassing, my alienation complete.

Like all universities, then and now, Nottingham University was a thoroughly middle-class institution, desperately aping Oxbridge. As a first-year female, I was assigned to a single-sex residence hall. Its pretensions I now recognize as merely that. Dressing for dinner was mandatory, and whereas some—including my reluctant roommate—had problems deciding what to wear, my choice was always the dress I hadn't worn the day before. I arrived at university proud of the two new dresses that my mother had made for me and that were the only dresses I had. Familiarity soon bred contempt—in me and in my fellow residents. My humiliation at my restricted wardrobe was compounded by the completely foreign experience of being "waited on." The opportunities for working-class girls to dine in restaurants were limited and for me, nonexistent, and I knew nothing about the niceties of dining etiquette. I shudder at the memories even now and become again an uncouth lout unsure about glasses and forks and bread and butter.

Bourdieu's concepts of cultural capital and habitus discussed earlier never rang truer. It was as though the other students of Nottingham spoke another language, and to some degree they did, as Bernstein's (1973) work on codes reveals. He argues that different social classes generate distinct forms of communication, that is, different linguistic codes. Whereas the working class generates a "restricted" code that relies on shared meanings and assumptions, the "elaborated" code of the middle class makes meanings explicit, specific, and highly individuated. If my feelings of dislocation were delayed and occurred at university rather than at school (as experienced by Bourdieu's and Bernstein's research subjects), I attributed it to the fact that during my time at school, because of its geographical location, I was surrounded by children from not too dissimilar backgrounds. At university, however, I was one of a very rare breed.

University caused me problems beyond class. I had no vocabulary to describe it in that way at the time, but Nottingham was an inherently sexist institution. We took turns to sit at the High Table over dinner, so that we would learn the Art of Conversation when our husbands brought home colleagues, the boss, or other important people. That we learned this art from the hall's unmarried female warden, who was pursuing an immensely successful academic career, added irony to the proceedings. Female students were not allowed to go into "digs" until their third year, and then only if the university deemed them suitable. Flats were never suitable. So as residents in an establishment quite archaic even at that time, we had to obey rigid rules and regulations that included no men in the rooms after 7:00 P.M. unless chaperoned, males outlawed altogether after 10:00 P.M., and a strict curfew of 10:30 P.M. unless special permission was granted. These rules applied exclusively to women's halls of residences; the men came and went as they pleased at theirs.

I did not have one female lecturer during my years at Nottingham.

I never felt I belonged and floundered trying to make sense of most of my study there and received very little guidance in my struggles. In fact, I got the opposite. At the end of my first term at university, I was asked by the warden of the hall if I thought I was suited to academic study. But I did complete the course and graduated with a mediocre honors degree in history. Only later, when I studied for a masters in education, was my love of study rekindled.

My aim in telling this tale is not to tell it as a success story but, rather, to emphasize the myriad obstacles that working-class children must overcome to be successful at school. Then there were the other costs, such as the pain of alienation from parents, families, and community and never quite belonging anywhere again. I am not convinced that much has changed. Thirty years later, working-class children certainly attend universities in higher numbers, but the percentage is still low, even in Australia, where I live now—a country thought to be egalitarian (Aspin 1993). Even when they do attend, they do so with a lower rate of success than their non-working-class peers. And they are more likely to withdraw from their studies and are much less likely to progress to higher degrees, as a detailed analysis of the statistics of my own university have shown (Planning Unit 1996). In my view, the tendency in the Western world to move tertiary education to a "user pays" basis makes the possibility of equitable access to and outcomes from tertiary education for the working class even more remote.

Bibliography
Arnot, Madeleine, and Gaby Weiner. *Gender and the Politics of Schooling.* London: Hutchinson in association with Open University Press, 1987.
Aspin, Lois. *Focus on Australian Society.* Melbourne: Longman Cheshire, 1993.
Barton, Len, Roland Meighan, and Stephen Walker, eds. *Schooling, Ideology, and the Curriculum.* London: Falmer, 1980.

Bernstein, Basil. *Class, Codes, and Control.* Vol. 2. London: Routledge & Kegan Paul, 1973.

Bourdieu, Pierre. "The School as a Conservative Force." In *Schooling and Capitalism,* edited by Roger Dale, Geoff Esland, and Madeleine MacDonald. London: Routledge & Kegan Paul in association with Open University Press, 1976.

———. *Reproduction in Education, Society, and Culture.* London: Sage, 1977.

Bowles, Sam, and Herbert Gintis. *Schooling in Capitalist America.* New York: Basic Books, 1976.

Crowther Report. Central Advisory Council for Education (England). London: HMSO, 1959–1960.

Dale, Roger, Geoff Esland, and Madeleine MacDonald. *Schooling and Capitalism.* London: Routledge & Kegan Paul in association with Open University Press, 1976.

Delamont, Sara. *Sex Roles and the School.* London: Methuen, 1980.

Douglas, James W. B. *The Home and the School.* London: MacGibbon and Kee, 1964.

Floud, Jean, A. H. Halsey, and F. Martin. *Social Class and Educational Opportunity.* London: Heinemann, 1956.

Gaskell, Jane, and Ann McLaren, eds. *Women and Education: A Canadian Perspective.* Calgary: Datselig, 1987.

Halsey, A. H., Jean Floud, and Arnold C. Anderson. *Education, Economy, and Society.* London: Free Press, 1961.

Jackson, Brian, and Dennis Marsden. *Education and the Working Class.* Harmondsworth: Penguin, 1966.

Kamin, Leon. *The Science and Politics of I.Q.* New York: Hallsted Press, 1974.

Kelly, Alison, ed. *Science for Girls?* Milton Keynes: Open University Press, 1987.

Kelly, Alison, Judith Whyte, and Barbara Smail. "Girls into Science and Technology: Final Report." In *Science for Girls?* edited by A. Kelly. Milton Keynes: Open University Press, 1987.

Lees, Sue. "The Structure of Social Relations in School." In *Gender and the Politics of Schooling,* edited by Madeleine Arnot and Gaby Weiner. London: Hutchinson in association with Open University Press, 1987.

Macdonald, Madeline. "Schooling and the Reproduction of Class and Gender Relations." In *Schooling, Ideology, and the Curriculum,* edited by Len Barton, Roland Meighan, and Stephen Walker. London: Palmer, 1980.

Planning Unit, University of South Australia. *Equity & Access in the University of South Australia.* Adelaide: University of South Australia, 1996.

Pratt, John. "The Attitudes of Teachers." In *Girl Friendly Schooling,* edited by J. Whyte et al. London: Methuen, 1985.

Robbins Report. Committee on Higher Education. *Higher Education: A Report.* London: HMSO, 1963.

Seabrook, Jeremy. *Working Class Childhood.* London: Gollancz, 1982.

Sennett, Richard, and Jonathan Cobb. *The Hidden Injuries of Class.* New York: Vintage Books, 1972.

Steedman, Carolyn. *Childhood, Culture, and Class in Britain.* London: Virago, 1990.

————. *Landscape for a Good Woman*. London: Virago, 1986.

Walker, Stephen, and Len Barton, eds. *Gender, Class, and Education*. New York: Free Press, 1983.

Walkerdine, Valerie, and Helen Lucey. *Democracy in the Kitchen*. London: Virago, 1989.

Whyte, Judith, et al., eds. *Girl Friendly Schooling*. London: Methuen, 1985.

Williams, Raymond. "Base and Superstructure in Marxist Cultural Theory." In *Schooling and Capitalism*, edited by Roger Dale, Geoff Esland, and Madeleine MacDonald. London: Routledge & Kegan Paul in association with Open University Press, 1976.

Willmott, Peter. *The Evolution of a Community: A Study of Dagenham After Forty Years*. London: Routledge & Kegan Paul, 1963.

Willmott, Peter, and Michael Young. *Family and Kinship in East London*. London: Routledge & Kegan Paul, 1957.

Young, Michael. *The Rise of the Meritocracy*. London: Hutchinson, 1958.

Maureen Dyer is an adjunct scholar at the University of South Australia, Magill. From 1994–97, she was director of the university's Centre for Gender Studies.

The Not-So-Distant Mirror: Teaching Medieval Studies in the Working-Class Classroom

Carolyn E. Whitson

When I was a graduate student supporting myself by teaching at a junior college, the faculty at both my university and the community college considered medieval studies, my field, to be "too hard" for junior college students. Or if my colleagues didn't say that it was too hard, then they would deem medieval studies "too irrelevant"—not only having no relationship to their lives as modern people but also having no use even as a mental exercise, such as reading Shakespeare might have. I began to wonder why medieval studies was considered a waste of time for junior college students but not for entry-level freshmen. And I wondered about all those people I saw at Renaissance and Celtic fairs who had more than a passing interest in and knowledge of the premodern who did not appear to be professors.

At the university where I studied and was a teaching assistant, medievalist scholarship and course work were tolerated but regarded by most of the more hip students and faculty as being the last bastion of elitism, of caring about what dead white males wrote when they were semiliterate and even more barbaric than they were thought to be now. None except those already in the know, or who had taken a course because it was held at a convenient time, had any idea that women, non-Europeans, non-Christians, gay people, or peasants might be feasible subjects of study in the medievalist's classroom. The events and artifacts of that time were at best curiosities, confirmations of a backward time that someone, one supposed, could spend time researching so the rest of us would know where we'd been, never to go back. Those who did study the medieval period were considered eccentric but perhaps admirably rigorous with themselves, since it was so pedantic and obscure a subject. Any students who wished to indulge in the impractical luxury of such studies were hoped to have parents who could support them. In sum, the attitude that the many nonmedievalists in the academy had toward medieval studies was that it was a suitable occupation for the idle rich, of whom it was primarily the study, anyway. Their sentiments about junior college students were that their skills

were too limited and they were too oppressed to appreciate or benefit from such a rarefied field.

The views of most junior college instructors were even more con-
descending: they felt that working-class students (and that's what most
of these students were) couldn't, nor should they, study anything so
difficult or so specific in literature that wasn't directly related to their
lives and the skills they needed for good jobs. To me, this smacked of
utilitarianism—don't waste the nonelite's time with elite culture. What
was fashionable in teaching was composition classes that invited students to psychologize themselves or reading and writing courses that
were designed to politically agitate the students. Over the years I had
dutifully and even enthusiastically taught such courses, but I found
that my students were not thanking me for such instruction—they had
come to learn something and didn't like being considered little
oppressed people who needed their condition explained to them by
some nice white lady graduate student.

In the spring of 1991, I decided to defy all the conventional wisdom
and base my composition course on medieval studies, in a course I
called "The History of Love and Selfhood." My intention was for my
students to consider and write about these two subjects, which in my
experience are of keen interest to them (particularly the young
adults), but rather than having the course devolve into a consciousness-raising session or a cross-gendered harangue, we would read
medieval works on romantic love between individuals and speculate
how such literature arose out of a tradition that had previously concerned itself with wars; having taken this in, we would explore how or
whether things had changed much in the ensuing centuries. What
actually happened in that course (and its subsequent incarnations)
was far more surprising and, to use a hackneyed word, empowering,
than any of us (I, the students, or my pessimistic colleagues) could
have predicted. This experience gave me a whole new education in
class and gender issues in pedagogy (both my own and the teaching I
received) and bears discussion here to show that students can lead a
course to a more inclusive, expansive, and fulfilling experience than
can all the educational theory and scholastic training of one teacher.

In designing the course, I had to examine carefully my own motives
for wanting to teach something against the grain of all my training and
experience. As a woman from a working-class family who had found
her way into academia, I often wondered why I myself had chosen
medieval literature, or even literature at all, over something my family would find useful and helpful to large numbers of people, rather
than something that seemed so frivolous, decorative. I came to

medieval studies through a series of happy and unhappy accidents, not the least of which was trying to find a Ph.D. adviser in literature who either was a feminist or at least liked women. At my institution, medieval literature was a venue in which I could have that. Even as an undergraduate, I had liked medieval literature because it held characters I could identify with and admire—the saucy and outspoken Wife of Bath, the smart-aleck-and-poor young scholar Handy Nicholas, the dreamy and earnest Piers the Plowman, the court jongleurs like Chrétien de Troyes who inserted their class commentary into their tales of how the privileged amused themselves. In medieval literature I found an abundance of social critique literature and debate as lively and thoughtful as today's (often more so) about gender issues, social transgressions of convention, religious freedom, and other kinds of injustice. In addition, I found a number of provocative women writers—something that survey courses in high school and college had never led me to expect. These studies gave me a long-range look at my place in society, my society's place in time, and the possibilities of knowing what had been tried and what had been found wanting.

I have used literary studies as a way to steal tools from the middle class to create a more inclusive and just world. I use the term *steal* because it was apparent throughout much of my education that people who came from the working world were supposed to stay there, to take out of education only a few points of etiquette and affectations with their job skills. Or you might be clever enough to join the middle class and "pass" as someone who fulfilled the American Puritan ideal of joining a congregation of elect individuals—anyone hardworking enough to succeed in this great, free land of ours. I found myself not wanting either to go back and be a good, literate worker or to turn my back on where I came from. So in the university, I looked for ways of thinking that I could share with students like me, that would create a community in charge of its own collective and singular destinies. Audre Lorde once said, "The Master's tools will never dismantle the Master's House" (110). I was not sure that I could dismantle it, or wanted to destroy all the achievements of that house, but I was intent on cutting some doorways, creating some ventilation—allowing currents and people to pass both in and out.

What were some of these tools that medieval studies in particular and elite education in general offered that I wanted to impart to my working-class students? They were the ability to sound out ideas for their inherent assumptions, prejudices, blindnesses; to recognize and circumvent manipulation; to meet an institution on its own terms, in its own coded speech, without buying into it; to read through history for alternative ways of life that the current day's focus of study buries, denies, and sidesteps—and to use it for one's own life design. The ability to see in art the practice of being creative in living, in shaping a future from choices not stated or established. Claiming options and changing what one has the power to participate in and create. Recovering from history the strategies that oppressed groups have used to effect social change. The ability to understand one's inner workings and passions without getting lost in narcissism or resignation. And not as a tool but as a basic human need: for beauty, harmony, and grace to be of value and to have a place in one's life.

The irony was not lost on me, then or now, that this was in many ways just a different approach to those two schools of teaching that my colleagues were using: psychologizing and politicizing. But the difference in my approach was to remodel these aims to fit an old, condemned model of educating—the symposium, the dialectic. I would invite students to explore these old ideas and to bring them together in community teaching and discussion of how these millennia-old issues described and informed their lives. At the same time, these studies would give them the analytic rigor and intellectual sophistication that would allow these students to engage in academic discussions—a possible passport to whatever they wanted from the middle-class world.

On the first night of "The History of Love and Selfhood," I had to take care of several orders of business before actually beginning the course, the most important of which was to assure the students that they were capable of reading something "old" and having something worthwhile to say about it. It seemed that they had been taught by their previous teachers that older literature was harder and less interesting; their teachers had extended their own prejudices and fears of the literature to the students and had instilled in them a learned helplessness that was more of an impediment than were any real issues of ignorance or cultural/temporal dissonance. Many students knew only that the course was "college composition" and had not checked the catalog to see what the course's subject matter would be—they were there for the credits and a convenient time slot. A few were quite angry that this course offered something different from the usual community college writing class, and some left, either intimidated or genuinely not interested. But with the remaining students I launched into a discussion of why the course would be useful to them, providing a shamelessly utilitarian list at first. I explained that the materials in this course were from eras in which writing to persuade and win arguments was a high art form—skills that would serve them well in business, school, and quite possibly at home, that being able to trace an idea through a few hundred years or more of thought would show them how to discern patterns and progressions in other events now happening around them. My two trump cards were that (1) most college teachers are secretly intimidated and impressed by anyone with a knowledge of older literature, so being able to list and discuss that material would give them a significant advantage in future classes and (2) a knowledge of the history of love and selfhood might be helpful in figuring out and managing creatively their own personal relationships. One or two of these things were motivating to the students, and from there the discussion moved to how they could work successfully with the material.

Some teachers complain that their students are shallow because they seem to be concerned only with getting good grades with as little work as possible, and not with the "higher goals" of learning. But working-class students usually are living a very different reality from that of their professors. Working-class students usually are working, and even if they are on scholarship, the institution itself has set up their educational possibilities in sharp capitalist terms—good grades mean continued support; hard courses threaten financial aid; bosses who are subsidizing their workers' educations are looking for measurable improvements in job skills, not a greater sensitivity of spirit. Moreover, the students are often cynical from years of high school busywork, admissions criteria that care more for scores and the ability to fill out a scan-tron than for what they actually think, and professors who grade according to how the students please them more than how they do the work. These students develop their behaviors and values in education out of feeling burned and needing to survive. In order for the students to engage in any of these more philosophical/psychological/political conversations, I had to demonstrate that I, as their instructor, could deliver the things that were of value to them in the course—those things necessary to their survival and success—so that they could relax enough to participate in and discover the joy of intellectual discussion.

This trust was partly won by my frank discussion about why the course would be helpful to them. The other way I tried to win their trust was by presenting them with a medieval text in translation that they could walk through with me to discuss its points, structure, and style. This piece was a fairly lengthy excerpt from Andreas Capellanus's *Art of Courtly Love*, which I prefaced by explaining its social realities—that Andreas was a court chaplain in an age when a powerful court was intent on institutionalizing love as a kind of intense game among privileged individuals and that he was likely commissioned to write the piece to instruct a young male noble in how to love "properly."

Students identify quite strongly with Andreas's assertion that "Love is a certain inborn suffering derived from the sight of and excessive meditation upon the beauty of the opposite sex, which causes each one to wish above all things the embraces of the other and by common desire to carry out all of love's precepts in the other's embrace" (28). They latch on to the words *suffering, excessive meditation, beauty, opposite sex, wish,* and *embrace*. But the sentence itself is abstract, formal, and (toward the end) obscure for them on the first reading. Our job at this point was to pick apart what was said there and assess it for accuracy.

When I had gay students who were both out and outspoken, they contested the stipulation that only opposite sexes could love—and later in the text Andreas asserts that this must be so, according to "nature." The ideas that love must involve beauty, suffering, and sex were also called into question. We then speculated on who Andreas—a priest with a vow of celibacy—was to say what love was, and asked what these rules were based on, anyway. Women in the class often pointed out that the passage suggested that love was something that men did and that women had visited upon them, or were used as props for, since this inborn suffering was predicated on the "sight and excessive meditation" on beauty, and little actual interaction.

At the end of forty-five minutes or so of our working as a group to figure out what was going on in this piece, I would point out to the students the structure of Andreas's argument, that he defined and regulated a topic by

> consider[ing] what love is, whence it gets its name, what the effect of love is, between what persons love may exist, how it may be acquired, retained, increased, decreased, and ended, what are the signs that one's love is returned, and what one of the lovers ought to do if the other is unfaithful. (Capellanus 28)

The chaplain's rhetorical form and style in the text are clear, and they speak volumes about how he views himself as a writer, how he views authority, and what he thinks will sway his young noble audience. In addition, the argumentative and rule-laden style of the treatise bothers students and often leads them to talk about how rules—like the one against homosexuality that clearly has no power whatsoever to stop such love—express fears and desires much more than what actually happens.

The passage in the excerpt from *The Art of Courtly Love* that elicits the most comment from students (and, indeed, was selected for just

that purpose) is entitled "The Love of Peasants," which was clearly
designed, as with the stricture against homosexuality, to make such
love impossible, not to show why it wasn't possible:

> [I]t rarely happens that we find farmers serving in Love's court, but
> naturally, like a horse or mule, they give themselves up to the work
> of Venus, as nature's urging teaches them to do. For a farmer hard
> labor and the uninterrupted solaces of plough and mattock are suf-
> ficient. And even if it should happen at times, though rarely, that
> contrary to their nature they are stirred up by Cupid's arrows, it is
> not expedient that they should be instructed in the theory of love,
> lest while they are devoting themselves to conduct which is not nat-
> ural to them the kindly farms which are usually made fruitful by
> their efforts may through lack of cultivation prove useless to us.
> (149–50)

This passage, even though it was written eight hundred years ago,
makes many working-class students furious, and this fury leads to the
issue I want to discuss—how workers are represented in literature, in
intellectual discourse, in the academy. Without any modern politicizing, consciousness-raising, or nosy inquiries into my students' personal
feelings, a passionate, text-based, and analytically sophisticated discussion can bloom. And the students' fear that they will have nothing
to say, to bring to, a discussion of medieval history of love and selfhood
evaporates. The political and personal connections soon become clear
as the students themselves do the analysis. As they introduce those connections to the classroom discussion, they demonstrate a sense of trust
in the classroom environment and in their own ability to articulate
their thoughts. If I or other students challenge them, the students
know that they themselves have invited the debate by raising the issues.

This controversial chapter of Andreas Capellanus's text concludes
with a how-to in sexual politics that brings female students—many of
whom did not consider themselves feminists—to offer arguments that
would do any women's studies classroom proud:

> And if you should, by some chance, fall in love with some of their
> women, be careful to puff them up with lots of praise and then, when
> you find a convenient place, do not hesitate to take what you seek
> and to embrace them by force. For you can hardly soften their out-
> ward inflexibility so far that they will grant you their embraces qui-
> etly or permit you to have the solaces you desire unless first you use
> a little compulsion as a cure for their shyness. We do not say these
> things, however, because we want to persuade you to love such

women, but only so that, if through lack of caution you should be driven to love them, you may know, in brief compass, what to do. (150)

Female students point to this passage as showing that Andreas is trying to create, not describe, an environment for his male audience in which differences in social station make love impossible (thereby maintaining and reinforcing the objectification and disrespect of women with a lower social status). Male students also agree that here Andreas must see the political implications of people of unequal relation being drawn to each other in equal feelings, for what he suggests as a remedy for what he portrays (probably dishonestly) as a rare, lamentable occurrence is guaranteed to kill immediately any actual love that might be present, nipping in the bud any breaking down of social barriers.

"The History of Love and Selfhood" course really began with a text that was not medieval—Plato's *Symposium*. I chose it as a representation of ways of exploring how, whom, and why to love that was quite different from the medieval paradigm whose assumptions remain, for the most part, in operation today.

The Symposium at first appeared to my students as a daunting text—its style of discussing an issue like love seemed stuffy and alien to them (this is as much the fault of pedantic translators as it is the students' preparation for such material). But once they had read far enough to reach the stories being told at the party, the students began to relax and enjoy the competition among the drinkers for the best panegyric to love. Informed by the issues raised in their discussion of Andreas, the students were curious to know who these people were who had no jobs (by their standards) and who had such bizarre drinking competitions. All were surprised by, and many attracted to, the Greeks' propositions about how to look at love, and especially to how one speaker made loyalty such a high priority.

Phaedrus frames love as an instrument that can make citizens of greater value to their culture—a conclusion quite the opposite from that of Andreas Capellanus centuries later. Phaedrus declares:

> The principle which ought to guide the whole life of those who intend to live nobly cannot be implanted either by family or by position or by wealth or by any other means so effectively as love.... I mean the principle which inspires shame at what is disgraceful and ambition for what is noble; without these feelings neither a state nor an individual can accomplish anything great or fine. (Plato 42)

Phaedrus then states that the most noble and effective army one could assemble would be an army of lovers, for they would do anything to avoid appearing shameful in their beloved's eyes and would have intense loyalty to each other. For many working-class students, this idea of fierce loyalty and embattledness struck a chord, for it reflected one of the greatest and most precious aspects of their life (their love relationships) as ennobling, motivating—not as the empty diversion that movies and commercials make them out to be. For the students working while they go to school at jobs they don't like, their love relationships—particularly with spouses and children—are the motivation for being "good," dedicated, for getting an education (after forty hours at the factory) in order to "better" themselves.

Not all students were quite so charmed with Phaedrus's speech; some were offended or incredulous when it became apparent that the army of lovers would be all men or that the state would have a cynical interest in using people's affections to its own advantage. Women, understandably, took issue throughout the text at the fact that ennobling love was the sole property of men and that women were used as bodies and were not considered capable of higher expressions of love. All this led to two weeks of discussion on how sexuality was and is institutionalized to create or foster certain values that benefit a ruling class or government. That men loving men was considered the height of masculinity in ancient Greece but is the depth of effeminacy (that this is an insult speaks volumes) in our time moved the students to thoughtful debate on how varying opinions on the same behavior over time could pertain more to a society's political needs than to any sort of truth. For Greek men, erotic relationships and loving devotion fostered a sense of equality and enhanced their public lives, whereas women had a use in private life and traveled in different spheres that gave them lives that little resembled in opportunity or values that of men. From this, love came to be a matter of relatedness or exchange that was about growth, a luxury that only free men could enjoy, whereas marriage was about maintaining a household and a dynasty. Students wanted to claim this male model of love for their own relationships (regardless of their sexuality), but they also wanted to take issue with its exclusionary, limited quality, its status as a privilege and not a right. In this respect, *The Symposium* did not offer anything better than courtly love.

By starting with a classical text, I was able to dislodge the concept that history is a steady, progressive trajectory toward a completely democratic and equal society. Students were shocked at the idea that they would prefer an older culture to a more recent one, that a culture so different from this one could offer something they preferred to their conventional romantic model. *The Symposium* gave me the opportunity to set up an array of ways of looking at love that challenged modern assumptions: it introduced the idea that we could apply some rational intentionality to love, that it wasn't something that just landed on us and entrapped us into a set way of being; it upset the assumption that love was only about relationships that could lead to the institutionally sanctioned passing on of wealth to offspring; it offered the idea that love could lead us to be productive in the world in a creative and responsible way, that it wasn't just a self-absorbing diversion; it differentiated love into loves for different times of life and for different kinds of enrichment (students were delighted to find a range of terms for love, whereas in their own language one bland word had to cover all kinds of feelings, from the erotic to the sublime to personal food preferences). All these models of love led the students to reevaluate the limited vision of how loves and selves are supposed to be in this culture—and, most important to them, who would have the privilege of enjoying or choosing from the widest range of possibilities for fulfillment. The text of *The Symposium* gave them a taste of how to discuss personal feelings in analytical, intellectual forms, so that in their papers they were eager to try this style of debating issues to argue with Plato and Andreas.

With *The Symposium*'s alternatives set in place, students were able to return to the medieval construction of courtly love with concerns and criteria that they could use to critique the stories. Courtly love occurs in the romances of Marie de France, Chrétien de Troyes, and Beroul as a game that idle married nobles played to pass the time. Moreover, the inherent deception and corruption that spring from these diversions made it difficult for even the most confirmed romantics in the class to support wholeheartedly lovers such as Tristan and Yseut, Guinevere and Lancelot.

I had two assignments for playing out my students' conflict over being all for true love but being against its use as an excuse to mistreat others. The first assignment was to divide the class in half and stage a debate over whether Tristan and Yseut (as portrayed in Beroul's *Romance of Tristan*) were justified in their betrayal of king, family, and country in the name of their love. In this debate, I did not let students choose their sides but arbitrarily divided the room, for (as I told them) the purpose of the exercise was to practice making arguments, not to assert beliefs. Having to work to see the reasoning behind a position with which they disagreed would, in fact, be an even better exercise for them if that was where they found themselves in the debate.

Making personal opinion in the matter a side issue allowed students to engage in this academic exercise as a game. My hope was that they would come to see how, as in *The Symposium,* intellectual discussions often contain that element, for this realization would give them freedom to approach more intimidating academic situations with more playfulness, with less feeling that they had to fight for their viewpoints as a struggle for survival or visibility in the classroom. Although that struggle may indeed have been taking place, to approach it with fear and seriousness would not ensure any more success than would learning how to "play the game."

The second assignment came at the end of the term when, after the students had read eight or nine courtly romances, I asked them to write a paper on whether courtly love was a destructive social force undertaken for selfish or diversionary reasons or a positive, revolutionary force that changed people's concepts of themselves as constituents of a society. I received the full gamut of answers. Those who felt that courtly love came out of real feelings, giving them a place in culture and literature but nonetheless undermining the social institutions they believed in (marriage, patriotism, religious morality), focused on lovers from the texts who abused others in the pursuit of their relationships. The most lambasted lovers were Beroul's Tristan and Yseut. Yseut plotted to silence Brangain—the loyal servant who offered her virginity to help Yseut conceal her infidelity on her wedding night—by having her murdered. In the tale, Brangain's humble loyalty so shames Yseut's selfishness that she is spared. Tristan not only cuckolds his own uncle but also maliciously murders anyone who seeks to expose his treason to King Mark. Both of them engage in elaborate games of theatrical deception and blasphemy, mocking the people they deceive. Students who condemned these courtly lovers pointed to these characters' attitude of being "above the law" or their "unearned sense of privilege." Some wrote excellent papers claiming that the true heroes of Beroul's text were Brangain and Governal, the lovers' servants, who offered their loyalty and self-sacrifice, in contrast to the egotistical nobles.

Those who felt courtly love was a revolutionary force for the good tended to defend Tristan and Yseut as caught in political machinations (arranged marriage, treaty making) that made their humanity subordinate to the desires of those in power. But those who wished to make a case for courtly love looked to *Erec and Enide* by Chrétien de Troyes. Erec and Enide are unmarried when they meet and fall in love, but their troubles begin when they continue to act like lovers after they are married. The students who used this story for their papers argued

that Erec's marrying Enide for love and admiration of her particular
qualities over her impoverished minor nobility and political anonymity
greatly improved Arthur's court and ultimately Erec's kingship. The
story moves from the beginning, when Erec has all the power and
Enide the beauty and wisdom, to when he enshrines her as his courtly
mistress (and his wife)—giving her power over him, to when they disagree over what their relationship is going to be—love or marriage—
and go off on a quest as two knights together, seeking a resolution in
which they can have both and, as anachronistic as it may sound, live as
equals. Working-class students identified strongly with Enide, who
emerges from the sewing room in a worn and poor tunic to greet Erec
and is then instructed by her father to "take [Erec's] horse and stable
it with those of mine. Take off its saddle and bridle and give it oats and
hay. Tend and curry it so it's well-groomed" (de Troyes 6). Even though
her father has rank (albeit low), Enide must work. But she is smart and
rhetorically savvy, and in most of the story, Chrétien and all his characters have to find a place for her wise voice at the court. Some students who argued for courtly love as a revolutionary force used Enide
to counter Andreas Capellanus's instructions that nobles use, not love,
women who work.

My working-class students interpreted these texts in ways that I
rarely encountered in my own training or study. They noticed characters who were minor: sharp-tongued dwarfs and lowly workers, perhaps just parodies of peasants who were largely invisible; servants who
displayed more courtesy than did lords and ladies; women stripped of
their status by men for some real or imagined transgression (often simple ugliness) who roamed the countryside giving knights prophetic
castigations; minor citizens incidentally liberated from sweatshops (as
in Chrétien's *Yvain*) or from being held hostage (*The Knight of the
Cart*), even though the main action centers on the nobles' pursuit of
love. Along with these characters, often sympathetically portrayed, who
gave those who work some presence in the stories of the grand drama
of the court, students noted when the nobility were ridiculed. In *The
Knight of the Cart*, Chrétien subtly mocks nobles at play while the kingdom is in turmoil around them: "In this meadow were maidens,
knights and damsels playing at various games, for it was a beautiful
place. It was not just frivolous amusements they were in engaged in,
but backgammon and chess, or, in other cases, dice games of different types" (207). There were hoots of derision in the classroom at the
idea of a serious game of backgammon. These small, seemingly throw-
away, moments in the writings of Chrétien de Troyes led us to conclude that Chrétien wrote for the nobility as a job but did not feel

compelled to subordinate himself to them and cater to their self-indulgence, as Andreas Capellanus did.

The students' discussions of love and work and their research on premodern life gave them a structure in which to consider concepts of a self that was essential to any discussion of love and society. The texts and topics I used in the course showed the importance of the external conditions of one's being (gender, age, class, birth order) in determining one's internal shaping. Marriage and early concepts of success in courtly love were predicated on one's looks, wealth, and position; only generosity and verbal skill seemed to be individual qualities that could make a difference in wooing. That observation provoked in students great concern about whether and how those external markers today have as much influence on internal traits.

Besides using texts to teach literary analysis, academic speaking, and composition to students, I added a series of guest speakers and performers to give the history a fuller scope and reality for them. I had colleagues come in to talk about how they used medieval history in women's studies and theology—to show them that medieval history wasn't just my own eccentric obsession. I also invited people in the Society for the Creative Anachronism, antique-weapons buffs, and Morris dancers to demonstrate crafts, fighting styles, music, and costume. These things, along with my own slides of medieval architecture, gave students a sense that an interest in history could take on a life outside books and the classroom.

The ultimate achievement of the course was the students' independent research and presentation on a topic of their choice in medieval or classical culture. What emerged from those projects were studies that vastly increased my knowledge of premodern cultures, for many students explored avenues of history that had some relationship to their own lives—and their lives were typically overlooked in university curricula. Students were encouraged to choose some aspect of their own life that was significant to them and to trace its existence back to the Middle Ages or ancient Greece. Presentations by Muslim students on the influence of Islam on medieval European culture gave us insight into courtly love, the history of mathematics, architecture, and music. Women students' presentations on the history of women's sexuality, marriage, and the laws affecting women drew the whole class into lengthy, animated discussions. Some might see these presentations as opportunities for students to engage in identity politics, but the spirit in the classroom was one of discovery and sharing, not indoctrination.

I received an education from my students in aspects of the Middle Ages that conventional university classes have seldom touched on: the

Spanish Jews' disputations with the Catholic church, peasant culture, women-run businesses, child-rearing practices, lay education and occupational literacy, and textile production. The "History of Love and Selfhood" class had an open structure that allowed students both to pursue their own intellectual interests that honored and used their own experiences and to participate in academic analysis in a way that allowed them to derive from the institution a satisfying learning experience that would prepare them to move in a middle-class and elite culture. My experience as a professor in the working-class classroom has led me to conclude that in most cases the students themselves point the way to a far more "cutting-edge" and intellectually dynamic curriculum than many universities, even those with commitments to diversity of representation in the curriculum, can imagine.

NOTE
My thanks to Valerie Ross at the University of California, Santa Cruz, for her numerous contributions to my thinking on this text and for her great lectures in my "History of Love and Selfhood" course over the years.

Works Cited

Beroul. *The Romance of Tristan.* New York: Penguin, 1981.

Capellanus, Andreas. *The Art of Courtly Love,* edited by John Jay Parry. New York: Columbia University Press, 1990.

Chrétien de Troyes. *Arthurian Romances,* edited by D. D. R. Owen. New York: Everyman Classics, 1987.

Lorde, Audre. *Sister Outsider.* New York: Crossing Press, 1984.

Marie de France. *The Lais of Marie de France,* edited by Robert Hanning and Joan Ferrante. Durham, NC: Labyrinth Press, 1982.

Plato. *The Symposium.* New York: Penguin Classics, 1951.

Carolyn E. Whitson is an assistant professor in literature, women's studies, and the humanities at Metropolitan State University. She writes a feminist book review column for La Gazette, *a central California women's newspaper, and has published poetry in* Matrix *and* Porter Gulch Review. *She is currently working on a book on critical approaches to working-class literature.*

Identity and Politics in the *Silent Worker* Newspaper: Print Publication and the Laboring Deaf Body

Terry Easton

> *Deaf indeed are they who do not hear the desperation in the voice of the people crying out against cruel poverty and social injustice. Dull indeed are their hearts who turn their backs upon misery and support a system that grinds the life and soul out of men and women.*
>
> —Helen Keller, Address at the Sociological Conference,
> Sagamore Beach, Massachusetts, 1913

It should come as no surprise to students of American politics and labor history that the title of the periodical *Silent Worker* changed to the *Deaf American* in 1964. Some particularly keen students, especially those sympathetic to the laboring or working classes, might even ask why the original title was kept for so long. This question elicits a framework for thinking about connections between disability and social class in the United States. At first glance, social class might seem disassociated from, or at least to some degree irrelevant to, an inquiry into disability. To the contrary, however, recent scholarship in the emerging field of disability studies illuminates symbiotic relationships between social class and disability. Statistics indicate, for example, that deaf workers are generally found in low-paying, unskilled, semiskilled, or otherwise manual jobs that pay only 72 percent as much as do similar jobs held by their hearing counterparts. In addition, a rather startling statistic shows that deaf women, on average, are 50 percent more likely to be unemployed than hearing women are.[1]

What do these facts have to do with the transformation of the *Silent Worker* into the *Deaf American*? The *Silent Worker* and the *Deaf American*—publications for, by, and about the deaf—have played vital roles in the way that the deaf community has located itself both within and against American society. My aim in this essay is to show how the *Silent Worker* and the *Deaf American* have located (and in some sense have created) deaf workers in the American workforce.

In 1891 the students and faculty at the New Jersey School for the Deaf began publishing a newspaper, the *Silent Worker*.[2] Besides providing a forum for the activities and news in and around the school, the newspaper paid particular attention to the role of work in the students' lives. By teaching students those skills basic to printing, woodworking, shoemaking, dressmaking, sewing, embroidery, and other manual activities, the school helped ensure the students' employability after graduation. Following up on this training, the newspaper's editorial pages and industrial page urged the students to become model workers and citizens by cultivating characteristics such as honesty, industriousness, reliability, temperance, and pride. Manual labor, then, played a major role in forming students' awareness of their identity in the deaf community while establishing their projected role in the workforce after graduation.

Robert Buchanan's 1993 article "The *Silent Worker* Newspaper and the Building of a Deaf Community: 1890–1929" offers readers a solid historical foundation for this publication's early years. Buchanan documents issues important to the New Jersey School, the *Silent Worker*, and the deaf community. In her article "Vocational Education in the Deaf American and African-American Communities" Tricia A. Leakey explains the similarities between vocational education for African Americans and deaf Americans in the late nineteenth and early twentieth centuries. Central to both articles, though not always stated explicitly, is the idea that deafness has been constructed as a stigma that must be overcome for acceptance into the hearing society. Neither of these articles deals specifically with the way that bodies, particularly deaf and laboring bodies, intersect with and are acted on by political, economic, and social forces.

Michel Foucault's notion that bodies are a battlefield heads in the right direction. Lennard J. Davis extends Foucauldian principles to disability studies, claiming that "the disabled body is not a discrete object but rather a set of social relations" (11). Without question, throughout recorded history the deaf body has been a site of contestation and evolving social relations. In the twentieth century, deaf bodies have been fought over by audist educators, medical "experts," eugenicists, legislators, captains of industry, and an array of middle-class "professionals."[3] For example, in March 1902, a *Silent Worker* writer questioned the findings of a doctor who had recently given a lecture in England entitled "The Survival of the Unfit." The doctor regarded with fear his findings demonstrating that "the deaf are not increasing in proportion to the general population, but at a much more rapid rate." The editorial response was typical:

If the deaf were less good, less thrifty, less law-abiding, less honest, or less fit, in any way, than those who hear, we might be tempted to look askance at [the doctor's] figures, but statistics do not show such to be the case, and until they do we may regard with complacency that the physical condition of deaf children is kept at its best in American schools for the deaf.

This example—only one among many—demonstrates how deaf writers and others have thought about the deaf body. Working against commonly held perceptions that the deaf were not fully human, *Silent Worker* writers cited examples, from a network of contributors around the world, of the individual and collective accomplishments of the deaf. Their strategies centered on the notion that the deaf could become fully engaged, functional, productive, and reproductive citizens.

Erving Goffman helps us think through disability as a lived process that is subject to evolving social relations: "The normal and the stigmatized are not persons but rather perspectives" (138). Clearly, residential school educators and *Silent Worker* writers felt that perspectives could be altered, shifted, and ultimately transformed. Based on the popular belief that labor power enhanced the likelihood of altering audist perceptions of the deaf, residential schools focused on training students in trades that would ensure employment after graduation. In July 1910, for example, the New Jersey School's superintendent, John Walker, stated that an "especial work of the school is to take the deaf child from the ranks of dependents and give it a foremost place among the wage-earning and self-supporting, and to this end every boy and girl is being given a knowledge of some useful trade" (*Silent Worker* 181). At the turn of this century, a direct link between vocational education and the labor market was firmly established. In November 1893, for example, a writer worried that students received only 2,880 hours of training per year, whereas "the ordinary working day of ten hours, for 310 days, which allows for Sundays, will make for 3100 hours" (4). In July 1914, a writer was concerned that residential schools were answering too quickly to the demands of industry by emphasizing job placement over the completion of schooling (96).

As did schools for other stigmatized or minority groups, residential schools linked education with training the body for industrial occupations. But one of the problems with this formulation, as Leakey pointed out, is that too often vocational education impeded the upward mobility of deaf workers (Leakey 76). True, deaf workers gained an economic foothold through vocational training, but as it turned out, they were less likely to hold positions necessary for establishing political power and gaining a policymaking status. In this sense, deaf persons may have lost one stigma only to win another—that of the laboring, working-class body. Buchanan makes this point when he tells us that not only were deaf laborers' job security sensitive to the rise and fall of employment during the war years but also "deaf laborers in the manufacturing sector and elsewhere may be underemployed, working in positions below their backgrounds and abilities" ("Silent Colony" 256–57). By this measure, a majority of deaf workers did not become fully functional and engaged citizens but, rather, cogs in a free-market system dominated by fierce competition, periods of unemployment, and occupational hazards.

Throughout history, the deaf body has been acted on, scrutinized, medicalized, politicized, and controlled. Although some of this control over the deaf body has been entirely physical—we might borrow Louis Althusser's notion of the repressive state apparatus to explain this—at other times, and most relevant to a study of the *Silent Worker* and the *Deaf American*, the deaf body has come under the control of various ideological state apparatuses. As stated earlier, at the turn of this century one of the main goals of education at the New Jersey School was training pupils in manual trades. In addition to reflecting these goals, the *Silent Worker* reflects the ways that through their newspaper, editors and writers aligned student production with the reproduction of workers for the industrial revolution in the United States. "Obey those who have a right to direct you . . . let us see no grumbling and no long faces, but prompt, cheerful obedience" exclaimed a *Silent Worker* writer on November 2, 1891. In this way, residential schools differed very little from hearing schools where reformers were "impelled by the desire to accommodate the young to the new industrial civilization through schooling that engendered 'respect for authority, self-control, self-discipline, self-reliance, and self-respect'" (Aronowitz 73). Of the available ideological apparatuses in the deaf community (schools, newsprint, church, home, peer groups, and the like), an educational institution and a school newspaper at the New Jersey School worked in tandem to create docile bodies that were "subjected, used, transformed and improved" (Foucault 136). Because residential school students lived on campus and because their social circles and contacts were smaller than those of hearing students, when compared with their hearing counterparts, deaf students may have been more deeply affected by these ideological apparatuses.[4]

The *Silent Worker* shows how labor and politics marked deaf bodies. A central story in the July 1904 issue of the *Silent Worker* discusses the aims of the New Jersey School, that the mere development of the mind, while almost the sole object in the speaking school, would in an institution for the deaf result in but comparatively little advantage to the child. The soul, the mind, the body, the industrial sense alike receive attention, and the effort is to bring correlation in these and the greatest perfection in each. (1)

The writer goes on to explain how deaf girls and boys are taught "some useful trade" so that they may "rise from the ranks of dependents" to gain "a foremost place among the wage-earning and self-supporting." As the writer indicates in the first passage, total penetration of the body and mind creates an "industrial sense"—a sense, I would argue, that serves first and foremost the interests of capital. Needless to say, it became a source of great pride and encouragement for residential schools that their vocational training programs were considerably more successful than those implemented at hearing schools during the nineteenth century.

Because the hearing society perceived the deaf as a stigmatized group, often associating them with "lunatics," "paupers," and "criminals," educators and writers worked hard to convince deaf students and readers that rising through the ranks of the working world was one of the few paths available to them for obtaining social legitimacy.[5] With the objective of assimilating students into mainstream society, *Silent Worker* writers and residential school educators directed students and readers to concepts sacred to the hearing community: hard work, temperance, patriotism, and religion. It is no surprise that two of these characteristics have a direct relationship to the body.

In his *Industrialism and the American Worker, 1865–1920,* Melvin Dubofsky examines some of the anxieties that industrialists faced during the shift from an essentially artisan-based workforce to an industrial one. Large industrialists, Dubofsky explains, were troubled by nineteenth-century work practices based on tradition, custom, artisan knowledge, and craft union rules. Anxious for increased production and concerned about the loss of efficiency, employers searched for ways to decrease "high labor turnover, excessive absenteeism, alcoholism, and avoidable industrial accidents" (84). The work habits and moral rectitude outlined in the pages of the *Silent Worker* confirm accusations that the roots of educational reform were located in industrialists searching for ways to increase their capital. The "Children's Code of Morals," printed in the April 1921 issue, states this case explicitly. Addressed to girls and boys, the writer says that "the Good American"

Tries to Gain and Keep Perfect Health: The welfare of the country depends upon those who try to be physically fit for their daily work. . . . [He] Controls Himself: Those who best control themselves can serve their country. . . . Is Self-Reliant. . . . Does His Duty: The shirker or the willing idler lives upon the labor of others, burdens others with the work which he ought to do himself [and] harms his fellow citizens, and so harms his country. (241)

Writers frequently correlated labor with concepts such as physical health, personal responsibility, and national unity. In the early decades of the twentieth century, Boy Scout leaders invoked similar concepts when preparing boys (and only a short time later, girls) for "productive" adult lives. Central to the Scouting philosophy was the idea that stern discipline coupled with physical fitness and an unquestioning obedience to authority made Scouts useful to employers specifically and the nation generally. Residential school administrators, like Scout leaders, readily accepted the role of preparing laboring bodies for the workforce.[6] "To march side by side with the hearing," one writer exhorted, "you need a good education and habits of industry" (November 1899, 25). Jonathan Kozol's belief that schools are in business to produce reliable people is all too pervasive here (Loewen 268).

In her turn-of-the-century articles entitled "Deaf Women and Their Work," Hypatia Boyd, a Gallaudet College graduate, offered advice and described various occupations open to women. Because she believed that a woman's "noblest position is in the home where she can advantageously wield her redeeming power and where she is sheltered from the hardening influences of the world" (September 1899, 11), Boyd's point of view limits our understanding of the way in which girls and women were perceived in the deaf community. Nonetheless, her descriptions of various occupations are revealing. For example, in November 1899, she writes that women "make life brighter and better for her fellow beings in ministering to their needs, just as the noble women of long ago ministered to Christ" (27). Against this backdrop, Boyd goes on to suggest that women, in whatever occupation, have the responsibility to "minister" to others. Clerks and typists, she suggests, might be good occupations for girls: "Such a business as the copying of manuscripts, circulars, or the addressing of envelopes, is a pleasant and profitable one, and, where desired, it can be carried on at home" (27). She closes by pointing out that these occupations can be performed both inside and outside the home, thereby showing girls that they have the option of choosing occupations that do not completely separate home and office. As the title of an article in the

July 1953 issue of the *Silent Worker* reveals ("Deaf Girls Prove Efficient Office Workers"), Boyd's advice retained relevance even at midcentury (9).

In this same article, Boyd also writes about some of the more labor-intensive occupations, such as printing, millinery, dressmaking, and laundry work. While recommending printing for its high wages and availability of positions (printing paid the highest wages and employed most of the deaf in this period and after), she also discourages it for those "whose eyes are weak" (27). Likewise, she tries to dissuade girls from seeking millinery and dressmaking positions because they "require a cultivated taste or talent in the combination, selection and effects of color" (27). Boyd is limiting earning potential (in the first example) and circumscribing class boundaries (in the second example) when making these suggestions. Offering only a short paragraph on these occupations (she writes at length about typists and clerks), she closes the paragraph with a rather telling warning regarding laundry work: "To work in a laundry," she exclaims, "one must be sure that one has a strong constitution, and is used to working all day long and often overtime" (27).

Even at this early stage in the *Silent Worker*, Boyd, like many other writers, warns against habits detrimental to production on the job. She ends this article, for example, with an anecdotal tale about a girls' after-hours business club. The women report to Boyd that they forget about work for a few hours so that "when we are back at work the next morning, we experience a delightful sense of feeling stronger . . . of course we do not overindulge in these evening pleasures too often, for in that case we would go to work worn out and sleepy" (27). To offer examples contrary to this would go against the well-understood rules of mainstreaming and maintaining exemplary images of deaf workers in the pages of the *Silent Worker*.

Boyd's writings fit comfortably within the parameters established by the growing cadre of deaf commentators. Even though she made public some of the problems plaguing industrial occupations, particularly issues women faced when working at factories before and after giving birth (September 1900, 11), she failed to recommend solutions to these and other problems. In an article entitled "As to Working in Factories," for example, she writes of "factory evils" in a manner that most Realist novelists would envy. Rather than offer solutions to the horrible working conditions, however, she concludes with a question: "Is it not much better to be a housekeeper or a chamber-maid rather than a factory hand?" (September 1900, 11). Boyd's suggestion merely shifts the burden of dangerous industrial work to others while channeling the read-

ers of the *Silent Worker* into what she considers a more appealing situation, the domestic sphere. Clearly, eliciting voices of radical dissent was
not the main objective in Boyd's writings. There were, however, other
candidates for radical thought.[7]

From December 22, 1892, until the early 1920s, Helen Keller's name
appeared sporadically in the pages of the *Silent Worker*. It was not until
well after 1909, when Keller joined the Socialist Party and then went
on to support the IWW (Industrial Workers of the World), that Keller's
radical thought entered the pages of the *Silent Worker*. A likely candi-
date for discussion in the *Silent Worker*, Keller emerged as an icon of
inspiration for the deaf in the closing decade of the nineteenth century. Although the *Silent Worker* writers invoked Keller's name whenever possible, particularly when the hearing community perceived her
in a positive light, they followed their habitual tendency to treat "controversial issues circumspectly," as Van Cleve and Crouch noted, and
especially so when Keller became politically active and visible (Van
Cleve and Crouch 104). With few exceptions, *Silent Worker* copy on or
about Keller focused primarily on her path from her birth in Alabama
to her accomplishments as a college graduate and public speaker. The
Silent Worker differed little from the hearing publications on Keller in
that they both presented her as "the deaf and dumb girl who over-
came." This, of course, matched the educational philosophy of residential schools, namely, that with "patience, industry, and steady work
habits, [one can] work to the top" (October 1918, 8).

In a short article entitled "Helen Keller's Complaint," the *Silent
Worker* brought to light the reporters' and book editors' lack of attention to Keller's social concerns and political beliefs. The author, Alice
T. Terry, reveals that in Keller's book *The World I Live In*, editors would
not let Keller publish her views on education, the tariff, labor, and
other big issues of the day. "Editors don't want that," Terry observes,
they would rather she "confine herself to her own soundless and sight-
less world."[8] Terry also reports that hearing editors "fail to grasp that
we are really and truly educated and normal-minded [and] able to
think along new lines" (n.d. [c. 1914], 113). Note the use of the word
normal, implying that this *Silent Worker* writer, though acknowledging
the different body of the deaf, nonetheless is arguing that their minds
function like those of "normal" persons. Foucault suggests that this
"constant division between the normal and the abnormal, to which
every individual is subjected," functions in the deepest sense as a dis-
ciplinary mechanism (199). Always struggling for acceptance by the
hearing society, deaf writers frequently invoked language that would
enable the hearing society to think of the deaf as fully functional, pro-

ductive, and "normal." Clearly, this device created a body of well-trained and disciplined youth willing to sacrifice their bodies to gain "normal" status in a hearing-centered society.[9]

Radical thought again entered the *Silent Worker* in a review of *Deliverance,* a film about Keller's life. In a review called "Courage, Comrades," the writer says that "it had been Miss Keller's intention to appear in person at the first performance, but she abandoned the plan because her sympathies were with the striking actors and she was unwilling to appear in a theater closed to them" (October 1919, 2). The writer goes on to say that Keller "did her bit" in arranging an agreement between actors and managers (2). By 1919 Keller's solidarity with workers was known throughout the United States and abroad. Indeed, many of her speeches and writings after 1909 focus on the ways that workers, particularly industrial workers, were exploited by industrialists. As this example shows, Keller's thoughts focused on the degradation of worker's bodies:

> The trouble is that we do not understand the essential relation between poverty and disease. I do not believe that there is any one in this city of kind hearts who would willingly receive dividends if he knew that they were paid in part with blinded eyes and broken backs. If you doubt that there is such a connection between our prosperity and the sorrows of the poor, consult those bare but illuminated reports of industrial commissions and labor bureaus. . . . In them you will find the fundamental causes of much blindness and crookedness, of shrunken limbs and degraded minds. (Foner 30)

It is not surprising that Keller's radical thought did not often make it into the pages of the *Silent Worker.* Although the *Silent Worker*'s writers and residential school educators extolled the virtues of hard work and selflessness to industry, Keller spoke out strongly against manufacturers who exploited workers. She was merely trying to bring to light what historians now tell us, that "the long hours and intensive labor practices combined to produce in the United States one of the highest industrial accident rates in the Western industrial world. From 1880 to 1900, 35,000 workers were killed annually and another 536,000 were injured . . . [and] between 1905 and 1920, no year passed in the coal mines without at least 2000 fatal work-related injuries" (Dubofsky 22).

Because Keller came out strongly against the United States' involvement in World War I, she was at odds with Walter M. Kilpatrick, superintendent of the New Jersey School for one school year (1916–1917).[10] The *Silent Worker* had strongly opposed military intervention in earlier

U.S. wars, so Kilpatrick's strong military background and support for the United States in World War I brought a significant shift in the newspaper's perspective. Keller writes that the

> future of America rests on the backs of 80,000,000 working men and women and their children. We are facing a grave crisis in our national life. The few who profit from the labor of the masses want to organize the workers into an army which will protect the interests of capitalists. . . . It is in your power to refuse to carry the artillery and the dread-noughts and to shake off some of the burdens, too, such as limousines, steam yachts and country estates. (Foner 75)

Kilpatrick and *Silent Worker* writers, however, eager to mainstream the deaf, saw things differently. The war gave them the opportunity to give the hearing society a positive portrait of the deaf, particularly of their industriousness and patriotism.

As it did for other stigmatized or minority groups, the war created numerous jobs for the deaf. The Firestone and Goodyear rubber factories in Akron, Ohio, for example, actively recruited deaf workers (both male and female) for full-time employment during the war years. In the December 1948 edition of the *Silent Worker,* J. O. Hamersly reports that the Firestone and Goodyear managements found deaf workers "highly efficient" and that "by the close of the war in 1918, nearly 700 deaf from every corner of the country had come to work in Akron's rubber industries" (9). In a move to retain the workers' loyalty, Firestone and Goodyear offered community activities such as sporting events, religious associations, and social clubs for deaf workers. Advertisements placed in the *Silent Worker* ("Firestone wants strong, energetic deaf workmen over 18 years of age and weighing over 140 pounds") kept a continuing supply of deaf workers headed for Akron (July 1919). In June 1919, a writer reported that "some will find the work sickening and uncongenial and go home knockers, while a large number will find it just what they love, and remain permanently" (177). Benjamin M. Schowe, a deaf Firestone employee hired to recruit deaf laborers, wrote in February 1921 that even though the Firestone operations in Akron were "exceptionally clean and free from accident or occupational disease hazard," the work was strenuous and "not always was it heavy work, but almost always it was piece work" which required "machine gun speed and accuracy" (153). Although the deaf were not allowed to serve in the front lines of the war, *Silent Worker* writers went to great lengths to demonstrate how the deaf in Akron (and throughout the country) were doing all they could to "fight the war at home." Ironically, the "war at home" meant something quite different to Keller.

Keller's views were often directly at odds with the fundamental principles and philosophies of the *Silent Worker* and the New Jersey School. While writers and educators praised individualism and encouraged a "pull yourself up by your bootstraps" mentality (readers were told that with patience, industry, and steady habits, they would get "to the top" and that "the deaf are to blame if they can't find employment"), Keller was working for collectivity and speaking out against capitalism and its dangers to the minds and bodies of workers (October 1918, 8). *Silent Worker* writers and residential school educators were doing their best to produce deaf wage earners while Keller, as a member of the IWW, was attempting to abolish the wage system.

As Keller's public life was drawing to a close in the 1920s, Alvin E. Pope (the hearing superintendent of the New Jersey School who replaced Walter M. Kilpatrick in 1917) began taking a larger role in the production of the *Silent Worker*. The paper acquired the physical appearance of a magazine when Pope published longer articles from outside sources and skipped reports about the activities in and around the New Jersey School. In response to current trends in the United States, the *Silent Worker* took an anti-Bolshevik stance while, not surprisingly, continuing its worship of "Americanism," no doubt partly because of assaults on radicalism and "foreignism" by the American Legion and the National Association of Manufacturers. In 1922, for example, the American Legion began a drive to make history textbooks "preach on every page a vivid love of America," while at the same time, the Veterans of Foreign Wars worked to eliminate "un-American textbooks" (Heale 86).

Woodrow Wilson's recommendation that the United States have one class of persons with a liberal education while another class of persons, a "much larger class of necessity in every society, to forgo the privilege of a liberal education and fit themselves to perform specific difficult manual tasks" works nicely with the educational philosophy at many residential schools (Loewen 198). Because deaf pupils were trained better in the "manual arts" rather than in the "liberal arts," they were consequently tracked into vocational occupations that offered fewer opportunities for gaining political and economic power.[11]

Continuing its drive to create reliable workers, the *Silent Worker* ran a series of editorials in 1921 that reaffirmed its commitment to the interests of business, civic associations, and textbook publishers. In a March editorial, "Theory of Pain and Pleasure," Pope suggests that nations thrive when laborers love their work and that a worker's relationship to work is determined solely by his or her "spirit within." He uses two poems to make this point clear. Represented in the first poem are those workers who find labor a form of drudgery:

> *With fingers weary and worn,*
> *With eyelids heavy and red,*
> *A woman sat, in unwomanly rags.*
> *Plying her needle and thread—*
> *Stitch! Stitch! Stitch!*
> *In poverty, hunger, and dirt,*
> *And still with a voice of dolorous pitch*
> *She sang the "Song of the Shirt."*
>
> *Work—work—work—*
> *From weary chime to chime,*
> *Work—work—work—*
> *As prisoners work for a crime!*
> *Band and gusset and seam,*
> *Seam, and gusset, and band,*
> *Till the heart is sick and the brain benumb'd*
> *As well as the weary hand. (198)*

According to Pope, the voice in this Thomas Hood poem asserts a troubling attitude toward work; that is, the narrative voice wrongly conflates work with a prison sentence.[12] The narrative voice in the second poem, however, offers readers a better understanding of Pope's aims:

> *Work!*
> *Thank God for the might of it,*
> *The ardour, the urge, the delight of it—*
> *Work that springs from the heart's desire,*
> *Setting the brain and the soul on fire—*
> *Oh, what is so good as the heat of it,*
> *And what is so glad as the beat of it,*
> *And what is so kind as the stern command,*
> *Challenging brain and heart and hand?*
>
> *Thank God for the swing of it,*
> *For the clamouring, hammering ring of it,*
> *Passion of labour daily hurled*
> *On the mighty anvils of the world*
>
> *To answer the dream of the master heart*
> *Thank God for a world where none may shirk—*
> *Thank God for the splendor of work! (98)*

This Angela Morgan poem (from which I quoted only a small portion) offers its readers the "correct" attitude toward work. No nation will last, Pope explains, if citizens do not love their work. He also states that "it is for each one to determine by his attitude towards his position in life whether he will be a slave of work or a master of work." Colin Greer's research indicating that "the real achievement of schools consisted in their ability to train children to accept the prevailing class structure and their fate as workers within the industrial system," comes to mind here (Aronowitz 74). Stanley Aronowitz describes this type of educational system as one that leads not to social advancement but, rather, to social stasis (*False Promises* 74).

Pope's concern with labor and production grew even more provocative in April and May 1921. In April, Pope relied on an unnamed French philosopher to distinguish three classes of people: "thieves, beggars and producers." "To which do you belong?" he asked readers (237).[13] In May, in an editorial entitled "The Pace That Kills," Pope tells his readers that recent investigations into ill health and work show that

> the pace that kills is the slacker's pace; that hard work produces long life and that people who work very hard are usually the healthiest and happiest, and when these very same people quit work and begin to lead easy lives, they soon die. A machine will rust away quicker than it will wear out. Few men overwork but they imagine they are overworked when they try to work and dissipate at the same time. (280)

Pope's comparison of the human body with a machine makes perfect sense. By 1921, experiments with the scientific management of bodies on the assembly line, or "Taylorism," were well under way in the United States. With speed and efficiency the top priorities in the industrial marketplace, the human body, as Pope maintains, must remain active, energetic, and industrious. Failing to do this would result in underuse or "rusting."

The national debate over methods of instruction (whether schools should use strictly oral methods or the combination of oral and manual methods) had, for the most part, been won by the oralists when Pope began his tenure at the New Jersey School in 1917. An advocate of oral methods of instruction (teaching and learning through speech instruction and lipreading), Pope was particularly strict with students whose oral skills were deemed deficient. In fact, the president of the New Jersey Alumni Association accused Pope of transforming the school into a medieval workhouse for "manual" students (Buchanan 186). Supporters of strictly oral methods of instruction (most of them hearing persons) believed that deaf educators and students must do all they could to move deaf students into "normal" society. One of the aims of oral methods of instruction, therefore, was to encourage deaf students to speak the language of hearing persons. Pope's advocacy of oral methods of instruction was at odds, however, with many of the *Silent Worker* staff, especially George Porter, the deaf printing instructor, editor, and single most significant person involved in the production of the newspaper.

Before Pope's arrival at the New Jersey School, Porter and the *Silent Worker* writers actively promoted manual methods of instruction at residential schools. Yet Porter and many *Silent Worker* writers also realized that oral methods of instruction could be beneficial to some deaf students. Because of this, many supporters of manual methods of instruction became advocates of the combined method. Combined-system advocates—by the 1920s a minority of New Jersey School teachers—believed that a combination of both manual and oral methods of instruction worked best for a broad range of deaf students. By using both methods, they argued, students might gain access to hearing society while still retaining their ties to an already established and thriving language community.

Porter and Pope got along amicably during the first few years of Pope's tenure at the New Jersey School, but their relationship became increasingly strained in the late 1920s as Pope stepped up his advocacy of oralism. The 1928–1929 school year proved a difficult one for Porter and Pope. Before the school term opened in 1928, Pope asked Porter to retire, accusing him of "slipping." After Porter hired an attorney and refused to step down, the school board granted him a one-year extension. The tension increased during the school year when Porter blamed Pope for overloading his classes with students who were "deficient in basic skills—whose intellectual development had been undercut by extended exercises in speechreading and articulation" (Buchanan 188). Pope responded by asserting that the *Silent Worker* interfered with Porter's teaching responsibilities. At the end of the 1928–1929 school year, Porter's one-year extension was over. Pope further undercut the possibility of manual methods of instruction when he fired five deaf teachers at the end of the school year, claiming that the instructors supported a "program of opposition" to oral instruction at the New Jersey School. Buchanan's research indicates that at the end of the school year, there were no deaf teachers employed in academic departments. Finally, at the end of the school year, Pope halted publication of the *Silent Worker*, believing that producing the newspaper "strained the school's budget, distracted printing teachers

from their instructional responsibilities, and disrupted the students"
(188). After Pope ended production of the newspaper at the New
Jersey School in 1929, the *Silent Worker* remained silent for nearly
twenty years.[14]

By the time the National Association of the Deaf (NAD) began publishing the *Silent Worker* again in 1948 (the New Jersey School took no
part in editing, publishing, or printing the periodical after 1929), the
American political landscape was such that *Silent Worker*'s editors and
writers took an increasingly more conservative stance on political
issues.[15] After the New Deal began running out of steam in the late
1930s, fear of communism and socialists (the "Red scare") began to
take hold in the United States. In 1938, the House Un-American
Activities Committee was formed, and as was often the case, labor
activists and other radicals were deemed suspicious, dangerous, and
"un-American" (Heale 122). Afraid of striking workers and a takeover
by "anti-American" elements, businesses and corporations began stepping up their role in public school education. The National Association
of Manufacturers wanted the "economic facts of life" to be a major
focus in the schools because as they pointed out, students were "too
often exposed to leftist philosophies" (Fones-Wolf 197). In addition,
in 1948 Frank W. Abrams of Standard Oil and the Committee for
Economic Development charged that if "our hope of an advancing
American economy involves reducing costs, increasing individual productivity, and devising better ways of doing things, we must consider
that we have a major interest in helping American Education" (Fones-
Wolf 198). In 1947, the Ford Motor Company contributed $40,000 for
an essay contest promoting the need for labor harmony. Elizabeth A.
Fones-Wolf notes that the titles of the essay topics were "Worker and
Employer, Partners in Business," "What Do Strikes Cost the Worker?"
and "What Free Enterprise Means to My Future" (203).

When taking into account the anticommunist and procapitalist sentiment from the late 1930s and continuing into the 1940s, 1950s, and
1960s, it is not surprising that many in the deaf community wished to
find a new name for the *Silent Worker*. In a letter to the editor, a government bacteriologist mixes humor with seriousness when writing
about the title of the *Silent Worker:*

> Is it necessary to have such a title as the *Silent Worker?* . . . with the FBI
> witchhunting, it is not amusing. My predecessor was fired when the
> FBI caught him selling narcotics, and now you are linking me with a
> Communist publication! Can't you picture me screaming at a row of
> test tubes: "Streptococci of the world, unite! You have nothing to lose
> but your virulence." (December 1948, 31)

Sporadically from 1948 to 1964, the proper title for the magazine—the newspaper had grown to the size and status of a magazine—was open for discussion in the editorial pages. Some readers did not like *silent* because it had both literal and figurative meanings, and others did not like *worker* because it brought to mind the *Daily Worker,* the then-defunct paper of the Communist Party in America.[16] The *Silent Worker* board of directors thus decided to hold a contest.

"Suggestions are pouring in," exclaimed the editors in October 1960 (2). Some people wanted the name to remain the *Silent Worker,* whereas others proposed different titles: "deaf Citizen," "Silent Monthly," "New Silent Worker," and perhaps the most conceptual, "Nadan," a palindrome demonstrating how the deaf and the National Association of the Deaf "look backward in history, but forward in achievement" (July 1949, 31). It was not until September 1964 that the new title, the *Deaf American,* was adopted.

When Helen Keller died in 1968, her obituary did not appear in the *Deaf American.* This may indicate that Keller's life, thoughts, and actions were no longer considered a model of emulation for the deaf community. In his study of textbook publishing and its relationship to anti-radical thought, James Loewen suggests that Keller remains an inspiration "only so long as she remains uncontroversial, one-dimensional" (25). Davis makes a similar argument: "We assume that our 'official' mascots of disability are nothing else but their disability" (7).

In their analysis of publications for the deaf, John Vickrey Van Cleve and Barry A. Crouch point out that establishing "cultural connections" and "cultural guidelines" played a central role in this vast body of documents (98, 100). Certainly, Benedict Anderson's notion of imagined communities helps us think through the power of newsprint as a medium of communication and cultural connection. Moreover, Clifford Geertz's assertion that culture is a "set of control mechanisms—plans, recipes, rules, instructions . . . for the governing of behavior" gives us a better understanding of how newsprint and periodicals transmit values and establish behavioral expectations (49).

If we think of culture as the "production and legitimation of particular ways of life," as do Aronowitz and Giroux, then we can safely say that residential schools and deaf publications create a culture specific to the desires and demands of many, but certainly not all, members of the deaf community (50). All these formulations lead us back to Foucault's belief that "discipline produces subjected and practiced bodies, 'docile' bodies. Discipline increases the forces of the body (in economic terms of utility) and diminishes these same forces (in political terms of obedience)" (138). Indeed, in the case of the New Jersey

School for the Deaf, the *Silent Worker,* and the *Deaf American,* the power of education and newsprint, two central ideological apparatuses in the lives of the deaf, worked in tandem to create truths that produced and reproduced laboring deaf bodies.

NOTES

Special thanks to Lennard J. Davis for making this essay possible. His graduate course at the State University of New York at Binghamton, "The Different Body: Postmodern, Disabled, Other," provided an environment in which I could think through disability, deafness, and the deaf community. His particularly insightful perspectives on class studies mark this essay throughout. Thanks also to Thea Arnold for offering challenging critique and for helpful comments on an early version of this essay.

1. These and other statistics can be found in Steven E. Boone and Gregory A. Long's *Employability Enhancement Needs of the Deaf,* 4–5.

2. I state this even though editions of the *Silent Worker* can be found dating back to 1888. It was not until 1892 that George Porter became a printing instructor in the vocational department and the editor of the *Silent Worker* that the paper became a regular publication at the New Jersey School. See the July 1928 issue of the *Silent Worker* for details of Porter's career at the New Jersey School for the Deaf.

3. For an insightful discussion of "audism" and "audists," I recommend Harlan Lane's *The Mask of Benevolence: Disabling the Deaf Community.*

4. As the language I use here indicates, this is mere speculation. To my knowledge, there have been no studies of this kind, and consequently, I have no conclusive evidence to prove my assertion.

5. Of interest here is that the association of deafness with subaltern institutions is not entirely without merit. For example, some residential schools for the deaf began in insane asylums and pauper houses.

6. Michael Rosenthal points out that the founding principles of the Boy Scouts were laden with class bias. Worthy of note here is the notion that the founder of the Boy Scouts, Lord Baden-Powell, wished to produce "out of the morally dubious, unformed lower-class youths, a kind of serviceable citizen for the [British] empire." See Rosenthal's *The Character Factory,* 6.

7. In the next part of this essay, I work through Helen Keller's radical thoughts and writings in relation to the *Silent Worker.* For more on some of the internal debates within the deaf community, see the *Silent Worker* from 1900 to 1915 for the writings of Zeno and cartoons by the Independence League of the Deaf.

8. For a brief yet illuminating discussion of the "silencing" of Helen Keller, see J. C. Quicke's "'Speaking Out': The political career of Helen Keller," *Disability, Handicap & Society* 3, no. 2 (1988): 167–71.

9. For a provocative analysis and history of the term *normal,* see Davis's *Enforcing Normalcy,* 23–49; and Douglas C. Baynton's *Forbidden Signs,* 138–48.

10. Kilpatrick was asked to leave after serving only one year at the New Jersey School. The administration did not react favorably to his attempts to create a military training facility for deaf youths at the New Jersey School.

11. For example, even though many schools for the deaf employed deaf teachers, very few deaf superintendents or principals can be found in the history of deaf education. Even less common were deaf persons on school governing boards. Consequently, as oralism increasingly supplanted manualism in the first quarter of the twentieth century, supporters of the manual method (most being deaf teachers and deaf adults) had limited political means of resisting the rise of oralism (Baynton 149).

12. Besides pointing out that this poem was a favorite propaganda piece for seamstresses and their supporters in the early nineteenth century, Christine Stansell suggests that the doggerel beat of this poem captures the drudgery of seamstressing. See Stansell, "The Origins of the Sweatshop," 90.

13. A recurrent antipeddlar and antibeggar stance is taken throughout the history of the *Silent Worker* and the *Deaf American*. Articles and editorials in both publications demonstrate a concern in the deaf community that beggars and peddlers were responsible for creating negative stereotypes of the deaf.

14. See Buchanan's "The *Silent Worker* Newspaper and the Building of a Deaf Community, 1890–1929" for a more detailed and nuanced interpretation of Pope's role as superintendent of the New Jersey School. Buchanan's meticulous research is responsible for the information in this paragraph. The demarcation between direct quotation and paraphrase is a troublesome one in this particular paragraph of my essay. Suffice it to say that most of this paragraph can be attributed to Buchanan's research.

15. It is not surprising that the NAD took over publication of the *Silent Worker*. In 1921 the NAD ceased publishing the NAD *Quarterly*, deciding instead to make the *Silent Worker* its unofficial organ.

16. *Silent Worker*, August 1960, 2; September 1964, 2.

Works Cited

Aronowitz, Stanley. *False Promises: The Shaping of American Working Class Consciousness*. New York: McGraw-Hill, 1973.

Aronowitz, Stanley, and Henry Giroux. *Postmodern Education: Politics, Culture, and Social Criticism*. Minneapolis: University of Minnesota Press, 1991.

Baynton, Douglas C. *Forbidden Signs: American Culture and the Campaign Against Sign Language*. Chicago: University of Chicago Press, 1996.

Boone, Steven E., and Gregory A. Long. *Employability Enhancement Needs of Deaf Persons: Model Interventions*. Springfield, IL: Thomas, 1988.

Buchanan, Robert. "Building a Silent Colony: Life and Work in the Deaf Community of Akron, Ohio from 1910 Through 1950." In *The Deaf Way: Perspectives from the International Conference on Deaf Culture*, edited by Carol J. Erting et al. Washington, DC: Gallaudet University Press, 1994.

————. "The *Silent Worker* Newspaper and the Building of a Deaf Community: 1890–1929." In *Deaf History Unveiled: Interpretations from the New Scholarship,* edited by John Vickrey Van Cleve. Washington, DC: Gallaudet University Press, 1993.

Davis, Lennard J. *Enforcing Normalcy: Disability, Deafness, and the Body.* New York: Verso, 1995.

Dubofsky, Melvyn. *Industrialism and the American Worker, 1865–1920.* Arlington Heights, IL: Harlan Davidson Press, 1985.

Foner, Philip S. *Helen Keller: Her Socialist Years.* New York: International Publishers, 1967.

Fones-Wolf, Elizabeth A. *Selling Free Enterprise: The Business Assault on Labor and Liberalism, 1945–60* Urbana: University of Illinois Press, 1994.

Foucault, Michel. *Discipline and Punish: The Birth of the Prison.* New York: Vintage Books, 1979.

Geertz, Clifford. *The Interpretation of Cultures.* New York: Basic Books, 1973.

Goffman, Erving. *Stigma: Notes on the Management of Spoiled Identity.* New York: Simon & Schuster, 1963.

Heale, M. J. *American Anticommunism: Combating the Enemy Within, 1830–1970.* Baltimore: Johns Hopkins University Press, 1990.

Lane, Harlan. *The Mask of Benevolence: Disabling the Deaf Community.* New York: Vintage Books, 1993.

Leakey, Tricia A. "Vocational Education in the Deaf American and African-American Communities." In *Deaf History Unveiled: Interpretations from the New Scholarship,* edited by John Vickrey Van Cleve. Washington, DC: Gallaudet University Press, 1993.

Loewen, James W. *Lies My Teacher Told Me: Everything Your American History Textbook Got Wrong.* New York: New Press, 1995.

Rosenthal, Michael. *The Character Factory: Baden-Powell and the Origins of the Boy Scout Movement.* New York: Pantheon, 1984.

Stansell, Christine. "The Origins of the Sweatshop: Women and Early Industrialization in New York City." In *Working-Class America,* edited by Michael H. Frisch and Daniel J. Walkowitz. Urbana and Chicago: University of Illinois Press, 1983.

Van Cleve, John Vickrey, and Barry A. Crouch. *A Place of Their Own: Creating the Deaf Community in America.* Washington, DC: Gallaudet University Press, 1989.

Terry Easton *is a doctoral student in the Graduate Institute of the Liberal Arts at Emory University.*

Representations of Working-Class "Intelligence": Fiction by Jack London, Agnes Smedley, and Valerie Miner, and New Scholarship by Carol Whitehill and Janet Zandy

Deb Busman

In the dominant ideology of a middle-class mythology that passes all too often as simply "how it is," unmarked in its bias and masking of privilege, intelligence is often represented as somehow belonging to the "educated" individuals of the owning class. In the social body of capitalism, the "head" is the intellect and reason of university-achieved privilege that rules the "body" of the "ignorant masses"—the workers. Encoded in that representation of "mind over matter" is the belief that the well-to-do are the smart ones—they have the education and the money; the poor are slow, stupid, and uneducated. They drop out of school and work like "dumb animals" because they are not "smart" enough to find their bootstraps.

This conflation of class status with intelligence is neither accidental nor benign. Denying and undermining the intelligence of certain groups of people has been a long-standing tradition in this country, a personal and institutionalized tactic of oppression used to deny the rights and humanity of women, people of color, and the poor and working class. Since these groups, of course, inevitably overlap, many people are forced to resist assaults on their intelligence made on multiple fronts of racism, sexism, and class oppression. While this essay focuses primarily on the particulars of "working-class intelligence," the workings of these three interlocking systems of oppression make it impossible to ever really isolate one strand, unravel it from the mass, and name it "class," separate and distinct from race and gender.

In part 1 of this essay, I explore some representations of intelligence in working-class literature and explain why working-class authors have both perpetuated and refused portrayals that equate intelligence with class status. In part 2, I look specifically at the university as a system that confers both class and intellectual status, focusing on the daily experiences of working-class students who find themselves directly in the belly of the beast of a university system that perpetuates privilege.

As a working-class student who was almost forty years old before I truly questioned the lies that had been told about my intelligence—I was too "slow," I wasn't smart enough to go on in school, I would never "amount to anything," higher education wasn't for "people like me"— I understand the damage that occurs when accusations of "stupidity" are internalized. Working as a writing tutor for SAA/EOP (Student Affirmative Action/Equal Opportunity Program) at the University of California, Santa Cruz, I saw the struggles of marginalized students who not only had to combat class and race bias on a daily basis but also had to fight the internalized messages of not being "smart enough," not being "worthy" of being "let into" the institution.

When intelligence is equated with class position, a number of things must happen. First, intelligence becomes something that people can be "born" into if they inherit enough wealth to purchase an education (and kept out of if they're poor). Second, when "being smart" carries positive value for a society and a privileged class claims that characteristic, then that class is elevated higher in status and the nonprivileged or working class becomes further degraded and "lacking" in that trait. Third, the values and actions of the privileged class become equated with intelligence, which is in turn rendered invisible in the values and actions of the poor. For these reasons, not only is there a general, predisposed tendency to view the working class as "ignorant," but obvious displays of intelligence also go unseen.

An example of this occurred when I worked as a press operator with a bright young African American man who was great at troubleshooting and finding chemical or mechanical solutions for printing problems. His ability was so striking that it could not go unnoticed, but how it was recognized happened in this way: "He sure is good with his hands, isn't he?" or "Boy, they sure do teach 'em good in the army, don't they?" Yeah, right! That my friend even survived the army, not to mention the racism of Mississippi in the 1970s and California in the 1990s, speaks to the creativity of his intelligence. Not to mention the fact that he was able to think at all after repeated ten-hour days of inhaling printing fumes and standing on concrete next to pounding machinery. What is going on when skill and intelligence in a working-class African American man are reduced to "being good with his hands," when we would never say that about an accountant, for example, whose hands fly over a twelve-key adding machine, or a surgeon, who had better be good with his hands?

Praise for the working class is most often coded in terms of physical attributes that also carry gender and racial bias. Silicon Valley female factory workers, especially Asians, are preferred "because their small hands are so good with details." The act of reducing workers to "bodies" that produce labor denies not only the person inside the body but also the impact of physical labor on the "person" and the "body." As we will see, representing the working class as "body, not brain" has serious political implications as well, because it impairs the creation and sustainment of a consciousness about class that is necessary for social change.

Part 1: Representations of "Intelligence" in Working-Class Literature: Acts of Replication or Resistance?

In literary representation, members of the working class are repeatedly portrayed in terms of their physical bodies and lack of intelligence and are often compared with machines and animals. This is especially common in literature written by middle-class authors about the working class, although working-class authors often employ such imagery as well. Jack London is a writer whose depictions of the working class tend to replicate rather than resist class-based stereotypes. In his semi-autobiographical novel *Martin Eden,* he starts out with a detailed description of Martin's awkward and ungainly physical presence as he enters Ruth's class-privileged house. His "legs spread unwittingly," his "heavy arms" hang loosely, he fears his "broad shoulders should collide with doorways," and he "lurches like a frightened horse" (31). He is "shamed," "ignorant," and "inarticulate," an "uncouth young fellow with lacerated hands" (40). As a working-class man, Martin does not "fit" into this house of privilege.

As hard as he is on himself, Martin/London is ruthless and racist when he compares the women of his class with the exquisite and educated Ruth:

> [H]e saw the weak and sickly faces of the girls of the factories . . . swarthy cigarette smoking women of Old Mexico . . . Japanese women, doll-like . . . full-bodied South Sea Island women . . . frowsy, shuffling creatures . . . gin-bloated hags of the stews . . . vile mouthed and filthy that under the guise of monstrous female form prey upon sailors . . . the scum and slime of the human pit. (36)

He holds up these images of what is female and poor against the vision of Ruth, "marveling at all the knowledge that was stowed away in that pretty head of hers" (39). He is deeply moved by the beauty of an oil painting, wistful and yearning at the sight of books on a table. "Here was intellectual life, he thought, and here was beauty" (40). For Martin, beauty, intellect, and class privilege become synonymous and collapse into one another, rendering the working class ugly, uncouth, and ignorant. At this point, he makes a passionate vow of upward mobility—"I don't know nothin' much about such things [poetry]," he tells Ruth. "It ain't in my class. But I'm goin' to make it in my class" (42).

Whereas writers like London often help reproduce images of the working class as "ignorant" but individually capable of upward mobility into universities and thereby intelligence (especially if, like Martin, they renounce their background and internalize the shame), some working-class writers challenge such biased ideology. Agnes Smedley, author of the autobiographical novel *Daughter of Earth,* is such a writer, providing us with the fierce feminist voice of a teacher and activist who critiques the trappings of upward mobility even as she demands and claims an education that allows her to access it. Part of the strength of this novel is that the protagonist, Marie Rogers, refuses to give up her working-class values as she gains mobility as an activist, student, and writer. She never believes that intelligence is the domain or prerogative of the privileged and so is able to control her own autonomy of judgment. She determines from her own experience and knowledge what is to be judged as "ignorant" and is as likely to use that term to describe the narrow-mindedness of teachers, police, ministers, and university-educated folks as she is to describe that quality in fellow members of the working class.

Because she locates in herself the authority to define and critique the social reality around her, Marie does not suffer the fragmentation and loss of self and identity that other characters, such as Martin Eden, experience when they leave "what they know" in order to acquire class-biased education. Marie does not hold "ignorance" as a trait or sin of the poor and so does not leave "it" behind as she gets an education and eases the shackles of poverty. In fact, the more she learns, the more likely she is to describe herself as ignorant, but that description comes more out of humility than self-deprecation. After years of university education, when she sits before the teacher Sardarji and laments, "It was a misfortune that I was too ignorant, too undeveloped to grasp the meaning of all he might have taught me" (269), she is criticizing the limitations of academic institutions as well as the "Americanization" that constrains her thinking. She does not equate "knowing" and intelligence with class status and so escapes the internalized shame of those who equate ignorance with poverty.

In one of my favorite scenes in this novel, Marie utilizes her "street smarts" when faced with a situation in which she lacks "education." She has been assigned to teach in a remote area of New Mexico and has no illusions about her own "schooling." Understanding the relative nature of learning, she admits,

> I was ignorant, yes, but I was learned compared with those about me. And I possessed a native cunning. When a smaller child could not do a problem in arithmetic, and I saw that I also could not do it, I called upon one of the older boys to demonstrate his knowledge before the classroom. He did it proudly, and all of us learned something. (118)

This passage is wonderful for a number of reasons. First, it demonstrates the egalitarian nature of Smedley's vision of education. Knowledge is not "private property" to be possessed and wielded over those who do not "have" it; knowledge is communal, to be shared and to benefit everyone from the sharing. The other reason I love this story is that it replicates the teaching experience of a friend of mine who was raised poor, dropped out of high school, and did physical work all her life until she went back to school and clawed her way through junior college and then the University of California, Davis. After being told she was "too smart to teach," she got a job teaching high school science in a rich neighborhood where the privileged white boys in AP chemistry listened to Rush Limbaugh and knew more than she did about much of the course material. She did exactly what Marie did, assigning sections of the course to various students who initially shared their arrogance but ultimately their knowledge. No one was shamed, and as Smedley writes, "everybody learned something."

Another working-class writer who insists on bringing the values and experience of her origins with her as she enters the privileged world of higher education and publishing is Valerie Miner, author of *A Walking Fire*. In this novel about a working-class daughter of a patriotic merchant marine, Miner explores the main character, Cora, and her struggle to maintain self and sanity as she goes off to college during the height of the Vietnam War, in which her father and two brothers are fighting. By situating Cora's involvement in the middle-class antiwar movement and by her questioning and claiming of "family values," Miner creates a novel that carries the tension of class conflict, betrayal, leaving home, and political and moral integrity. *A Walking Fire* also questions the idea of "knowledge:" who has it, who can say what is considered knowledge, and which knowledge "counts," the experiential knowledge of her father and brothers—Vietnam War soldiers who served "in the trenches" yet got their information from television—or the disembodied "superior" thinking of war protestors who are almost entirely race and class privileged.

In the battle over which knowledge counts, Cora is positioned between her family and the university. Her dad has a sixth-grade education ("and I did OK, didn't I?" he asks her). Cora's brother George goes to electrical school before joining the army. They scoff at the "knowledge" Cora is gaining at the university. "College pap," George calls it, taught by "Commie professors." When Cora begins to question her country's involvement in the war, her pop "practically laughed her off the phone" (26). "Didn't she know we were just supporting the Vietnamese people until they got back on their feet? Didn't she understand that Ho Chi Minh was backed by Peking? Didn't they teach her anything about the domino theory in college? What was she studying— underwater basketweaving?" (26). Cora's dad has "done OK" in terms of upward mobility and helping make a better life for his children. He has been employed by the U.S. government, "risen above" his sixth-grade education, and provided a nice home and television for his family. He is invested in defending his life (and the system) from criticism and feels deeply betrayed when his daughter becomes involved in the antiwar movement. He is the patriarch and his knowledge should count.

As Cora learns more and more about the United States' involvement in Vietnam (gaining more insight from the university than what was provided on her pop's TV shows), she is thrown into a crisis of intellect and identity that threatens her sanity. Becoming estranged from her family's "knowing" and their support, Cora becomes increasingly isolated and thinks of her mother's mental breakdown. "Mom's trips to the hospital were always preceded by times of isolation. Cora was more afraid of craziness than anything. She would have to sort out her ideas about the war some other way" (27).

> She . . . wished she hadn't listened to stories about soldiers destroying villages. Wished she hadn't heard those lectures about American international ambitions. Wished she could go back to the last year and take different classes and make different friends. She did not want to know what she knew. She was beginning to understand that the most real person in her life didn't know everything about the real world. (26)

In these passages, Miner brings together the interconnected nature of complex issues that working-class students face when they leave home for the middle-class domain of college. The knowledge they bring with them to the university is often discounted. They are made to feel stupid for not possessing the same kind of information that class-privileged kids "have." Even though Cora is passionate about gaining a better understanding of how the world and war work, she is also made acutely uncomfortable by the class bias inherent in these "understandings." The rich and middle-class kids she works with in the antiwar movement on campus are blind to their overprivilege. They have access to lawyers, college deferments, and a guaranteed place in the corporate world, whereas the working-class kids like Cora's brothers see the military as "the way out of unemployment or dead-end jobs." Rather than incorporating a class analysis into their critique of U.S. government policy, these "radical" students actually blame the oppressed for becoming soldiers. Speaking of the "rednecks" at the community college, one middle-class student regrets the "hopeless consciousness there," and Henry Rhinehart calls them "pathetic . . . naive bastards. Like lambs to the slaughter." (31) This linking of blame and ignorance in middle-class representations of the poor is a highly political act that serves both to undermine the working class and to "keep them in their place."

Miner problematizes "knowledge" and "intelligence" in this novel by exposing the values and bias inherent in knowledge and also in her characterization of Cora's mother as highly intelligent—and crazy. Her mom is always reading and excited about knowing things. She had to drop out of high school after two years to support her family, but she pursues knowledge in every way available to her as a working-class mother and wife. She "reads the dictionary for fun," explaining to her sister-in-law, "'You learn that there's so much you don't know.'" Aunt Min, the rock that holds the family together, responds, "And there's so much you don't *need* to know" (117).

For Aunt Min, the pragmatist, certain knowledge can be dangerous when one does not have the economic agency of class privilege. She watches her sister-in-law grow increasingly "crazy" as Cora's mother's mind seeks more and more information that her circumstances don't allow her to integrate. When Cora goes off to college, she gains both an economic and intellectual lifeline, yet she pays a huge price for it in terms of estrangement from her family of origin. As Miner puts it, "College was where the world became unbridgeable, where the world had cracked open for her" (164). Eventually, Cora partially heals her fractured world of family, politics, and sanity, understanding that she carries with her traits from both her mother and father. She comes to see her opposition to her father's position on the war as acting out of, rather than against, the value system he has taught her: "In truth, she was just expressing her values—his values—in light of new information" (164). The struggle then becomes what to do with what she has learned to save her father and brothers' lives, fight the class bias of her middle-class "comrades," deal with the pain of her family's disowning her, and not go crazy as her mother did. And also do her schoolwork. What Miner seems to suggest here is that sanity and survival for the working-class student mean a delicate balancing and interweaving of the "values" of origin and the "new information" gained from education.

**Part 2: The Conflation of "Smart" and "Educated"—
or Why I Don't Feel Smart Enough to Write a Paper on Intelligence**

In her doctoral dissertation, "Issues of Entitlement," lecturer and psychologist Carol Whitehill looks at the intellectual experiences of reentering working-class women at the University of California, Santa Cruz. In her examination of how issues of entitlement affect these students' self-perceptions of "intellectual competence," Whitehill notes the cultural differences between their class and gender identities and their current academic experiences at an extremely privileged university. Drawing on interviews with twenty-four working-class female students, as well as on psychological and sociological studies, Whitehill's work deconstructs the value-laden but often invisible assumptions of bourgeois discourse equating "intelligence" with a college education.

Although working-class students may come to the university with a sense of self-worth in regard to competence, skills, and abilities—especially reentering women who often have raised families and earned a living in the "real world"—many feel that although "it was good and possible to have 'common sense' . . . 'intelligence' was reserved for middle-class people who had gone to college." According to Whitehill, in working-class cultures that value "common sense," "street smarts," and the knowledge that comes from experience, "intelligence is suspect in itself, for it connotes book learning, which can be far removed from daily life. . . . They believed more in those people who had personally experienced something and could pass on this trusted knowledge, than in anything written in a book by unknown people" (59). Here we are reminded of Miner's portrayal of Cora's working-class family's perspective—the distrust of book learning.

As anyone who has entered the privileged domain of academia knows, however, the "trusted knowledge" of experience (at least the experience of the oppressed) doesn't count at the university level. Because what is valued at institutions of "higher learning" is a disembodied theorizing about something other than the thing itself, working-class students are often placed in the absurd and crazy-making position of being silenced while a middle-class academic lectures to them about class issues in America. (And that is on the rare occasion when class is even mentioned.)

An example of this privileging of academic theory over the knowledge of lived experience can be found in the story of a friend of mine who is working class, white, and a single parent on welfare. When she challenged an economics professor on his racist and sexist portrayal of welfare recipients as "black women who keep having babies to collect extra welfare payments," she was told to keep quiet and not interrupt the lecture. But because as the quarter went on, she persisted in reintroducing her "personal" experience and analysis into the class discussion, she was "restricted" to speaking only once per class session. After all, the teacher had done his graduate work on the "subject" of welfare, and therefore he possessed the expertise.

In her study, Whitehill defines "Perceived Intellectual Competence" as

> the belief that one's mind is adequate to take in new knowledge, to understand and integrate aspects of this knowledge, and to express this knowledge in appropriate ways as in writing, speaking and sharing ideas. . . . It has both an internal psychological component involving self-perceptions and a social interactive component involving communicating to others. (66)

It is easy to understand why working-class students might feel somewhat less than "intellectually competent" in a system that not only devalues and eradicates the "ways of knowing" they bring to the university but also silences them if they attempt the "social interactive component involving communicating to others."

The university is the "gateway" to class privilege, and it is important to understand that it comes complete with all the trappings of the dominant ideology. The process of passage for middle-class students through these gates of privilege is radically different from that of students from a working-class background. When middle-class kids enter the university, their journey through the gates is part of an economic and cultural continuum they are expected to follow, and when they are given new "knowledge" to take in, it generally does not disrupt the previous "knowledge" into which it is "integrated."

When working-class students approach these gates, however, they are expected to leave behind their previous ways of knowing. They are stepping out of their cultural and historical body of knowledge, "rising above" their class status, "overcoming" their background. Part of the deal for being "let in" (for those who don't "belong") is that they will leave behind where they came from. As Valerie Miner notes in her article "Labor Pains, the Loneliness of the Working-Class Writer," "We acknowledge our working class past only when we want to demonstrate how far we have progressed."

As we can see, virtually every part of Whitehill's definition of "intellectual competence" (though itself a viable definition) is value laden and problematic for working-class students. "The belief that one's mind is adequate" is not something that can be presumed for those who come from the "ignorant masses" with a "body of knowledge" they must leave behind; "to take in new knowledge" can also present problems when that "knowledge" is laden with class bias and often directly contradicts these students' own life experiences; and "to understand and integrate aspects of this knowledge" is almost impossible when working-class students are required to eradicate the experience and knowledge into which this new knowledge is supposed to be integrated. It is like being up a creek without a paddle . . . or a boat.

In the introduction to her book *Liberating Memory,* Janet Zandy writes about the problems of working-class writers (and students) when they attempt to make meaning and to bridge the chasm between their own experience and understanding and that of the dominant culture and ideology: "It is dangerous work because dominant bourgeois culture is hostile to working class identities. They are perceived as too rough, too loud, too dirty, too direct, too 'uneducated.' They are valued—if at all—as requisite labor and service, but not valued as intelligence and knowledge" (2).

Just as working-class writers must struggle to bring their experience, analysis, and vision into a literary canon that discounts and undermines their "reality," working-class students also face the battle of holding on to their knowledge, of bringing it with them to the university rather than checking it at the gates, as they are instructed. Even if working-class students (or writers) somehow manage to sneak in their class "experience," the system is such that this experience will be reduced to a "text" that is then interpreted (and thus controlled) by the privileged.

As a writing tutor for the SAA/EOP program, I learned an important lesson early on about the complexities and dangers of telling one's "story," relating one's experiences in papers that will, in most cases, be read by faculty who have race and class privilege. Most of the students I worked with came from high schools where they were actively discouraged from expressing their opinions or writing about who they were and what their lives were like. Then at UCSC, they were asked in their composition classes to write about their background. All these students experienced a profound panic at this request, as though they were being asked a trick question but hadn't yet figured out what the trick was.

At first, I encouraged them to "find their voice," to "tell it like it is," to introduce the experiences of the race and class oppressed into the "literary canon" of UCSC classes. I was operating out of the ideology of refusing to be silenced and made invisible, of challenging the middle-class dominant discourse with the "realities" of the "oppressed." What I quickly discovered, however, was that the race and class bias went deeper than overt "silencing" (although that certainly was taking place as well) on a liberal campus that paid lip service to dynamics of oppression and that the students were absolutely right in their caution and distrust. One particular student's experience clarified my understanding of the subtleties of oppression.

This working-class, mixed-race student turned in an analytical paper that represented her ideas and best thinking. It was a fairly well written paper that questioned assumptions made in the class discussion. Her teacher returned it with a poor evaluation, saying that "perhaps she should consult a writing tutor." Her next paper was not very well written. She told me she ran out of time and so just wrote about her "experience," told what she called her "mixed-race story." When I asked her how that paper was received, she said, "Oh, he sucked it up, loved it." What is going on when a poorly written paper telling a "story" of an "experience" of oppression is praised, and a well-written paper offering a working-class student of color's "analysis" of a subject is criticized? Well, racism, classism, and sexism to begin with, as all of a working-class woman's knowledge and analysis are reduced to a "story." As Zandy reminds us, "Reality is not merely a text" (5).

We can see from this student's experience that it is not enough simply to "insert" a piece of one's story into the dominant machinery of oppression. As long as those in positions of power control the "making of meaning" about experience, the status quo will not be disrupted. When a working-class student makes her own meaning, creating from her knowledge and personal experience of oppression an analysis that critiques the status quo, then the trouble begins. She is put in her place: she is of the race and class that may be written about, objectified, commodified; she may tell her story, but she is not authorized to analyze it. She can produce a commodity for the instructor's consumption, but she may not question the machinery that consumes it.

It is interesting to note that in the first paper, neither the student's argument nor her analysis was critiqued or responded to; it was her "writing ability" that the instructor commented on. One of the first papers that I wrote at UCSC was for a feminist theory course that was expounding on the value of "theory" over "experience." In my introduction (which was, admittedly, a long, run-on sentence), I argued that the kind of theory we were discussing was not, as it represented itself, outside or superior to experience; rather, it came directly out of experience—in this case, the experience of privilege. I knew this argument was going to be a problem, since the teaching assistant was a very well-to-do academic theory-head who adored disembodied thinking, but I wrote it anyway. When I got the paper back, I saw that she had circled my introduction and written beside it, "This is not a paragraph!" There was no engagement with my argument, simply a dismissal that implied that if I weren't even capable of writing a proper paragraph, then clearly I wasn't bright enough to appreciate the wonders of Foucault. Her remaining comments suggested that with time and effort, I might come to see things differently. The material, she admitted, was "difficult."

Based on my own experience and that of my students, it is clear that the university is set up by the class privileged as a means of perpetuating and controlling access to that privilege. Working-class students are frequently reminded that they have been "allowed in" provisionally and perhaps by error. They are surrounded by middle-class students who do not see college as a privilege at all but, rather, just as something they have always known they were entitled to. As "college material" from day 1, middle-class students can take for granted their intelligence and entitlement, whereas working-class students have to struggle for both.

In her article "'Upward' Mobility and the Working Class Student in the University," Renny Christopher writes extensively about working-class students' struggles in academic institutions that both mask and perpetuate privilege. She quotes UCSC sociology student Cheryl Gomez:

> The problem with letting academics make the definitions is that they can say this is the better world and yours is a worse world; they can say working class people can't talk, can't think, and although you and I know that's bullshit, we're being asked to accept the whole thing, definitions and all, and therefore to reject our old world, rather than changing their definitions. (250)

Gomez shows how the "meaning making" of knowledge (which is power) is held in the hands of the privileged—academics whose "definitions" are value laden and biased. To succeed at the university, that is, to "get" intelligent, working-class students must reject not only the world they came from but especially the way they "talk" and "think" (two critical elements of Whitehill's definition of intellectual competence). The class dynamics in this country (and the university) are designed to deflect the accountability of those in power and to place personal, individual blame on those oppressed. A major part of the myth of "upward" mobility is that "anybody" can achieve middle-class status and that the inability to do so is a personal rather than societal failure. To achieve "success" in an institution of overprivilege, working-class students must leave behind their cultural and familial worlds and values and submit to the terms and lies of academia. In her dissertation, Whitehill writes about the difficulties that students have when locating themselves in university discourse:

> In the kinds of academic discourse these women were encountering, authority is not so defined [as having power over people and using that power in an inhumane way] but rather is allied with knowledge. Questioning in this discourse demands a degree of autonomy of self, of individualism . . . [and] redefining ideas about authorities in order to position oneself as an equal. In this way the territory of the discourse and the position one takes in that territory are linked. (252)

Here Whitehill critiques the values assumed by academic discourse as necessary for "success." By removing "authority" from the realm of social power over people (with which working-class students can identify) and allying it with knowledge, academia requires students to engage in a process favoring those who identify as "individuals" who can "position" themselves as "equals." Guess which class of students these would tend to be? And guess who is disadvantaged and made crazy when they try to position themselves (uprooted, culturally disenfranchised, and intellectually discredited) as "equal" to overprivileged folks who wield knowledge like a weapon? Under the class system of capitalism, it makes sense that knowledge has become privatized, privileged, and possessed in the institutions of academia that are designed to enforce and bestow class privilege, but it is nonetheless annoying.

Whitehill suggests that working-class students find a place of "location" in the university discourse in order to survive and maintain a validated identity. She notes that all the women she interviewed "qualify their entitlement to be at the university with either previous economic and social limitations or with idea that they are not smart enough"

(261). Those who were most successful in surviving academia either had integrated their past and present situations in ways in which they could feel comfortable with values of individualism and autonomy, or they had developed "an understanding and respect for [their] social background as representative of a territory different from the university" (257).

Whitehill's descriptions of these women's struggles and strategies remind me of Gloria Anzaldúa's writings on "mestiza consciousness"— the ability and practice of locating oneself not only in multiple identities but actually in the "borderlands," the places of intersection. Like Anzaldúa, many of the students discovered that the marginality that initially seemed to restrict and disempower them as working-class women actually became a powerful location to occupy. To use the margins as a location of power and resistance, students must take advantage of community support outside the location of the university— professional, cultural/familial, or political communities.

Returning to the discussion of literary representations in part 1, we can see how the two characters who most successfully resisted the degradation and co-optation of middle-class ideology were Miner's character, Cora, and Smedley's protagonist, Marie, both of whom established a political and social base or location. Martin Eden, on the other hand, sucked up the middle-class values of privilege so as to profit personally from them, thus succumbing to rather than critiquing systems of power and class inequity.

According to Whitehill's study, the most confident respondents were those socially established in a community other than the university, which provided values and identity separate from the university.

> All . . . had a broader vision of the uses of their knowledge and saw the university as a place to gain more tools. These communities provided another location in which respondents had already begun to develop a voice and gain new recognition and feelings of self worth. The respondents who are most confident of their thinking abilities . . . have overcome some shame and silence before entering the university. They are, however, angry. (262)

Anger is an appropriate response to a system that (1) sets up "intelligent" as equal to "educated"; (2) defines the terms and conditions of entrance into the means of "getting" an education; (3) undermines the cultural, social, and intellectual location of identity for working-class students; and (4) implements a curriculum of "knowledge" that students must "learn" if they are to become "intelligent" yet that is completely value laden with a middle-class ideology that overvalues and glorifies the class and race privileged while shaming and personally blaming the underprivileged. The working-class students and writers who seem most successful in simultaneously challenging and succeeding in this system are the ones who refuse to internalize the personal blame and have a social and political framework for directing the anger outward toward the system and those who profit from it. And they seem to be the ones who refuse to leave behind their working-class background.

In Christopher's article, "Working Class Students," she quotes reentering student Jessie Virago's response to the comment by a literature professor with a Ph.D. from Yale when she mentioned her social background and years spent working as a secretary: "He replied, 'But you always knew you were smart, right?' Hear how the conjunction 'but' juxtaposes smart with secretary or smart with working class. I consider the equating of social class position with intelligence to be one of the most common, egregious, and offensive examples of classism in America" (251).

Virago goes on to explain how uncomfortable she is made by the praise she receives at the university:

> I know I am not brighter now than I ever was. What that means is that I was this bright when I was a nurse's aide; this bright when all my books fit into the headboard of my bed; this bright when I spent over half a decade in a windowless office filling in little blanks in insurance claim forms; this bright when my boss sexually harassed me and put his dirty spoon in his out-basket for me to wash . . . More than that, it means that my sister and cousins, and legions of other working-class sisters and cousins, are every bit as bright as I am and remain just as trapped as I was. (253)

The resistance in Virago's insights is profound and deeply rooted in her class background and values. By questioning the "praise" of her professors, she is challenging the value-laden ideology of the institution and refusing its assumptions. Her "brightness" is not something she "obtained" at the university. Intelligence was not somehow "bestowed" on her as she gained passage into the middle class. She carried it with her always, in every menial job she held as a working-class woman. By problematizing the individual praise, Virago also makes the political move of refusing to be isolated from her family and "working-class sisters." She doesn't allow herself to be the "exception," who has "risen above" her background but, rather, claims community and political solidarity. She may be "different" in that she is no longer "trapped" in the same ways she was without the privilege of education, but who she is not different from who she was, nor is she different from those who remain trapped. And she makes it clear that the trapping of working-class women is a result of social discrimination rather than of a lack of intelligence.

In the same article, Christopher provides an example from her own experience as a graduate student. She tells the story of a conversation with two friends, also graduate students, who are impressed at how well she does at literary theory and joke that she must not really be from a working-class background but that, in fact, her father is "probably a professor of Philosophy at Harvard!" Christopher breaks down the "joke":

> The reasoning goes like this: if my father really is a carpenter, I couldn't possibly be as smart as I am. So, in order for me to be as smart as I am, my father must be a professor at Harvard. This means that we have not a class system, but a caste system—no working class kid can be smart, and upper middle class kids will always be smart. Meanwhile, I feel doubly undercut—either I'm not really working-class and am faking it, for reasons I can't imagine, or I'm a phony in school, and I don't belong. Either way, I lose. (251)

As these stories point out, even "positive" experiences such as receiving praise from professors or flattery from friends often carry a class bias and can undermine a working-class student's sense of self. The implications of a working-class identity as devoid of intelligence (not to mention morality and virtue) are profound and painful for students who are expected to renounce and conceal their family of origin in order to "succeed" at the university.

A student I worked with told me about one of the most painful and crazy moments she encountered when coming to the university. As an entering freshman, she had to take the "Subject A" writing placement exam, an essay test that determines the classes that students are allowed to enroll in. The exam gave a little fictional story of a girl trying to decide which clothes to wear and then asked the students to respond to the story and write about all the things that went into their own decisions regarding clothes. They were asked to explore what it meant to make a "fashion statement."

This student was the daughter of a migrant farmworking family in Watsonville. She had never worn a dress that had not been previously worn by her two older sisters. She was expected to take care so that her clothes could be worn by her younger sister in the future. She sat there in the examination room completely unable to write a word. She knew that she could not tell "them" the truth because "it wouldn't answer the question" about "fashion," and besides, she knew better than to talk about her poverty. She was trying to "pass," to gain entrance into the university. As time ran out, she tried to write what she imagined someone she had seen on TV once might have written, but it "made her crazy" and her "head felt like it was going to explode." She failed the exam and eventually dropped out of school, in part because, as she put it, "Shit, I figured if I wasn't smart enough to even pass the damn dumbbell writing test, I'd never make it in the university."

This was a student who had maintained an A average through secondary school while working in the fields and frequently moving. She graduated with honors from high school and had been senior-class president. But all her life she had been told in one way or another that she was "a dumb Mexican" who would never be "college material." Racist and class-biased epithets such as this are not only shaming and demeaning, but they become internalized and stay in the body and mind. When working-class students are faced with class-biased entrance exams and a curriculum that is purported to be "objective" but in fact is loaded with painful assumptions of privilege, they understandably feel "crazy." Fortunately, they often also feel angry, deciding to stay and fight it out or, like the student above, return to the university and complete their education, refusing, as this student put it, "to let the turkeys get me down."

Zandy writes about the struggles of working-class authors trying to publish their work in a society of class-privileged domination. She sees the task of working-class authors, in part, as "bringing the knowledge of physical labor into the cultural work of organizing, teaching, painting, photographing, writing poetry, and publishing" (11). The silencing that working-class writers face in a capitalist society is the same as what seeks to silence working-class students entering the university. The resistance strategies also are the same. Zandy speaks of how she "learned how language could be a weapon to demolish and oppress; and still later . . . recognized language as a tool to reconstruct and reclaim." She sees memory as a "bridge between the . . . private and unprivileged circumstances of individual lives . . . and the collective history of class oppression" (4). The thinking abilities of oppressed peoples must be fostered rather than disparaged and discredited. The knowledge and memory of working-class lives and experiences must not be erased and silenced but, rather, insisted on and continually reintroduced as "story," "history," and social and political analysis. Institutions of "learning" that represent only the "knowledge" of the privileged can only replicate systems of oppression.

Works Cited

Christopher, Renny. "'Upward' Mobility and the Working Class Student in the University." In *Multicultural America,* edited by Betty Ch'maj. Lanham, MD: University Press of America, 1995.

London, Jack. *Martin Eden.* New York: Penguin, 1967.

Miner, Valerie. *A Walking Fire.* Albany: State University of New York Press, 1994.

———. "Labor Pains: The Loneliness of the Working-Class Writer." *Village Voice,* January 5, 1988, 49–50.

Smedley, Agnes. *Daughter of Earth.* New York: Feminist Press, 1973.

Whitehill, Carol. "Issues of Entitlement." Ph.D. diss., Fielding Institute, 1990.

Zandy, Janet. *Liberating Memory: Our Work and Our Working-Class Consciousness.* New Brunswick, NJ: Rutgers University Press, 1995.

Deb Busman is currently in the creative writing graduate program at Mills College, Oakland. She is an English instructor for the Mills Upward Bound program.

The Self-Manufactured Woman: Working-Class Identity in the Academy

Eileen Bresnahan

Growing up female and feminist and lesbian and working class and Catholic in the South, the main thing I wasn't sure of was why people didn't like me. That they didn't like me, I accepted as a given. But it was too hard to sort out all the variables, to try to figure out in a given case what the cause of their distaste was.

That was then. Now I'm grown and more, though no longer Catholic, no longer Southern—except in those moments when I run across another with these legacies and we compare notes on what they told us. Or stand in solidarity against the Yankee masses who think Southerners are stupid by definition. In these times, I've seen even race recede in the face of the necessities of the times. Together we defend the South, though the only praise I still ever can manage of Catholicism is that it gave me a good general education and lots of great stories to tell, even while willfully misinforming me on matters of sex and faith.

In those times of solidarity, it is so warming to belong and to get a sense of what it must be like to fit, to be part of the jolly crowd, to share the same understandings as one's companions. What being working class does, too often, is to isolate the sufferer. She is not one of the group, but neither is she a member of another group. She has had to define herself against the rest, and so she does this even with those like herself. She cannot identify with them for the same reasons that she cannot be identified with: because they are shabby and slow and too serious and have little fun to offer. Were she to identify with them, she would have to admit she is one of the despised. So instead she despises the others, despises those like her—and despises herself. Internalized oppression, I've long since known it's called. Franz Fanon, blah, blah, blah. In high school it matters little; in high school you just want to fit in.

Now, of course, that admission seems tawdry. Now as a feminist, I'm expected to have analyzed the situation all along. Now I listen to women who have never in their lives been really different, praise difference as though it were manna while at the same time extolling community, ditto. We vamp around in clothes meant to be cool, costing more than a working-class family can afford to spend on Christmas. Working class means shopping at Kmart and Wal-mart, not just for toiletries and lawn furniture, but for an entire wardrobe, including shoes. One dress a year. In teen years, it means making do with what you can scrounge from your siblings, your parents, and the thrift stores, trying to look cool on no money, and sometimes, by dint of talent and nerve and lots of failed effort, succeeding; more often becoming an object of curiosity or derision. "Not our kind, dear." "What could she have been thinking?"

Working class means looking working class in ways that are not cool: having bad teeth and bad skin and bad hair—all reminders of a childhood of neglect and poor nutrition and emotional stress. Working-class parents commonly have the same legacy that they have given to their children—they grew up poor. Though they may love their children, their own self-loathing can get in the way of really liking them. You may have read black women's remembrances of their mothers, keeping house all day for privileged white families and coming home at night full of stories of the achievements of their "other babies," stories of all that their own neglected children could never be. This injury of race is also an injury of class: many white working-class parents also let their children know they would like them better if they were someone else, someone richer, someone prettier, someone who has had more advantages. A lot of women have known the feeling that some cherished relative would prefer that they were male. For working-class women, it rarely stops there.

Of course, many working-class parents—perhaps because they are especially intelligent or unusually politically aware or remarkably kind—do manage not to allow their own self-loathing to damage their children, either because they have somehow defeated it within themselves or have somehow kept from passing it on. But if we truly acknowledge the injuries of class and face up to what it does, what legacy it leaves, we have to admit that these triumphant ones are exceptions to the rule. They somehow have seen through the evil of society's construction of values according to a hierarchy of class; most, however, just accept those values. Indeed, it is arguable that in a capitalist society, to raise your children working class is by definition to neglect them, since you will never be able to give them everything they must have to succeed. They will start behind; they will learn along the way to serve; and before anybody knows it, they will be raising their own children in the wrong neighborhoods, dressed in the wrong clothing, going to the wrong schools.

Feminist, lesbian, Ph.D.—each a step away from who you were meant to be when you were growing up, each a critique of that former self as inadequate, making them right all along. Now she who was you is an embarrassment to those around you. You see them react to new versions of what you used to be and remember being that. You know you would not be that now, no matter what, and wonder who you were when you were that person. She is Other, so you are your own Other— a schizophrenic place to be, to be sure. Defined against, you have left everything behind to remake yourself.

But the women tell you that you have no self and that the woman as such does not exist. What, then, is this thing that you have made, for which you have struggled so long and hard? Fashioning an identity out of the bits and pieces of the culture is not a project that everyone must take on. Identities may be given for those who fit, but they are not for those who do not. These must remake themselves, to try to repair the "problems," to try to become acceptable to others—one of the requirements of mothering, we're now told—though in the working classes, apparently, too often left undone. And this not for lack of trying, but because a working-class mother can produce an "acceptable" child only by making her middle class; self-replication equals failure.

Was it my mother's fault that I wasn't "acceptable" growing up? Or my father's mother's, immigrant wife of a tenant farmer on the silent plains of North Dakota? She reared a son fit for those plains, gave him an eighth-grade education, and sent him out to spend a war in the engine room of a battleship in the South Pacific. He became my father, fresh from technical school in his marine uniform, married to my mother eleven months before I was born. She was twenty-nine, he thirty-one, and they went on to have ten more, without a breather. The oldest, I would see people in passing cars count heads as we went by in the station wagon we didn't even own. A company car, the one real perk he got, to travel the "territory": Florida, Georgia, and some of Alabama at first. He was always gone, making a living. "Your father works so hard," they said, and you couldn't argue. He did.

And my mother? I remember begging her to have no more children. First crying, then raging, then threatening. "You'll never see me again, if you do. When I'm grown, I'll go, and never come back." And it came true. I'm gone forever; we are strangers, beyond all healing hope. I didn't really mean it when I said it, but somehow it's one of the truest things I ever said.

Feminism saved my life—it did. I fought for it in order to exist. In order not to become a woman like my mother, who let life wash over her like ocean waves and drifted with the tide. It made me who I am. But now I feel I have to fight women who call themselves feminists, to fight them in order to be at all. My students ask me why we're reading what we are, and I have no answers. But I have to find the answers, beyond "I had to be competent in this to get and keep my job. Personally, I think it's crap, but we have to know it now." How did we get here? We start the course with excitement and lively discussion and end with depression and confusion and frustration and discouragement. I do know how to teach—why can't I teach this stuff? Why does it repel my students, when the Redstockings still excite them; W.I.T.C.H. turns them on; and Solanas leaves them laughing? Where does that energy go, and in whose interest is it that it leave? It's the politics, stupid. The students know their lives are crap; they're looking for answers that speak to them in language they can understand, because the people writing that language understand their lives because they live them, too. Can I write like that and publish? If so, I have yet to find the key, the magic way to unlock that heavy door. I'm frustrated along with them. I love them for their budding feminism and want to help them, but I can't even help myself.

Always in danger of crumbling, the edifice I've made rises on the spot where I once stood. It's quite a mix of styles—different periods of construction and all that. Patched over where the seams show through, passable for what it is, though anyone with eyes can see that it was cheaply made. Am I comfortable with it, or is it all I can afford? I know it's mine, but whose am I?

If I expose this, is it knowledge? Is my personal political? It seems so self-indulgent to demand recognition of one's own experience, but feminist epistemology has often depended on such methods. And in American feminism today, consciousness of class is very low. Words like *style* and *taste* and *manners* conceal judgments formed by class; a realization of that might help us recognize the power they embody. But style and taste and manners also enhance lives, enrich living, and smooth the way. Am I to be congratulated for realizing this or condemned for being too weak to live as the class in which I was born? If the former, why not, then, a sex change? Start out one way, live another. Is there a difference?

Integrity, for me, inheres in trying to be who I would choose to be. But to achieve that freedom, I have given up a lot; to be true to myself has meant being false to everything I was reared with. In the academy, by learning a new language and a different way of life, I have found a home in which I cannot feel at home. This all is the cost of gaining a voice, but even then it is difficult to be heard. The expected academic forms are alienating and class specific, but can anything else be understood as knowledge? Surely in feminism, if anywhere, it might be so.

Eileen Bresnahan is an assistant professor of political science and women's studies at the University of Utah.

Tangled Threads: Two Novels About Women in the Textile Trades, *Call the Darkness Light* by Nancy Zaroulis and *Folly* by Maureen Brady

Julia Stein

Two recent novels that deal with women working in textile factories are Nancy Zaroulis's *Call the Darkness Light,* about a woman textile worker in Lowell, Massachusetts, in the 1840s, and Maureen Brady's *Folly,* about North Carolina garment workers in the 1970s. Before I compare changes in the roles of proletarian heroines from the 1840s to the 1970s, I will look at other literature about textile work.

When did literature on the textile trades begin? There has been much written about women's preindustrial textile work.[1] In 1994 Elizabeth Wayland Barber published *Women's Work: The First 20,000 Years,* on women's work with cloth in early times. Barber claims that when humans settled into Neolithic farming communities in the Middle East and also in the Americas, they developed the first looms, which empowered them during the Neolithic Age. Barber analyzes Homer's *Odyssey,* in particular the episode of Odysseus' visit to the island of the Phaiakians, a society much like that of Minoan Crete. The Phaiakian women's creation of "delicate well-spun draperies," as described by Homer, empowered them (Barber 121).

Women weavers remained empowered for the next two thousand years, particularly in the English weaving villages. In his book *Rebels Against the Future,* Kirkpatrick Sale describes the English Midlands where thousands of cottage weavers lived and women "work the same machines (as men) and earn an equal social status" (36). However, in the late eighteenth century, Watt's steam engine, the spinning jennies, and the power looms all were organized in a factory system imposed on the English Midlands that largely destroyed the village weaving culture, first in England and then in America.

American women, unable to support themselves as handweavers, found work in the new factories. In his book *Beneath the American Renaissance,* David S. Reynolds maintains that the factories inspired "the literature of women's wrongs . . . [which] portrayed the miseries of American women, usually working-class women brutalized by dissolute men or exploited in the workplace" (351). This mid-nineteenth-century literature is the first generation of fiction about working-class women, to which even Herman Melville contributed. In 1855 he published in *Harpers* his sketch "The Paradise of Bachelors and the Tartarus of Maids," showing rich men feasting while New England women workers silently suffered in the new paper mills. Melville, letting his readers draw the obvious conclusion regarding the male economic exploitation of women workers, offered no solutions. Reynolds argues that for two decades before Melville's piece, American authors had written factory-girl novels and stories about suffering seamstresses and that "'The Tartarus of Maids' was a literary culmination of a rich tradition of fiction about women factory workers" (353).[2]

The second generation of women's proletarian fiction began after 1900. Between 1900 and 1920, the feminist and labor movements combined to produce a mass organization of more than 100,000 working women and also a new generation of radical fiction writers and literary critics. These critics first used the term *proletarian literature* to describe the new novels dealing with the working class. In *Labor and Desire*, Rabinowitz comments that the "term 'proletarian literature' had been used by the socialist editors of *The Comrade* as early as 1901 and that Floyd Dell used it in connection with John Reed and Jack London in *The Masses* in 1919" (21). Interestingly enough, Dell used the term in connection with Reed, an author from the middle class, as well as London, a writer born in the working class.[3] I will follow Dell's practice and include authors from both the middle class and the working class when I refer to proletarian literature.

Novels about garment sweatshops published after 1900 include Theresa Malkiel's *Diary of Shirtwaist Striker* (1911), Florence Converse's *The Children of Light* (1912), and Zoe Beckley's *A Chance to Live* (1918). Jewish working-class immigrants Anzia Yezierska and Theresa Malkiel wrote fiction about garment workers in New York City from the viewpoint of the workers.[4] In Malkiel's novel, the collective action of the women strikers improved their lives. The huge wave of labor militancy in the Northeast before World War I convinced many garment and textile factory owners to move their factories to the nonunionized Southeast, but southern women soon began to organize.

The 1929 Gastonia strike of textile workers in North Carolina inspired six novels published during the 1930s—the third generation of proletarian fiction. In these works, as in Malkiel's text, the strike is central. Women wrote four of these books: Myra Page's *Gathering Storm* (1932), Grace Lumpkin's *To Make My Bread* (1933), Mary Heaton

Vorse's *Strike* (1930), and Fielding Burke's *Call Home the Heart* (1932).[5] Lumpkin, Page, and Vorse all were southern white middle-class women. Page's father, for example, was a physician, and Lumpkin came from an aristocratic but not wealthy Georgia family. E. A. Schachner, a leading 1930s Marxist critic, lauds their novels and "argues that the southern white male culture, which constrained elite white women within the double standard, created a sensitivity among these privileged women to the plight of black and white workers" (Rabinowitz 26). Both Page and Lumpkin had experience organizing textile workers in the South, which they used in writing their novels. Page and Lumpkin as well as Vorse and Burke placed "strong female protagonists at the center of their texts" about the Gastonia strike (Lumpkin xxiv).

Zaroulis's and Brady's novels are the fourth generation of women's fiction about textile factories.[6] Glyn Hughes's 1987 novel *The Rape of the Rose* is another contemporary work dealing with textile work. Hughes's book deals with both the weavers' resistance to the factory in the short-lived Luddite rebellion of 1810–1811 in Britain and the impact of the factory on women's lives. The foremen in Hughes's novel use physical violence to keep the women and children workers in line. Furthermore, factory work was so hated that factory hands were hard to get. Orphans from the workhouse were made to work, as they were prisoners in the mill. In this book, Margaret, a nine-year-old workhouse child, is indentured when her starving mother agrees to this condition. Later, Mr. Horsfalls, the mill's owner, rapes Margaret. Hughes brilliantly shows the connections between females' total economic dependency and their becoming victims of sexual violence and physical abuse.

In Nancy Zaroulis's novel, *Call the Darkness Light,* about the Lowell textile mills in the United States during the 1840s, the heroine, Sabra Palfrey, must live in a boarding house at Lowell; the factory dominates the physical space of both her work life and her personal life. In the book, English textile towns have a reputation for dissipation, gin drinking, and prostitution. American mill owners obtain their first labor force by convincing farm families to allow their daughters to work in the mills, boasting that they "offer our females a dignified life free of old world degradations" (Zaroulis 124). A patriarchal system of boarding houses was instituted where the girls had to stay; matrons policed the girls' behavior; and the boarders had to obey curfews.

In Maureen Brady's novel *Folly,* the garment factory, the biggest employer in town, also dominates both work space and personal space. Folly, the heroine, lives—as do many textile workers—in a trailer court near the mill in Victory, a company town in North Carolina where the factory dominates the residences of its employees. Just as Sabra faces repression in her personal life in the boarding house, in *Folly* the women have repressed personal lives, as two important characters, Martha and Lenore, are both in-the-closet lesbians.

Although Sabra Palfrey lived in the 1840s and Folly in the 1970s, they share some striking similarities. As young women, both seek to escape their working-class lives by becoming romantically involved with men who symbolize escape. They never think of escaping by going to school or having a career, as a bourgeois heroine might. Sabra marries Silas Blood, a young man dedicated to raising money to start a utopian colony; Folly marries Barney, who takes her for rides on his motor scooter and plans to escape their little southern town. Both men do escape, leaving the women alone to raise the children: Sabra has one, and Folly has three. Both women then are forced to work in the factory to support their children.

Both these novels describe intense ethnic segregation in their heroines' towns. In the 1840s, the mill owners hire only Anglo-American women, refusing to hire the new Irish immigrants, who are forced to live in the Irish ghetto. In the 1970s, both white and African American women work in the garment factory; the African Americans are forced to live in a ghetto, and this residential segregation carries over into social segregation on the job. The heroines of both novels are able to cross over, developing connections with "the other." Sabra rescues a starving Irish girl whom she brings into the boarding house; later destitute herself, Sabra goes to live in the Irish ghetto. In the 1970s, when organizing a strike of both white and African American women, Folly is the first white woman to empathize with the black women's complaints during the organizing drive. As she grows to overcome her white chauvinism, she changes her organizing strategy.

Besides describing ethnic segregation, both novels describe difficult working conditions. The corporations in the 1840s increase the number of looms each woman has to tend from two to three, with only ineffectual resistance from the workers. In the 1970s, the owner tries to increase production, but Folly circulates a petition against the increase, which stops it. Both novels describe how the unsafe workplaces cause illnesses in the workers: in the 1840s, the girls get "cotton lung" from breathing in the cotton lint. In the 1970s Folly looks at her friend Daisy, in her sixties, with arthritis: "This was the arthritis that everyone got at the factory eventually from pushing material through the sewing machine" (Brady 33).

These two works also use the labor history of their periods to tell of the attempts by the women at labor organizing. When Sabra's friend

Betsey Rudd circulates a petition for the ten-hour day, she is fired and blacklisted. Sara Bagley, a union agitator, actually lived in Lowell, organizing women into the Female Labor Reform Association, which agitated for the ten-hour day. Bagley and her followers, though brave, could organize only 3 percent of the women in Lowell. In contrast, Folly in the 1970s successfully started a strike and brought a union to her factory. During the 1970s, the women in the South were, after fifty years of failed attempts, finally able to unionize, as in Brady's novel. Why did unionization fail in the 1840s but succeed in the 1970s?

One huge difference between the two periods, as Zaroulis showed, was that in Lowell, patriarchal assumptions about women's role prevailed. Gramsci's concept of ideological hegemony is useful: the corporations had ideological hegemony in Lowell. In Zaroulis's novel, the organizer Sara Bagley complains that most female workers feel that their reputations would be ruined if they were to join a union. In the novel, Bagley says that one woman she asked to join a union said she couldn't because "Father would never approve" (336). Bagley maintains that the corporations "depend on the women to shackle themselves. . . . We insist on being perfect ladies, we agree among ourselves that it is unsuitable conduct to complain about our wages" (335). The corporations sponsored the *Lowell Offering,* which printed literature by mill women and helped the corporation define factory work as beneficial for women. In 1853, in his novel *Spiritual Vampirism,* C. G. Webber had a character criticize such publications as the *Lowell Offering:* "which consisted in poetico-rural pictures of the joys brought home by the factory-girl, to some father or bedridden grand-papa" (Reynolds 353). Bagley could never break down the corporation's ideological dominance.

The patriarchal ideological hegemony finally was broken at the beginning of the twentieth century. Theresa Malkiel's *Diary of a Shirtwaist Striker* deals with this problem directly. When Mary, the heroine, strikes, she must endure the hatred of men on the streets, her fiancé's telling her to quit the strike, and her father's hatred of her actions. After Mary's father throws her out, she goes to live with one of her women striker friends in a tenement. These strikers create female spaces both in the tenement and on the streets in their picket lines where they support the strike. After the women win the strike in Malkiel's novel (as in real life), the fathers and boyfriends finally approve the women's actions. Malkiel's novel is important because it shows how women's solidarity and a successful strike break down patriarchal assumptions about women's place.

Folly is quite different from the earlier novels. When Cora, one of the workers, is at her job, her child dies at home. Then the factory manager sends her home and calls the police, who arrest her. Cora's arrest sparks the strike. The women have their own ideology of fairness; when their female ideology is violated, they are enraged and start a wildcat strike. The narrator describes how the picketers articulate their ideology: "They didn't talk money. They talked about Cora and principles and being treated like shit" (Brady 29).

The strike in *Folly* is reminiscent of strikes in 1930s fiction. For sixty years, there has been a critical dialogue about proletarian novels of the 1930s. In *The Radical Novel in America 1900–1954*, Walter Rideout describes four main types of such novels: "(1) those centered about a strike; (2) those concerned with the development of an individual's class-consciousness and his conversion to Communism; (3) those dealing with the 'bottom dogs' the lowest layers of society; and (4) those describing the decay of the middle class" (171). Rideout cautions that these types are not exclusive and that "the conversion frequently comes by the way of strike" (172).

The four women's 1930s novels about Gastonia are classic strike novels. In *Labor and Desire*, Rabinowitz notes that Josephine Herbst's Trexler trilogy traces the decay of a middle-class American family. Rabinowitz then adds two more plots that 1930s women novelists used: a working-class girl child growing up, as in Tillie Olsen's *Yonnondio*; and a young college-educated woman who, after joining the workers' struggle, rejects her confining middle-class upbringing, as in Tess Slesinger's *The Unpossessed*.

Do Rideout's and Rabinowitz's categories for 1930s novels pertain to books written in the 1970s or 1980s? Nancy Zaroulis's *Call the Darkness Light* follows none of the six patterns. There were no strikes in the 1840s because labor was too beaten down to strike. Sabra does not change her political consciousness. The Irish, not the Anglo, factory girls were the "bottom dogs." There are no parents because Sabra is an orphan, so this story is not about the decay of a middle-class family; Sabra does not rebel against a middle-class upbringing; and this is not a story about growing up in a working-class family.

Zaroulis's novel does not follow any preconceived pattern outlined by Rideout or Rabinowitz, but *Call the Darkness Light* does have features in common with Harriet Wilson's *Our Nig*, Agnes Smedley's *Daughter of Earth,* and Anzia Yezierska's *Bread Givers*. The heroines in all four books are working young women on their own, without families. In Wilson's *Our Nig* (1859), the first novel written by an African American, the heroine is an orphan who runs away from the brutal household where she works and tries to survive on her own. Yezierska's heroine ran away from her overbearing father, and Smedley's heroine loses her

mother while quite young. All four heroines have difficulty supporting themselves; they survive loneliness or unfortunate marriages
and/or sexual traumas. Wilson, Zaroulis, Yezierska, and Smedley have
created a new proletarian woman's novel about a young woman who
is alone in the world struggling to survive. Reynolds says that by the
end of Wilson's novel, the heroine has learned "'to assert her rights
when trampled on' as she is thrown on her own resources and left only
with faith in herself" (361).

Although Zaroulis's book does not follow any of Rideout's or
Rabinowitz's patterns, Maureen Brady's *Folly* does resemble one of
Rideout's categories—a strike fiction in which the strike leads to the
protagonist's conversion. Lesbian feminist consciousness in the 1970s
novel has replaced the communist consciousness of the 1930s. In
Grace Lumpkin's 1930s novel *To Make My Bread,* the main female character is an Appalachian mountain woman named Bonnie McClure.
Bonnie is modeled after Ella Mae Wiggins, a mill worker, organizer,
and balladeer at Gastonia who was murdered by company thugs before
"fifty witnesses" for trying to organize black as well as white mill hands
(Lumpkin xxvi). In *To Make My Bread,* Bonnie McClure is shot and
killed when she is speaking at a rally to the strikers; her death cements
her brother John's conversion to communism at the end of the novel.
In contrast, Folly is never even threatened with violence in the 1970s
during her strike.

Folly in the 1970s is exceptional, just as Bonnie McClure was in the
earlier fiction. Both women have courage, strength, dedication, and
leadership ability. Both Bonnie's and Folly's consciousness develop as
they organize a union. Both are able to develop close working relationships with African American women. Both authors, Lumpkin and
Brady, are concerned with white women and black women bridging
the racial divide in order to work together for the union.

The lesbianism is new as well as the stress placed not on class solidarity but on female solidarity. Through her love for her co-organizer
Martha, Folly is able to change her feelings about lesbians, from fear
to acceptance. While organizing, she even breaks through her own sexual repression by making love to Martha. After the strike succeeds, she
comes out to her daughter Mary Lou. Folly learns to listen to and
respect her African American co-organizer Mabel. In organizing, she
learns lessons of female solidarity. Folly says that the main way in which
she is better off after winning a union contract is that "it had brought
her closer to the other women" (191). After the women go back to
work as union women, Folly's lover Martha is docked by the boss for
taking time off after her mother's funeral. This incident ignites Folly's

dream of having a women-run cooperative mill where the women would be in charge of their work lives. Folly has a newfound feminist consciousness at novel's end that allows her even bigger dreams of female empowerment—of women being in control of making textiles. One theme, the mother-daughter bond, does continue from the 1840s through the 1930s to the 1970s. In *Labor and Desire*, Paula Rabinowitz claims that the "relationship of mother and daughter appears crucial to narratives of female working-class subjectivity" (136). The mother-daughter bond also is key in *Call the Darkness Light*. Although Sabra's one goal is to provide a better life for her daughter, she is unable to stop her daughter Clara from going to work in the Pemberton Mills in nearby Lawrence. The Pemberton Mills collapsed in 1860 in one of the worst workplace disasters in the nineteenth century. Zaroulis's description of this disaster, the climax of the novel, is both horrifying and moving. Clara is inside the mill when it collapses but survives, mute and wounded. Sabra's inability to save her daughter from this suffering is, I think, an accurate depiction of the lives of nineteenth-century working-class women. For a year and a half Sabra nurses her mute, unmoving daughter, always hoping for her recovery, until one day her daughter at last registers her mother's presence: "It was Clara come back again" (Zaroulis 560). Sabra has become a heroic proletarian mother who has nurtured her daughter back from death to life.

Brady's novel has two important mother-daughter relationships. Folly's best friend Martha can't save her mother from having a stroke and dying at the end of the novel. The second mother-daughter relationship is that of Folly and her teenage daughter Mary Lou. At the beginning of the novel, Folly worries about her daughter but feels there is little she can do. But after Folly organizes a strike, Mary Lou supports the family by working at the supermarket, which ends her mother's carping. At the end of the novel, after Folly's union gets the workers a raise, Folly encourages her daughter to continue in school and go to college. The impotent, worrying mother at the beginning of the novel is replaced by a more self-confident mother at the end. In addition, Daisy has left her daughter Martha $20,000 in insurance, which allows Martha and Folly to begin planning to open a cooperative mill. Two generations of women are encouraging their daughters to have dreams of empowerment. Although Sabra was never able to encourage her daughter's intellectual aspirations, Folly can encourage her daughter to have a life based on intellectual development and not on drudgery.

So far the nineteenth-century proletarian heroine has been compared with the twentieth-century one. But how do the heroines of *Call the Darkness Light* and *Folly* compare with the bourgeois heroines in American fiction or nonfiction? In 1844 Margaret Fuller published *Women in the Nineteenth Century,* "an uncompromising demand for women's complete mental self-reliance. . . . Fuller asked women to devote themselves to truth, to the pondering of ultimate questions and the full development of inner capacities" (Reynolds 350). In addition, in her 1855 novel *Ruth Hall,* Fanny Fern describes a bourgeois heroine who evolved "from tearful victim to aggressive author and businesswoman" (Lauter et al. 1:1948). After Fern's novel, many bourgeois heroines in American fiction had expectations for fulfilling work, their own voice, and female autonomy. In the nineteenth century, the bourgeois heroines' aspirations were "often in conflict with society's. . . . Some version of this conflict underlay a whole series of important postwar fictions by writers from Rebecca Harding Davis and Elizabeth Stuart Phelps to Charlotte Perkins Gilman, Frances Harper, Kate Chopin and Mary Austin" (Lauter et al. 2:17).

These aspirations of bourgeois American women, however laudable, were seen by some nineteenth-century feminists as ignoring the realities of proletarian women. Reynolds states that during the 1850s, the suffrage newspaper the *Una* published the novella "Stray Leaves from a Seamstress's Journal," which criticized Fuller: "Could Fuller look into seamstress' comfortless homes and see them toiling fourteen to sixteen hours a day, . . . she would then realize how difficult, how impossible is self-development, when there is only the means of keeping body and soul together" (351).

In *Call the Darkness Light,* Sabra is too busy trying to "keep body and soul together" to think about self-development. As a Lowell factory worker, she thinks she lacks talent or ability to escape the factory: "I will never get free. . . I have come back because I had no choice and I will never get free again" (328). She has two bourgeois women friends whose aspirations are higher: Rachel Bradshaw, whose father managed a textile mill, becomes a schoolteacher and a feminist, and Mrs. Wetherbee, supported by her accountant husband, becomes a writer. The harshness of Sabra's life constrict her aspirations for both herself and her daughter. When she loses her factory job after a botched illegal abortion, her attempt at running her own dressmaking shop fails. When her wealthy friend Rachel Bradshaw begins to encourage Sabra's daughter to dream of having a career, Sabra thinks about ending Rachel's visits—aspirations are, to Sabra, dangerous nonsense.

In the beginning of Brady's novel, Folly also lacks aspirations for herself as a young woman, following her mother into the garment factory. She has vague dreams of her daughter Mary Lou going to college but is unable to talk about these dreams to anyone. Winning the strike, though, changes both her and her daughter's aspirations. She tells Mary Lou for the first time that she wants her to go college, and she tells her lover Martha she wants financial independence by starting a cooperative mill. The proletarian heroine, through developing self-confidence from the successful strike, has begun to develop aspirations similar to a bourgeois heroine's.

Unlike *Folly*, Sabra does not make her way as a heroine in a bourgeois realistic novel should. Zaroulis's *Call the Darkness Light* is reminiscent of the huge novels written by Tolstoy or Dickens during the nineteenth century. The panorama is large, the history accurate, and the characters many. Sabra is blown hither and yon and, like a heroine in Victorian melodrama, needs to be rescued at critical moments. It would be only the most exceptional working-class woman who could act as a heroine, first having dreams and then creating her own destiny. Thus what we think of as melodramatic shifts actually may be accurate portrayals of the majority of women dealing with a social order offering them only low-paid jobs of drudgery for twelve or fourteen hours a day.

Folly covers a much shorter span of time, less than a year, and is, according to critic Bonnie Zimmerman, a "realist lesbian feminist novel." Folly and her wildcat strikers say they know nothing about unions, but that presupposes there is something to know—a knowledge that is lost and can be gained. They do contact a union organizer who helps them conduct the strike and negotiate a contract. By 1970, the labor, feminist, and civil rights movements had built a social structure that had a sufficient support system for working-class women for them, too, to begin to control their own destiny. They could begin to be heroines struggling to fulfill their dreams in a realist novel. They could begin to have aspirations for both themselves and their daughters.

Bonnie Zimmerman, a critic of lesbian feminist literature, faults Brady for her underdeveloped African American characters. Zimmerman's position is very close to that of Marxist critic Georg Lukacs. According to Terry Eagleton in *Marxism and Literature*, Lukacs in *Studies in European Realism* thought that

> a "realist" work is rich in a complex, comprehensive set of relations between [hu]man[s], nature and history; and these relations embody and unfold what for Marxism is most "typical" about a particular phase of history. By the "typical" Lukacs denotes those latent forces in any society which are from a Marxist viewpoint most historically significant and progressive, which lay bare the society's inner structure and dynamic. (Eagleton 28)

The civil rights movement and the women's movement had a great impact on southern working-class women, and the dialogue between black and white women was key to organizing in the southern mills. The civil rights, union, and feminist movements are the historical progressive forces in Lukacs's theory. If Brady had linked the women with "the social whole and informed each concrete particular of social life with the power of the 'word-historical'" moment, her novel would have been richer (Eagleton 28).

Call the Darkness Light teems with characters involved with the reform movements important in American life in the 1840s and 1850s: utopians, Shakers, abolitionists, union agitators, and feminist activists. Zaroulis also includes German and Irish immigrants, Irish nationalists, and anti-immigrant mobs. She has created living Irish characters and two sides to Lowell—an Anglo side and an Irish side. Sabra is close friends with Rachel Bradshaw, an abolitionist and feminist; John Prince, the union agitator, is her lover. Sara Bagley agitates for the women workers, and Sabra's friend Klaus Hartman runs an abolitionist newspaper and fights for the Union in the Civil War. Zaroulis has succeeded, as Lukacs advises, in creating "typical" characters who embody the "historically significant and progressive" forces, and she fleshes them out in concrete characters and actions (Eagleton 28). *Call the Darkness Light* is a brilliant novel.

In conclusion, *Call the Darkness Light* and *Folly* are part of a literary genre that has lasted for 170 years. American women and men first wrote factory novels in 1815 and continue to write them in the 1970s and 1980s. This literary history brings up many questions. In the nineteenth century, could only bourgeois fictional heroines seek fulfilling work and female autonomy? Were these aspirations unrealistic for most nineteenth-century working-class women? In the twentieth century, do proletarian fictional heroines have higher aspirations? Is this a result of successful political movements that raised the aspirations of proletarian women? How do Rabinowitz's or Rideout's theories about 1930s novels fit nineteenth-century proletarian fiction or early- or late-twentieth-century novels? For example, Rideout says that "the strike novel" is an important type in both the pre–World War I period and the 1930s. Yet some decades, such as the 1840s and the 1960s, are not dominated by strikes but by reform movements (Reynolds 80). So working-class novels about the 1960s, such as Alice Walker's *Meridian*, are naturally focused on the black civil rights movement, just as *Call the Darkness Light* is focused on the reform movements of the 1840s.

Are novel forms connected with particular social structures or social movements or changes in technology? In what ways? How do these forces shape a proletarian heroine's role and expectations? To answer these questions, we need to study further all four generations of fiction about textile work in factories and fiction about preindustrial textile work. These novels and stories may not be marginal but central to an understanding of American women's lives and of American literature, as they help us see where we have been in the long history of women and textiles. At one time, women gained power and pride in their creation of weavings and quilts. In the future, women might regain control over textile technology, and then their creations of weavings and garments would again be empowering.

NOTES

1. Many American women have written fiction about preindustrial textile work. Nancy Hoffman and Florence Howe's anthology *Women Working: An Anthology of Stories and Poems* (Feminist Press, 1979) contains two fascinating stories. New England writer Mary Wilkins Freeman (1852–1930) wrote in the 1890s "The Bound Girl" about an indentured white girl in 1753. Dorothy Canfield Fisher's (1879–1954) "The Bedquilt" was included in her first collection of short stories, *Hillsboro People* (1915). The story is about a rural spinster aunt who proves her worth to her family by making a splendid bed quilt. Quilting also is an important motif in Okie/Native American poet Wilma McDaniel's book of poetry *Primer for Buford* (Hanging Loose, 1990). Alice Walker's short story "Everyday Use," from her 1973 collection *In Love and Trouble: Stories of Black Women,* explains why quilts create memories for African American women. Elsa Barkely Brown's "Afro-American Women's Quilting: A Framework for Conceptualizing and Teaching African-American Women's History" appeared in *Signs* (summer 1989).

2. Reynolds mentions Sarah Savage's novel *The Factory Girl* (1815), which painted a rosy picture of factory life; the 1834 pamphlet poem *The Aristocrat and Trades Union Advocate, a Colloquial Poem . . . by the Working Women of Boston* was staunchly trade unionist; Mary Andrews Denison's 1847 novel *Edna Etheril, the Boston Seamstress* showed the misery of these women; the novella "Stray Leaves from a Seamstress's Journal" appeared in the feminist newspaper *The Una* during the 1850s, in which "a tone of militant feminist anger has entered the seamstress genre" (Reynolds 353–56).

   Two white Protestant middle-class women wrote novels about mill work that continued this literature of "women's wrongs." In 1862, West Virginian Rebecca Harding Davis published *Margaret Howth*, a novel about an Indiana textile mill with both white and African American workers. Davis inspired New Englander Elizabeth Stuart Phelps to publish *The Silent Partner* in 1871, about women in the New England textile mills. Both Davis and Phelps saw Christianity and individual efforts at reform as the answer to the suffering of mill women. In *The Growth of American Thought,*

Merle Curti said that these "works showing humane sympathy for the underdog and criticizing sharply the ways of the rich were merely the beginnings of a crop of novels . . . in the 1880s and 1890s" critical of the business class (511).

Mill women wrote autobiography, poetry, and journalism. Lowell mill worker Lucy Larcom published poetry and an autobiography, *A New England Girlhood, Outlined from Memory* (reprint, Northeastern University Press, 1986). Benita Eisler edited *The Lowell Offering: Writings by New England Mill Women (1840–1845)* (Lipincott, 1977). Sara Bagley published articles in the labor newspaper *The Voice of Industry*. In 1898, former mill worker Harriet Hanson Robinson published *Loom and spindle: or Life among the early mill girls with a sketch of "The Lowell Offering" and some of its contributors* (Crowell, 1898), in which she describes the strike she saw in Lowell as a child in 1836.

3. Rideout is referring to T. K. Whipple's study in which Whipple states that Jack London came from the lower middle class (Rideout, n. 15, 302).
4. Anzia Yezierska wrote about garment workers in her novel *Bread Givers* (1925; reprint, 1975, Persea) and in her collection of short stories *Children of Loneliness* (1923; republished as *How I Found America: Collected Short Stories of Anzia Yezierska*, Persea, 1991). Two books about the 1909 shirtwaist strike are Arthur Ballard's *Comrade Yetta* (1913) and James Oppenheim's *The Nine-Tenths* (1911). Yiddish writer Sholem Asch deals with the garment industry in his novel *East River* (English language ed., 1946). Important union organizers of garment and textile workers who published autobiographies are Elizabeth Gurley Flynn, *I Speak My Own Piece: Autobiography of "The Rebel Girl"* (reprint, 1973, International Publishers); Rose Pesotta, *Bread upon the Waters* (reprint, 1987, ILR Press); and Rose Schneiderman, *All for One* (1967, Paul S. Erickson).
5. In the 1930s, six novels were written about the Gastonia strike of 1929. Women wrote four of these books: Myra Page, *Gathering Storm* (1932); Grace Lumpkin, *To Make My Bread* (1933); Mary Heaton Vorse, *Strike* (1930); and Fielding Burke, *Call Home the Heart* (1932). The two male novelists were Sherwood Anderson, *Beyond Desire*, and William Rollins, *The Shadow Before*. Fielding Burke is a pseudonym for Olive Tilford Dargan.
6. In 1982, Meredith Tax published her novel *Rivington Street*, about Jewish immigrant garment workers at the time of the Triangle factory fire, and a sequel, *Union Square* (1988). Glyn Hughes's 1987 novel, *The Rape of the Rose*, is about the weavers' Luddite uprising in the English Midlands in 1810. The heroine of Nancy Zaroulis's novel *Call the Darkness Light* is a mill worker in Lowell in the 1840s, and Maureen Brady's *Folly* deals with the organizing of a union during the 1970s in a North Carolina garment shop.

There have been so many contemporary poets who continued to write about the Triangle factory fire that critic Janet Zandy has dubbed this poetry "Fire Poetry." Zandy edited the "Working-Class Studies" issue of *Women's Studies Quarterly* (June 1995), which included two of these fire poems: Carol Tarlen's "Sister in the Flames" and Safiya Henderson-

Holmes's "rituals of spring." Chris Llewellyn wrote a whole book of poetry about this tragedy: *Fragments from the Fire* (1986). Mary Fell's long poem "The Triangle Fire" is from her book *Persistence of Memory* (1984).

Contemporary fiction film and documentary also deal with textile work. Sally Field starred in the movie *Norma Rae,* about the organizing of a strike in a southern textile mill. Half a million southern textile workers went on strike in 1934; "Uprising of '34," a POV/PBS documentary, is about this general strike in the southern mills.

Bibliography

Asch, Sholem. *East River.* New York: Putnam, 1946.

Barber, Elizabeth Wayland. *Women's Work: The First 20,000 Years: Women, Cloth and Society in Early Times.* New York: Norton, 1994.

Brady, Maureen. *Folly.* New York: Feminist Press, 1994.

Curti, Merle. *The Growth of American Thought.* New Brunswick, NJ: Transaction, 1995.

Dargan, Olive. *Call Home the Heart.* New York: Longmans, 1932.

Davis, Rebecca Harding. *Margaret Howth.* New York: Feminist Press, 1990.

Eagleton, Terry. *Marxism and Literary Criticism.* Berkeley and Los Angeles: University of California Press, 1976.

Hoffman, Nancy, and Florence Howe, eds. *Women Working: An Anthology of Stories and Poems.* New York: Feminist Press, 1979.

Hughes, Glyn. *The Rape of the Rose.* New York: Simon & Schuster, 1987.

Lauter, Paul, et al., eds. *The Heath Anthology of American Literature.* 2 vols. Lexington, MA: Heath, 1994.

Lumpkin, Grace. *To Make My Bread.* Urbana: University of Illinois Press, 1995.

Malkiel, Theresa. *Diary of Shirtwaist Striker.* Ithaca, NY: ILR Press, 1990.

Melville, Herman. "The Paradise of Bachelors and the Tartarus of Maids." In *The Heath Anthology of American Literature.* Vol. 1, edited by Paul Lauter. Lexington, MA: Heath, 1990.

Olsen, Tillie. *Yonnondio: From the Thirties.* New York: Delta, 1989.

Rabinowitz, Paula. *Labor and Desire: Women's Revolutionary Fiction in Depression America.* Chapel Hill: University of North Carolina Press, 1991.

Reynolds, David S. *Beneath the American Renaissance: The Subversive Imagination in the Age of Emerson and Melville.* Cambridge, MA: Harvard University Press, 1988.

Rideout, Walter B. *The Radical Novel in the United States 1900–1954.* Cambridge, MA: Harvard University Press, 1965.

Rosenfelt, Deborah S. Afterword to *Daughter of the Hills,* by Myra Page. New York: Feminist Press, 1986.

Sale, Kirkpatrick. *Rebels Against the Future.* Reading, MA: Addison-Wesley, 1995.

Smedley, Agnes. *Daughter of Earth.* New York: Feminist Press, 1987.

Wertheimer, Barbara. *We Were There: The Story of Working Women in America.* New York: Pantheon, 1977.

Yezierska, Anzia. *Bread Givers.* New York: Persea, 1975.

Zaroulis, Nancy. *Call the Darkness Light.* New York: Soho Press, 1993.

Julia Stein *has published two books of poetry,* Under the Ladder to Heaven and Desert Soldiers. *She writes reviews and literary criticism about women's and working-class literature.*

Blood on the Carpet

Carol Tarlen

In my two-room apartment, I am banished to a narrow piece of foam on the kitchen floor while my grandchildren occupy my bed like a small peacekeeping force, sweeping aside sheets and blankets in the arid heat of an Indian summer night. The windows are closed against the screams of motorcycles and fights hurled from the bar across the street. Lack of humidity inspires my grandson's nose to spurt blood. I bring him a cloth as he leans over the toilet, red stigmata swirling into the commode. In the morning, blood stains my carpet.

My sister sends me a birthday card two days late, writes that work is hard, she now has eighty people to supervise. She works eleven-hour days, doesn't get home till nine. Her two children make their own dinner, watch television alone until bedtime. Her best employee left work one night, drove to his ex-wife's apartment, shot her boyfriend, then put a bullet in his brain. The company has decided not to replace him.

When I was laid off the job I'd had for the last fifteen years, I couldn't even be rude to the boss. I needed a good recommendation. I was soon replaced by a twenty-six-year-old college student willing to do full-time work for half-time pay. Although I got another job in the same institution, I had to take a $400 a month pay cut and was put on a six-month "trial period," a euphemism for getting fired for no reason. "You just aren't what we're looking for. It's a bad match," are the reasons most often given. What this means is, "You're fucked. Apply for unemployment immediately." "Just smile a lot and don't say anything," a friend advises. Although I've lasted four months now, I'm nervous. I forget to be silent. Servility escapes me.

My brother calls, says he can't make my poetry reading. Sunday's his only day off from the factory. He has to fix his car, then visit Mom, fix dinner, watch the playoffs with her. She had wanted Cincinnati to win the National League pennant. During the Depression, Daddy played for one of the Reds' farm teams. She can still remember the past, some of it at least; now it's the present that's defeating her.

My brother says he's got too many responsibilities. Varicose veins are throbbing in his legs as he stands all day on a concrete factory floor making tiny, intricate wires for medical equipment. A friend of his got a bad review at work and shot his supervisor. Job stress and murder, the new way to downsize the American workforce.

It's Saturday. I'm allowed to relax. I ignore my carpet's demands for a cleaning and read the *Village Voice:* an article about a working-class leftie who infiltrates an upstate New York militia. The white, frightened, unemployed members own a lot of weapons. His black friends are predicting a race war. He writes that when he volunteered to fight famine in Somalia, he was kidnapped twice, shot at, had to hire a bodyguard, so he bought a Colt .38 police special made in Cleveland. The head of the food program was an Algerian journalist tortured by the French during the revolution. He saw the gun's wooden handle sticking out of the writer's pants. "Fucking Americans and their guns," he said.

When the O.J. verdict came in, all the clericals at work were bent over radios. The black secretaries cheered. The white women were silent, grim. The Latinas and Filipinas didn't give a shit. The next day, one by one, all the honkies talked to Eunice, the African American who answers the phone. They had decided the acquittal was just, even the Irish guy who gets lots of personal phone calls. Our supervisor insisted over and over again that she refused to read or watch anything about the trial. "I did like what Domminick Dunne wrote in the *New Yorker,*" she said. Eunice nodded sympathetically.

I thought about the verdict for twenty-four hours, all the time it really seemed worth putting in for a rich guy. Then it hit me. "Eunice," I said when I relieved her for lunch, "people aren't still talking about that Kennedy cousin who was acquitted of rape. Isn't he in medical school now? Hope he isn't planning on specializing in gynecology."

A few days later a friend called Eunice. I could hear her discussing O.J. "You should have seen the pale faces around here," I heard her say. Then she laughed.

My daughter takes me to dinner for my birthday. We order beer. "Make a wish," she says as we raise our glasses. For about twenty years now, I've wished for world peace, an end to racism, economic justice. I raise my glass. "My wish is to pass my probation and keep my new job."

Alicia works at a national corporation that makes a profit by competing with the post office for express mail and underpaying and exploiting its workforce. She was blackmailed into signing a statement against a coworker that management wanted to fire. They politely brought up her attendance record. She has two kids, one of them learning disabled. She has to take off work a lot.

"Screw the bastards," she answers. "Screw 'em good."

Carol Tarlen *is a clerical worker at the University of California, San Francisco, and a member of AFSCME 3218. She reads her prose and poetry and speaks at labor conferences and festivals, poetry readings, and feminist cultural events. Her work can be found in* Liberating Memory *(Rutgers University Press),* Calling Home *(Rutgers University Press),* For a Living *(University of Illinois Press), and the literary journal* Long Shot.

"These mill-hands are gettin' onbearable": The Logic of Class Formation in *Life in the Iron Mills* by Rebecca Harding Davis

William L. Watson

> *The working class did not rise like the sun at an appointed time. It was present at its own making.*
>
> —E. P. Thompson

Since The Feminist Press reissued Rebecca Harding's 1861 novella *Life in the Iron Mills,* scholars have read it in a variety of contexts without seeing that its publication and composition coincide with a key moment in the process of American class formation.[1] If one looks closely at this context for the novella, a rather startling parallel comes to light. For beginning on Washington's Birthday, February 22, 1860, perhaps as many as thirty thousand shoemakers began "the greatest strike in American history before the Civil War"(Taylor 284).[2] This strike shook New England for six weeks, idling half the workers in New England's largest industry. Mass-circulation newspapers and periodicals all over the United States covered the strike. According to the dean of American labor historians, Phillip Foner, "for a generation . . . [it] was recalled with the vividness and frequency people usually reserved for earthquakes or hurricanes" (*History,* 256).[3] Nor was the Great New England Strike an isolated occurrence: following the panic of 1857, the solidarity and militancy of urban workers became increasingly widespread (237). For instance, a demonstration of unemployed in New York's Tompkins Square in 1857 drew around fifteen thousand people, who then marched on Wall Street and paraded around the stock exchange demanding jobs (239). The shoemakers of Pennsylvania won a statewide strike in May 1859, overcoming attempts to split them along ethnic lines. The typographers, nail makers, and ironworkers in Harding's native Wheeling, Virginia, where half the population of sixteen thousand was composed of industrial workers and their dependents, had unionized in 1859–1860 (Williams 52).[4] And strikes in

Pennsylvania coal mines, New England textile mills, and on western railroads testified to a growing militancy by American workers on the eve of the Civil War (Foner, *History,* 227–40). Recent scholars have noted that *Life in the Iron Mills* transforms the literary traditions it inherited from the 1850s.[5] As of yet, however, no one has noted that Harding's groundbreaking representation of workers evolved at a time when workers were seeking, on an unprecedented scale, to represent themselves.[6] Viewed on such a terrain of evolving class consciousness, *Life in the Iron Mills* asks a timely question: How are American working people to be represented in relations with their employers, in law and politics, in belles lettres and popular culture?

National newspaper coverage of the Great New England Strike provides evidence that it was very much a part of the national experience (Huston).[7] Some northern papers viewed the strike from within the Jefferson-Jackson populist tradition and castigated "cunning capitalists" while lauding self-reliant workers who had "rebelled against . . . oppression" (Huston 200). More often, however, the strike was ammunition in the sectionalist war of words that would soon be resolved by civil war. Democrat newspapers, such as the *New York Herald,* cited the strike as evidence that radical Republican ideology was dangerous to civil order. While lurid *Herald* headlines described "The Revolution at the North," "The Rebellion Among the Workmen of New England," and the "Beginning of the Conflict Between Capital and Labor," the paper editorialized against women's rights and abolitionism, claiming that those ideas were now behind the unrest in Massachusetts. Similar editorials in other Democrat papers saw the strike as presaging a northern economic recession caused by the partial southern boycott of Yankee manufactured goods, a boycott begun in late 1859 (Huston 198; Foner, *Business and Slavery,* 158–64). Proslavery southern papers, such as the *Charleston Mercury,* cited the strike as evidence that free-labor society was on the verge of class warfare because the iron law of wages kept free workers on the verge of starvation (Huston 199–200). Free-labor and laissez-faire Republican papers (the *Wheeling Intelligencer,* which employed Rebecca Harding, was one such paper, although I found no editorials about the strike) argued that far from pending class revolution, the cordwainers' rebellion demonstrated their economic parity with employers and revealed political liberties not found among southern slaves (Huston 204). These papers commonly held that free-market forces would solve the labor problem, often advising that migration to frontier homesteads would ease the oversupply of labor causing depressed wages in shoemaking.

A recent survey of public reaction to the 1860 strike concludes, however, that Republicans and Democrats shared "a view of labor relations [that] was nearly identical" in accepting the tenets of classical liberal political economy (Huston 206, 212). Nowhere in the political debates spawned by the strike are there reservations about the hegemony of supply and demand. The only real challenge to laissez-faire was raised, and widely, by industrial workers and artisans who had been radicalized by hardship after the panic of 1857. These workers commonly argued that something was wrong with a system that meant wealth for a few and poverty for the many.[8] Such workers, however, were "nearly bereft of aid" in "their quest for a change in the laws governing economic endeavors"(211–12).

Placed within this debate, Rebecca Harding's representation of workers' hardship does tender such aid. It critiques the classical liberalism that had such a stranglehold on the labor debate. It distinguishes itself in the 1860 strike controversy by seconding organized labor's critique of laissez-faire. This critique animates those graphic descriptions of working people's degradation that have commonly been seen as something new in American literature. And it hits hardest in the lampoon of the cold, calculating mill owner's son, Kirby, who boasts about controlling the votes of his workers and who, upon being interrogated about their misery, sneers, "Ce n'est pas mon affaire" (34).[9] In Kirby, the free-labor ideology of Republicans and Democrats alike is divested of all Jacksonian cant. And through Kirby, it is suggested that those paeans to workers' dignity and social mobility that filled the air in the 1860 election served merely to camouflage a heartless social Darwinism (Huston 202–3).[10]

But for all its empathy with oppressed workers, *Life in the Iron Mills* appears surprisingly indifferent to the agenda of the striking shoe workers themselves, an agenda that was known and debated from Maine to Mississippi in the spring of 1860. Harding reveals what, historically, was done *to* workers and suggests what could be done *for* them, moral education and social uplift. But she cannot reveal what workers, historically, did *with* what was done to them. Workers' historic attempts at self-representation and self-protection—which were making national news in 1860—comprise an interesting absence in an otherwise detailed portrait of workers' lives. Although it may seem strange to charge such a gritty, "realistic" narrative with a kind of sin of literary omission, I will argue, in fact, that *Life in the Iron Mills* is shaped by just such an unwillingness to disclose workers' strengths.[11] Such omissions, or "gaps," become evident when the novella is read in the context of the Great New England Strike. These gaps helped determine the characterizations, narrative structure, and imagery of Harding's novella and identify it as one of the earliest formulations of class difference and class identity in the industrial United States.

Driven by a logic of class formation, the novella often abets the very injustices it seems to denounce. For example, when Hugh Wolfe, Harding's proletarian protagonist, is convicted of robbing an upper-class visitor to the mill, he received quite a harsh sentence, nineteen years. This sentence registers not only the particular theft but also some unknown depredations committed by the other mill hands, who are "gettin' onbearable," as a jailer says (51). Have there been strikes? Assaults? Demonstrations? Other thefts? The narrative does not elaborate. Hugh and his cousin Deb hope the stolen money will permit Hugh to leave the mill and develop his artistic talents, but if their attempt to redistribute wealth is part of a more widespread collective action by the other "mill-hands," the narrative is not clear on what it is. Thus not only is the unrest of "these mill-hands" unbearable to the property-owning class, it is also un-*bare*-able—what cannot be laid bare—by the graphically detailed narrative of workers' lives itself. The jailer's censure of those workers as "onbearable" slips on a metaphor of vision—"to lay bare"—likening what the bourgeoisie cannot stand and what this germinal example of American realism does not, and perhaps cannot, picture. Certain details of the lives of workers are thus absent from a narrative that has entered literary history precisely because it so convincingly details industrial life. And contradictions such as this are not limited to the jailer's speech.

For instance, both Judge Day's fictive sentence and Harding's characterizations of Hugh and Deb can be seen as glosses on a strategy that the antebellum courts used to respond to labor militancy. Historians of labor law call this strategy "conspiracy doctrine." Conspiracy doctrine evolved in the eastern United States between 1805 and 1842. In at least sixteen trials, strikes, unions, and union boycotts were deemed illegal conspiracies against trade and commerce (Yates 8–9).[12] In *Iron Mills,* Judge Day's response to some unseen and "onbearable" workers' unrest is to make Hugh a synecdoche for the more widespread conspiracy against trade that is absent from both the narrative purview and the legal docket. He hopes to control it by isolating and controlling Hugh. But the novella itself makes Deb and Hugh into synecdoches of life in the abyss by isolating them from their fellow workers, primarily in terms of their gender. The androgynous "Mollie Wolfe" may work and live alongside virile, rowdy iron puddlers, for instance, but his artistic nature makes them distrust and dislike him. And Deb is temperate, chaste, and lovelorn, a kind of True Woman *manqué* surrounded by profanity-spewing, half-clothed, and wholly drunk factory women. Thus the depiction of their resistance—as feeble, individual, and isolated—traces the ideological limits of literary realism. Compared with the epic scale with which it details workers' victimization—the infernal iron mill scenes, for instance, echo Milton and Dante and anticipate *Germinal* and *The Jungle*—the narrative paints Deb's and Hugh's ability to resist as a pathetic miniature. Although the Wolfes' isolated, individual theft signals the merest glimmerings of political awareness, mass resistance is "onbearable" to both power and the narrative. Thus, *Life in the Iron Mills* translates Judge Day's legal strategy for controlling workers into a similar narrative and descriptive strategy. Both Judge Day and the narrative "make an example of them" for a readership made newly alive to issues of social class by the Great New England Strike of 1860.

The March 17, 1860, *Frank Leslie's Illustrated* covered the strike and published one of the most famous pictures in American labor history. It shows a mass parade of striking female shoe factory workers in Lynn, Massachusetts, on March 7. They are marching through a snowstorm led by a company of armed, uniformed militia, a company that was probably also composed of shoe factory workers (Dawley 77; American Social History Project 361). The women are well dressed in the large hoopskirts and bonnets of the time and carry a banner on which is clearly written "American Ladies Will Not Be Slaves" (American Social History Project 361). The early pages of *Iron Mills* depict a procession of workers, too, one of the earliest in American belles lettres. But these workers–a "slow stream of human life creeping past, night and morning, to the great mills. Masses of men, with dull besotted faces bent to the ground, sharpened here and there by pain or cunning"—sharply contrast with the vigorous, assertive Lynn strikers (12). For instance, whereas Harding's "besotted" workers evince a kind of criminal "cunning," the workers' militia cannot be mistaken for criminals; the *Leslie's* artist depicts them as the out-and-out Jeffersonian revolutionaries their speeches and songs proclaimed them to be (Blewett 76–87; Dawley 82; Foner, *History,* 242). Furthermore, various newspapers reported the workers' sobriety; in Lynn, Massachusetts, workers even attempted to prohibit the sale of beer and liquor by local shopkeepers (Foner, *History,* 242). So, at a time when workers' temperance was being nationally publicized, Harding's "besotted" workers are notably *in*-temperate.

Similarly, the women in the shoemakers' march differ significantly from the women workers who first appear in Harding's book. The former are respectably dressed, imbued with communal purpose, and

Women's strike procession, Lynn, Massachusetts, 7 March 1860. Taken from *Frank Leslie's Illustrated Magazine*, 17 March 1860. Courtesy of Cornell University Press.

Women workers organize, Lynn, Massachusetts, 28 February 1860. Taken from *Frank Leslie's Illustrated Magazine*, 17 March 1860. Courtesy of Cornell University Press.

carry placards written in forceful, standard English. Harding's "crowd of half-clothed women"(15), however, is quite drunk and speaks a regional-ethnic dialect ("Inteet, Deb, if hur'll come, hur'll hef fun"[16]). They are distinctly Other to the genteel readers of the *Atlantic*. By contrast, the Lynn shoe workers pictured in *Leslie's* emulate genteel sobriety and modesty even as they violate the Cult of True Womanhood's stipulations that "women should not venture beyond kitchen hearth and church pew" (Dawley 82; also Welter 21–42). They complicate the construction of sympathy that marks the novella, as does another image of the strike published in the March 17 *Leslie's*. This lithograph of a women's strike meeting identifies the strikers as at once decorous and dangerous. It implies a certain evangelical fervor at the meeting, yet the women appear dignified and well organized, and except for the fact that a woman occupies the podium, the pictured women resemble church parishioners more than revolutionaries or criminal rabble. Thus while Deb Wolfe and her afflicted sister workers evoke pathos in the genteel reader, the Lynn shoe workers in *Leslie's* emulate and complicate the respectability of that reader. The *Leslie's* picture almost invites the protofeminist genteel reader— someone who may already be involved in abolition, suffrage, or temperance reform—to recognize her similarity to these impressively organized working women. At the same time, it shows women representing themselves in the debate over worker's rights that has caught the national attention. Tillie Olsen and Jean Pfaelzer noted that the emotional power of *Iron Mills* results from how deeply the author imagined parallels between the sufferings of workers and the oppression of housebound genteel women. It is entirely possible that newspaper coverage of women in the Great New England Strike suggested such parallels.

In contrast to *Leslie's* lithograph, which complicates easy class distinctions, Harding's workers immediately advertise their Otherness. The novella appropriates workers as Other by emphasizing the dialect and foreignness of "drunken Irishmen"(11) and "Welsh emigrants" who "skulk along like beaten hounds"(15). For instance, when one of them asks, "Where's Kit Small, then?" she is answered, "Begorra! on the spools. Alleys behint, though we helped her, we dud" (16). Again, this act of appropriation names itself when read in the context of the 1860 strike. In *Iron Mills,* ethnic origins and social class indicate each other in a way that became familiar later in the century when immigrants made up the majority of industrial workers. However, Harding's tale of the Welsh immigrant Wolfe cousins, Hugh and Deb, is set "nearly thirty years" (15) before the moment in which it is narrated, well before the Irish and German diaspora of the 1840s. The narrative presumes that the pronounced ethnicity and foreignness of the industrial working people in 1861 have been an accomplished fact for more than a generation. The setting for the novella is thus historically bifurcated. In 1860, the narrator gazes out at a "slavish" stream of downtrodden workers, but the downtrodden workers whose tale she narrates inhabit the 1830s. One effect of this narrative sleight of hand is to suggest that thirty years of industrial development have had no effect on the ethnic composition of workers because the plight of workers is somehow timeless or natural. But the way that Harding insists on the ethnicity of her ironworkers is also notable because the striking Lynn shoe workers almost self-consciously resisted any attempt to paint them as un-American.

They are able to refuse wage slavery because of this identity, for instance. "*American* Ladies Will Not Be Slaves"(italics mine) their placard proclaims. They begin their strike on Washington's Birthday, aligning it with the earlier attempt to define a national identity against Great Britain. Moreover, their songs and slogans lay claim to the national identity forged in that earlier revolution. For instance, the tune of one of their strike songs is "Yankee Doodle," and "several hundred Natick workers . . . marched through the streets singing" it in the days directly before the strike (Foner, *History,* 242). The chorus goes "Up and let us have a strike/Fair Prices we'll demand/Firmly let us all unite/Unite through out the land" (Foner, *Songs,* 73). The melody aligns the Massachusetts shoe workers with earlier revolutionary culture, and thus the song associates nationwide worker militancy with patriotism: "ye jours and snobs throughout the land,/tis' time to be astir:/the Natick boys are all on hand,/and we must not demur" (73).

The men of the Lynn strike also resist any rhetoric of Otherness because they cast themselves in the mold of the Jacksonian "Common Man": self-reliant, competent, industrious, and "manly." Harding's characterization of protagonist Hugh Wolfe as emasculated, meek, and without vigor—"he was known as one of the girl-men: 'Molly Wolfe' was his *sobriquet*" (24)—should be read as a class-interested commentary on the assertive masculinist rhetoric of the striking New England cordwainers. Hugh is described as having "lost the strength and instinct vigor of a man, his muscles were thin, his nerves weak," and he is most emphatically not "a good hand in a fight" (24). The Lynn workers, conversely, call themselves "men of pluck and nerve" (Foner, *Songs,* 73). In another song, they warn the Massachusetts bourgeoisie that the strikers *are* good hands in a fight, defining their virility in the very way that the denatured Hugh Wolfe cannot: "You feed upon us working-men/And drink your cobblers too;/But we're rough men, so think again,/We're neither faint nor few"(Foner, *Songs*, 73). The same song drapes the strikers in the trappings of a patriotic masculine patrimony: "So on the Anniversary/Of our Great Father's birth/You must allow how much the vow/of "greasy jours" is worth"(Foner, *Songs*, 74). Thus the strikers came forward as the rightful inheritors of a tradition of distinctly "manly" resistance to tyranny. They represented themselves as strong-handed men who embraced activism as a patrimony from their "Great Father."

Life in the Iron Mills substitutes the androgynous "Molly" Wolfe for the Lynn strikers' assertive masculinity. This artistically inclined "girl-man" represents workers at a time when male workers' resistance to industrial dehumanization featured a self-consciously masculine discourse. Harding thus both identifies gender as a point of contention in the industrial controversy—as do the Massachusetts cordwainers—and inverts the gender orientation of the striking journeymen. Furthermore, even though Hugh's softness and sensitivity are atypical in the iron mill, his rough-and-tumble fellows seem not to have inherited any linked ideals of masculine identity and resistance to tyranny from a revolutionary "Great Father." Instead they fight one another, not their masters, and their violence endangers the artist nature immanent in Hugh Wolfe more than it does the status quo. In contrast, when the Lynn strikers promised "an awful fuss twixt you and us" to those "Gentlemen of Haverhill and Lynn," it seems fair to infer that class battle lines were being drawn in the most industrialized part of the United States at the time of Hugh Wolfe's creation (Foner, *Songs*, 74).

Deb Wolfe, Hugh's hunch-shouldered, unmarriageable cousin, indicates a similar erased threat to the status quo. In an initial scene, Deb refuses to join the drunken woman cotton mill operatives in a carouse. Several of them grab at her, but Deb is defended by an Irish comrade: "Let Deb alone! It's ondacent frettin' a quite body" (42). From the very moment she appears, the narrative asserts that Deb *must* be a very singular proletarian, "a quite body," in some way segregated from the unruly mass of fellow workers by her temperance and sobriety. Here is an answer for a question that has not been asked. Why must Deb be "quite"? One reason Deb's hunch-shouldered body must be quiet is because her sexual desire for Hugh cannot be channeled into marriage, as is emphasized by Hugh's indifferent "kindness" to her, despite her love for him, and by the way that Hugh is attracted to his conventionally pretty neighbor, Janey. This surplus desire is expressed when Deb steals Mitchell's wallet, an act of nascent class consciousness:

"Money, money . . . it wud do all" she tells Hugh (42). To quiet Deb's unquiet body of desire, the narrative contrives a conclusion in which Deb conforms to the leading tenet of the Cult of True Womanhood: Piety, "the core of woman's virtue" (Welter 21). In the Quaker settlement, piety anchors Deb's body of potentially revolutionary desire: "There may be in her heart some latent hope to meet there (in heaven) the love denied her here,—that she shall find him whom she lost, and that then she will not be all-unworthy" (64). Contemplation of heavenly *caritas* absolves Deb of the earthly crimes of desire and class consciousness and ensures her absence from the arena of social unrest.

Deb is described as a "woman much loved by these silent, restful people; more silent than they, more humble, more loving" (63–64). The Quaker settlement encourages Deb to become doubly silent, so that she accedes to the representation effected by the narrative. This overdetermined insistence on Deb's quiescence, however, occurs at a time when workers' protests were publicized "from Maine to Florida" (Foner, *History,* 240). It is not necessary to provoke that Irish worker's appraisal of Deb ("a quite body") to see that twenty thousand militant workers are *quite a body* of workers. In its attempt to picture a worker whose dialect clearly proclaims her Otherness to the genteel reader, *Life in the Iron Mills* reveals the particular historical dialectic of that Otherness. Quite a body of workers—women most famously—may be making a revolution in Massachusetts. However, Harding's literary narrative of workers concludes with Deb's being sequestered far from the barricades and deprived of her ability to resist power. Read in the context of the Great Strike, Deb's seclusion and powerlessness reveal their own artificiality.

In the aftermath of the Great Strike of 1860, Rebecca Harding was historically poised to fulfill Georg Lukacs's requirement for a great "realist." She writes *Life in the Iron Mills* in "a great historical period . . . of transition . . . of crisis and renewal, of destruction and rebirth" (Lukacs 10). However, she ends up both reporting that moment and not reporting it. In a very real way, American realism—in Lukacs's sense of a discourse that "opposes . . . the destruction of the completeness of the human personality" and seeks to counter the "excessive cult of the momentary mood"—is stillborn in Harding's novella (Lukacs 6). For even though it offers the Wolfes as sociohistorical "types" in which "all the humanly and socially essential determinants are present on their highest level of development," this ostensibly revolutionary "type-making" is itself a by-product of the emerging middle class's quest for self-fulfillment and identity (Lukacs 6). The workers whom Hugh and Deb "typify"—antebellum industrial workers—

appear in and disappear from Harding's narrative according to a certain logic of class formation. In brief, *Life in the Iron Mills* reveals workers only when it serves the interests of nonproletarian social groups to do so. This class logic structures the central symbol of the novella: Hugh Wolfe's enigmatic "korl woman" sculpture.

Sculpted from slag in the rolling mill, Hugh's sculpture causes Mitchell and Dr. May to encourage Hugh to pursue his gift. Their advice, however, also forces Hugh and Deb to realize that such a pursuit is nearly impossible, leading to the fateful theft of Mitchell's wallet. Furthermore, because the narrator has acquired it and placed it in his or her study, the scene of writing of the tale, the statue inspires the narrator with a sense of the urgency of that vocation. Intrigued by the mingling of physical power, spiritual hunger, and interpretive possibility in the korl woman, feminist critics have remarked on its autobiographical significance. Thus, whereas ironworkers made and modeled for the korl woman that lurks in the narrator's study, the outlines of a woman author have been seen to inform its "mighty hunger, its unfinished work" (64). As Jean Pfaelzer put it, the statue "assumes the frustrations of Rebecca Harding Davis's own life: unfinished, hungry and eager to know" (243). And in the sculpture's "rough, ungainly" lines, Tillie Olsen detects a ready analogue for the author's fiction, whose imperfections were spawned by a demanding domestic life (Olsen 68, 114). By these accounts, the author's genuine empathy with working-class women, who shoulder the double burden of industrial and domestic work, arose from how she, too, suffered a double burden, of literary work and housekeeping.

To unravel this complex central symbol, a symbol of genteel women's and workers' similar hunger for a better life, one must place such autobiographical readings in the context of working-class history. Here is one way to do so. The korl woman statue, an attempt by a fictional worker at cultural production, should be juxtaposed with the culture of the antebellum workers he represents. The striking Massachusetts workers adumbrate the type of cultural solidarity that Herbert Gutman, Mary Blewett, and others saw among American workers during the early industrial revolution.[13] Herbert Gutman, for example, found the nineteenth-century worker to be "the sum of a total culture [who] . . . had distinct ways of work and leisure, habits, aspirations, conceptions of America and Christianity, notions of right and wrong, and traditions of protest and acquiescence that were linked together . . . by extensive voluntary associations and other community organizations" (Gutman, "Joseph McDonnel," 121). Accordingly, the Lynn shoe workers had their own newspaper, *The Awl*, which was similar in tone, form, and content to the other Boston-area workers' newspapers, *The Voice of Industry* and *The Mechanic*. These combined community news with utopian musings, union propaganda, poems, songs, and editorials by artisans, factory hands, and their supporters (Foner, *Songs*, 46–74). In addition, the Lynn workers' neorevolutionary songs and activism were symptomatic of persistent cultural formations. "The strike processions . . . emerged from the customs and traditions of preindustrial society. They were festivals of the old artisan way of life presented in the context of the new system of industrial capitalism" (Dawley 81). Similarly, as Sean Wilentz found, the symbol-laden parades and festivals of New York artisans played a distinctive role in the cultural life of that city for three-quarters of a century before the Civil War (87–92). The 1860 strike processions, then, are the tip of the iceberg of a distinctive, well-established workers' culture that provided widely known alternatives to industrial commodification of labor, culture and leisure.

The importance of such alternatives is driven home when one realizes that the social criticism in *Iron Mills* derives much of its force from a supposed opposition between culture and labor. By the logic of this dichotomy, if Hugh Wolfe continues to labor as an iron puddler, his fine gifts for *culture*—so evident in the korl woman sculpture—will be destroyed by the "grossness and crime" that determine workers' lives. Graphic details proclaim that there is no worker culture besides cockfights, dogfights, drinking, and fisticuffs. Hugh dies because he cannot be a genteel artist, end of story. Knowledge of a distinctive *workers'* culture, however, undercuts Harding's social criticism by expanding the menu of cultural practices from which workers, such as Hugh Wolfe, can choose. Their songs especially ("Up and let us have strike") define a viable culture that is neither genteel artistic nor degraded, and they define it in terms derived from indigenous American traditions. "Them vile songs of the mill" (52) that Hugh Wolfe's jailer says are sung by imprisoned workers are thus very different from those sung by workers themselves in 1860, and the novella insists on this difference in contradiction to workers themselves. The shoe workers' processions bespeak a collective solidarity that is a vast improvement over the animal-like swarm that *Iron Mills* depicts. And their newspapers, their nationalism, and attempt to enforce temperance all indicate that they are capable of managing themselves collectively to resist the "grossness and crime" that Hugh Wolfe, failed artist, cannot.

If the product of Wolfe's artistic labor stands for the worker culture that was publicized by the cordwainers' strike, then it also disavows that culture. Recovered knowledge of worker activism requires a reexamination of the politics of Harding's novella and its reception, including those autobiographical readings of Pfaelzer, Olsen, and others. To credit these readings, the korl woman sculpture is a by-product of both iron making and Harding's self-creation as a writer. Thus the korl woman symbol practically invites the reader to see that literary production shares the techniques and materials of industrial production. *Iron Mills,* then, both deploys a symbol of exploitive class relations and fears that symbol. For even though the artifact of the industrial abyss cements the narrator's credibility as a reporter of proletarian lives, it also symbolizes the workers' unglimpsed power, the danger they pose to genteel standards of decorum, gender, and culture. In response to this mingled desire and fear, the statue is both present—since the narrator tells the reader about it—and absent, since the narrator keeps it "hidden" behind a screen. Similarly, although the narrator occupies a vantage point from where potentially revolutionary workers may be surveyed, the danger they pose is neither absent nor present, the onlooker neither impervious to it nor paralyzed by it. The narrator's second-floor library, the scene of writing of the tale, perfectly symbolizes this contingent point of view and identity. Even though the house has been gentrified, changed, the library is upstairs from the Wolfes' former dwelling; it is soiled by the insidious mill smoke that both stifles the narrator and hides the industrial inferno from view; and there the korl woman figure of incipient worker unrest is hidden behind a screen, but dangerously present nonetheless.

To explain these contradictions I would argue that more than it encodes the desires and travails of the individual author, the korl woman indicates a certain set of ideas on the role of the author in an industrializing society. Specifically, the korl woman signifies how the processes of class formation and literary creation overlap. It points to how the literary vocation must negotiate with social forces that call it into being and threaten it. Amy Kaplan, for instance, identifies Gilded Age realism as a "strategy for defining the social position of the author" and points out how, to secure this author-position, realist writers "imagined and managed" potential threats to the social order (13). Similarly, Michel Foucault challenges the assumption that "the coming into being of the notion of 'author' constitutes the privileged moment of *individualization* in the history of ideas, knowledge, literature, philosophy, and the sciences" ("What Is an Author," 141). When this "privileged moment" is grounded in historical knowledge, Foucault concludes, the author is not so much the "genial creator" of an "inexhaustible world of significations" as he or she "is a certain functional principle by which . . . our culture . . . impedes the free circulation, free manipulation, free composition, decomposition and recomposi-

tion of fiction" (159). Such an "author function" is essentially peno-
logical, a way of holding the author culpable for fiction's inherent ability to "imagine and manage" alternative realities. "Authors became
subject to punishment," Foucault conjectures, "to the extent that discourses could be transgressive"(148). Rebecca Harding, I would argue,
discovered literature's transgressive potential when she seconded militant workers' critique of laissez-faire, and her novella negotiates
between this danger and her desire to be an author.

The self-consciously genteel narrator in *Iron Mills* thus has a stake
in what Foucault discerned as a general attempt to impose a
"sequestered and observed solitude" on the type of dangerous workers who trudge by his or her window (Foucault, *Discipline,* 204).[14] The
social construction of authorhood takes place when Harding imagines
and manages workers at a moment when real-life workers, in Lynn and
elsewhere, seem unmanageable. Simultaneously both the object and
the subject of the discourse of knowledge and power, the managerial
realist is neither safe from worker revolt nor hidden from the general
surveillance in the industrial city.[15] *Iron Mills* constructs an "author
function" that simultaneously transgresses and courts success through
the representation of workers at a moment of danger. Thus the korl
statue achieves the rich, Hawthorne-like ambiguity that has intrigued
critics for twenty-five years precisely because the Massachusetts strikers issued such a bold, public challenge to the idea of literary ambiguity itself. Through her reticence about the events in Massachusetts,
Harding fashions a conceptual space in which the vocation of letters
is still possible. Her nuanced ambiguity about the "meaning" of the
korl woman and her portrait of workers as uncultured "victims" censor the unbearable events in New England and create breathing room
for belles lettres in what the narrator calls the "stifling" industrial
miasma. The polluted atmosphere that Harding pictures, then, also
signifies the conceptual and economic environment in which genteel
literature of the *Atlantic* type finds itself. It exists uneasily between the
philistine mass-production aesthetic of emergent capitalism and the
danger that militant workers might abolish capitalism, genteel literature, and culture altogether in one fell swoop. *Life in the Iron Mills*
responded to this contradiction. It impeded the free circulation of
information about worker power and self-determination—that is, the
Great Strike—while putting forward images of American workers that
at once disturbed and reassured a genteel reader. The korl woman is
the veritable sign and gauge of this cultural work. As does *Life in the
Iron Mills* generally, it both documents industrial barbarism and dis-
guises literature's role in maintaining it.

A rather stern interrogation of the novella becomes almost irresistible when one considers the extent to which literature and criticism have omitted the Massachusetts strikers. If Hugh Wolfe's powerful sculpture is an artifact of the process by which Harding fashioned herself into an author, then do not the fictional sculpture, its fictional producer, and the vocation of letters thus fashioned all contain and disguise the workers' labor that composes them? As a social and historical phenomenon, does not *Life in the Iron Mills* participate in the general commodification of labor that it decries? Moreover, although *Life in the Iron Mills* advances a timely social criticism through its critique of laissez-faire economics, does it not, at the same time, employ industrial workers to create a managerial "author function" distinct from and above those workers? If so, then the favorable reception of *Iron Mills* makes economic and political sense. The *Atlantic* publication of the novella briefly made Rebecca Harding a literary cause célèbre and launched her long, prolific career. After the novella's publication, she toured the literary shrines of New England, met Hawthorne and Emerson, and was lionized by the *Atlantic* circle, who had experienced mass-worker unrest of unprecedented force the year before. What better rationale for acclaiming Harding than that her novella provided them with a language to understand the class violence they had known firsthand?[16] Furthermore, might not this language also allow Boston's literary Brahmins to preserve the sense of vocation they had inherited from less turbulent and less industrialized times? *Life in the Iron Mills* was certainly suspicious of the economics of literary and industrial production, in other words, but working-class studies should consider the extent to which the novella abetted the cruel stratification of industrial society that it documents.

In conclusion, *Life in the Iron Mills* represents workers because by doing so, literary writing created for itself a timely new role as the representative and manager of workers' lives and labor. But a profound anxiety haunts the text as well, the fear that militant workers, through widespread attempts to represent themselves, threaten the culture and social identity that the managerial writer would construct. In response to this linked fear of and desire for workers, Rebecca Harding introduced American workers to the readers of James Field's *Atlantic* as victims par excellence. Harding's disempowered, denatured worker-victims beckon bourgeois social "reform" to shape the representation of working people to its own ends. At much the same moment, the Great New England Strike revealed militant workers who emulated, transfigured, and threatened hegemonic definitions of femininity, class, and national identity. Only when read in the context of working-class culture and activism can *Life in the Iron Mills* be seen to reveal that far from being the helpless victims Harding imagined, militant workers were very much present on the scene of their literary (un)making.

NOTES

1. *Iron Mills* was published anonymously in the April 1861 *Atlantic*. At that time the author went by the name Rebecca Blaine Harding. In deference to common bibliographic use (and to avoid misunderstanding), I use the name Rebecca Harding Davis in the title of this essay, and then, throughout the text of this essay, Rebecca Harding. Although scholars have not yet conclusively established when *Iron Mills* was composed, Harris's recent investigation into the evolution of Harding's use of irony concludes that in *Iron Mills*, Harding perfected techniques of irony that had been less than effective in some of the editorials and book reviews she wrote for *The Intelligencer* in the 1850s. I am less interested in positing the strike as a direct influence on Harding than I am in understanding the strike and her novella as indicative of how all Americans—workers included—perceived workers and the formation of social classes. *Iron Mills* has received a growing number of critical treatments in the past quarter century. Most notably, given the present topic, Amy Schrager Lang compares Davis's approach to class with Stowe's treatment of race in *Uncle Tom's Cabin* and argues that through its extensive use of irony and consistently ironic address of the reader, the text advertises its unwillingness to "appropriate" the subject matter of working-class life, rejects "all modes of representation as forms of appropriation," and thus exposes both the "artless" romancers and the "erudite literary men" who are Harding's contemporaries as "members of the possessing class" (141) Certainly, the narrative breathes irony. But even though Lang sees a stern reappraisal of the politics of antebellum literature in Harding's rejection of "all modes of representation," she does not account for the context of proletarian self-representation in which the story was written and received. The Great New England Strike in particular signals that the debate on class has jumped off the pages of genteel publications, such as the *North American Review*, where Lang discerns it, and is instead being decided through mass action in the streets of suburban Boston. To me, it seems curious to insist that Davis's interrogation of mimesis so thoroughly determines the work, for readers and critics from Davis's time to the present have found the work to be a remarkably detailed and compelling account of working-class degradation. If it *dis*claims its account of these things, as Lang argues, it also *pro*claims them quite well. Sharon Harris, for instance, argues very persuasively that the novella is remarkable precisely for its willingness to show the underside of American industrial life. Lang does not account for the split between the self-imposed lack of credibility of the narrative and its repeated reception as deeply credible. Also, although the novella voices doubts about the compatibility of genteel sentimental reform to the working-class ghetto, middle-class domestic ideals were very

important to the temperance, social work, and settlement house movements—social movements that often provided middle-class women their
only avenue into public life—through which Gilded Age America
attempted to relieve the misery, and subvert the revolutionary potential,
found in workers' ghettos. So *Life in the Iron Mills* is remarkably prescient
in its use of sentimental strategies to depict, confront, and understand
working-class life. Although it is not my purpose to argue this here, the
novella may well mark the moment when the genteel middle class of the
antebellum period became invested in a social identity and position that
serve as buffer between the proletariat and capital and have become synonymous with the great American middle class.

2. Thirty-year-old Rebecca Harding submitted *Life in the Iron Mills* to the
Atlantic Monthly at a time when according to Sharon Harris, she was working at least part time as a reporter on the Wheeling, Virginia, *Intelligencer.*
Although coverage of the strike by this paper was limited, the strike gets
several mentions, including a report dated March 17 describing the
march of six thousand strikers led by a company of militia; the famous
lithograph in *Frank Leslie's Illustrated Weekly* offers the same image, as is
discussed in the text. I am grateful to the staff at the West Virginia
Historical Society in Charleston for finding these references in micro-
fiches of the *Intelligencer.* As someone on the information track of her day,
reporter Harding was well positioned to appreciate how the force of the
strike "was felt from Maine to Florida" (Foner, *History*, 256) and comprehend how it "marked the beginning of a new era of industrial conflict" (A.S.H.P. 361–62). For an exhaustive survey of the almost
innumerable contemporary reactions to the strike in newspapers,
speeches, and political debates, see Huston.

3. See also Dawley 80–88 for a sense of the meaning of the strike in local
memory.

4. In Wheeling in 1860, "more than 5,000 German, Irish and other immigrants augmented the labor supply" (Williams 52). For more information,
albeit scanty, on the unionizing of Wheeling's industrial workforce in the
late 1850s, see Doug Fetterling, *Wheeling: An Illustrated History* (Wheeling,
WV: Windsor Publishing, 1983); and Earl Chapin May, *Principio to
Wheeling, 1715–1945: A Pageant of Iron and Steel* (New York: Harper Bros.,
1945), 138.

5. For instance, Amy S. Lang discerns a forceful interrogation of sentimental domestic fiction in the novella, and Sharon C. Harris sees in it the earliest instance of realist descriptive strategies in the United States. In
Beneath the American Renaissance, David S. Reynolds briefly discusses how
Harding's novella adapts elements of subversive women's writing from
the 1850s.

6. The worker essay on self-representation evidenced by the 1860 New
England Strike had a literary component as well. The period between
1857 and 1861 witnessed an explosion in the publication, distribution,
and sales of story papers and dime novels aimed at working-class readers,

the so-called cheap stories, dime novels, and yellowback books. In Michael Denning's account, these genres emerge as a contested terrain on which various signs of social division—of class itself—became the site of rhetorical struggle. This rhetorical struggle mirrored and influenced the escalating social tensions over industrialization—such as were exemplified by the Great New England Strike of 1860—and helped shape the world being made by industrialism. Although not self-consciously political or ideologically doctrinaire, cheap stories inscribed the "concerns and accents" of workers and promulgated a violent, subversive, and sensational picture of urban life and the relations among the classes (Denning 4). They frequently depicted strikes and unions and were sometimes written by labor activists. The most famous examples of this genre, for example, are the work of the Philadelphia radical George Lippard, *The Quaker City* and *New York: Its Upper Ten and Lower Million*. Labor newspapers such as the *Workingman's Advocate* and the *Labor Leader* commonly ran cheap stories as a way of enticing workers to learn to read and thus take a greater role in their own political and social advancement (Denning 4; also see 43 for a quotation from Gilded Age proletarian writer Martin Foran's essay on the ameliorative impact of reading cheap fiction on workers). The cheap-stories industry appealed to, and perhaps may be said to have defined, a proletarian interpretive community quite removed from that reached by expensive publications such as *Atlantic*. Cheap stories brought lurid subject matter to a potentially radical readership that could afford only the lowest prices. They introduced worker-friendly alternatives to American exceptionalism. It is no wonder, then, that the 1860 description of his visit to the enormously popular *New York Ledger* by the genteel Brahmin Edward Everett alternates between gentle bemusement and genuine horror (Everett 480–89). Cheap stories problematized basic, often unexamined, notions of what America and Americans were all about. Furthermore, these alternatives were widely read and distributed. Such publications as the *New York Ledger*, the *New York Weekly*, and the famous Beadle's dime books, studied by Henry Nash Smith in *Virgin Land*, enjoyed a crest of popularity in the years after the panic of 1857, taking advantage of developments in mass printing and transport to reach hundred of thousands of readers (Denning 11, 19). The expansion in this literature for workers mirrored the expansion of genteel readership that made Harriet Beecher Stowe an international celebrity in the 1850s.

7. James Huston examined the journalistic record of this strike and found that knowledge of it was almost universal in the eastern United States. In addition to in the newspapers of New England, Boston, New York, Newark, Philadelphia, and Baltimore, Huston found editorials and coverage of the strike in newspapers from Charleston, South Carolina; Jackson, Mississippi; Augusta, Georgia; Raleigh, North Carolina; Richmond, Virginia; Chicago; Detroit; Springfield, Illinois; Indianapolis; and Pittsburgh. Huston's work, I believe, indicates that knowledge of the Great Strike was extensive and feelings about it deeply held.

8. This period following the 1857 panic saw a resurgence in labor militancy and an unprecedented number of strikes. See Foner, *History,* 227–40; and Huston 203–4.

9. The challenge by *Life in the Iron Mills* to the industrial order has been documented best by Amy Schrager Lang, Tillie Olsen, and Jean Pfaelzer. The editors of the *Heath Anthology* point out that Kirby's comment echoes Pontius Pilate, but they do so without noting that Kirby also mouths the truisms of Adam Smith and David Ricardo.

10. See also Abraham Lincoln's speech on free labor delivered during the Massachusetts gubernatorial canvass during the strike, in Basler 24–25.

11. To categorize the resulting discourse as genteel middle-class realism has a certain precedent, but such categorization tends to minimize the ongoing historical processes by which social categories are constructed and which render them contingent. As E. P. Thompson put it, class is not a "'structure,' nor even a 'category,' but . . . something which in fact happens (and can be shown to have happened) in human relationships." In Thompson's definition, the experience of class arises from a specular relation between social groups: "Class happens when some men, as a result of common experiences (inherited or shared), feel and articulate the identity of their interests as between themselves, and as against other men whose interests are different from (and usually opposed to) theirs" (Thompson 9).

    If class should be thought of as a relationship, it becomes more significant that the tale of Deb and Hugh Wolfe is framed by another narrative, that of the erudite, ironic, genteel intellectual who gazes out on the blighted industrial town from his or her study window, exhorts the readers' attention, tells the tale, and then returns the readers' attention to the study in which the tale was written. *Life in the Iron Mills* may have staked a place in literary history based on its graphic depiction of that industrial town, in other words, but as is the case with the framing narratives of midcentury southwestern humor, Harding's local characters are always seen from the point of view of a narrator who is manifestly not one of the locals.

12. See also Marjorie S. Turner, *The Early American Labor Conspiracy Cases. Their Place in Labor Law: A Reinterpretation* (San Diego: San Diego State College Press, 1967).

13. In the past half-century, most Americans have come, almost instinctively, to consider strikes and other trade union activities as purely economic activities. But this narrow economistic definition simply does not hold up when one examines the antebellum and Gilded Age worker. See Gutman.

14. In particular, Foucault's investigation of the "panopticon"—put forward in *Discipline and Punish*—is germane to Harding's novella. First, certain characteristics of the novella, especially its painstaking attention to the details of industrial life, are symptomatic of the widespread investigation of industrial workers, soldiers, and inmates narrated by Foucault. Second, the novella raises the issue of how workers are to be managed at a his-

torical moment when because of worker militancy, this issue has seized national attention. In the panopticon, as Foucault describes it, "the crowd, a compact mass, a locus of multiple exchanges, individualities merging together, a collective effect, is abolished and replaced by a collection of separated individualities." As I argued earlier, Harding's characterization of Hugh and Deb as alienated, unpopular proletarians also does just this. It separates them from the "onbearable" mill hands and makes of them individual examples by which the costs of industrialism may be read.

15. The machine of surveillance, or "panopticon," has "an apparatus for supervising its own mechanisms," and the fate of the "master of the panopticon" is tied up with the performance of the institution. If the "collective effect" of the inmates' massed subjectivities is not shattered, the master of the panopticon will be the first victim of the uprising (Foucault, *Discipline*, 204).

16. It is noteworthy that although the original publication of *Iron Mills* in the *Atlantic* was anonymous, Harding's name become attached to the publication during a tour of New England, the site of the strike and also the crucible of the American literary Renaissance. It is as if because *Iron Mills* was so potentially "transgressive," as Foucault put it, an author had to be found who was "subject to punishment." Given the mode of circulation and production of this era, anonymity was not an option for the managerial realist.

Bibliography

American Social History Project Under the Direction of Herbert G. Gutman. *Who Built America? Working People and the Nation's Economy, Politics, Culture and Society.* Vol. 1. New York: Pantheon Books, 1989.

Basler, Roy P., ed. *The Collected Works of Abraham Lincoln.* Vol. 4. New Brunswick: Rutgers University Press, 1953.

Blewett, Mary H. *We Will Rise in Our Might: Workingwomen's Voices from Nineteenth-Century New England.* Ithaca: Cornell University Press, 1991.

Buckley, J. F. "Living in the Iron Mills: A Tempering of Nineteenth-Century America's Orphic Poet." *Journal of American Culture 16* (spring 1993): 67–72.

Davis, Rebecca Harding. *Life In The Iron Mills and Other Stories,* edited and with a biographical interpretation by Tillie Olsen. New York: Feminist Press, 1985.

Dawley, David. *Class and Community: The Industrial Revolution in Lynn.* Cambridge: Harvard University, 1977.

Denning, Michael. *Mechanic Accents: Dime Novels and Working-Class Culture in America.* London: Verso, 1987.

Everett, Edward. *The Mount Vernon Papers.* New York: Appleton, 1860.

Foner, Phillip S. *American Labor Songs of the Nineteenth Century.* Urbana: University of Illinois Press, 1975.

———. *Business and Slavery: The New York Merchants and the Irrepressible Conflict.* New York: Praeger, 1968.

———. *History of the Labor Movement in the United States.* Vol. 1. New York: International Publishers, 1969.

Foucault, Michel. *Discipline and Punish: The Rise of the Penitentiary.* New York: Vintage Books, 1979.

———. "What Is an Author." In *Textual Strategies: Perspectives in Post Structuralist Criticism,* edited by Josue Harari. Ithaca: Cornell University Press, 1984.

Gutman, Herbert. "Joseph McDonnel and the Workers' Struggle in Patterson, New Jersey." In *Power and Culture: Essays on the American Working Class,* edited by Ira Berlin. New York: New Press, 1987.

———. *Work, Culture and Society in Industrializing America: Essays in American Working-Class and Social History.* New York: Random House, 1976.

Harris, Sharon M. *Rebecca Harding Davis and American Realism.* Philadelphia: University of Pennsylvania Press, 1993.

Huston, James L. "Facing an Angry Labor: The American Public Interprets the Shoemakers' Strike of 1860." *Civil War History* 28 (1982): 197–212.

Kaplan, Amy. *The Social Construction of American Realism.* Chicago: University of Chicago Press, 1985.

Lang, Amy Schrager. "Class and the Strategies of Sentiment." In *The Culture of Sentiment: Race, Gender, and Sentimentality in Nineteenth-Century America,* edited by Shirley Samuels. New York: Oxford University Press, 1992.

Lukacs, Georg. *Studies in European Realism.* New York: Grosset & Dunlap, 1964.

Olsen, Tillie. *Silences.* New York: Delacorte, 1978.

Pfaelzer, Jean. "Rebecca Harding Davis: Domesticity, Social Order, and the Industrial Novel." *International Journal of Women's Studies* 4 (1981): 234–44.

Rose, June Atteridge. "Reading *Life in the Iron Mills* Contextually: A Key to Rebecca Harding Davis's Fiction." In *Conversations: Contemporary Critical Theory and the Teaching of Literature,* edited by Charles Moran. Urbana, IL: National Council of Teachers of English, 1990.

Seltzer, Mark. *Bodies and Machines.* New York: Routledge, 1992.

Taylor, George R. *The Transportation Revolution, 1815–1860.* New York: Holt, Rinehart and Winston, 1962.

Thompson, E. P. *The Making of the English Working Class.* London: Victor Gollancz, 1963.

Welter, Barbara. *Dimity Convictions: The American Woman in the Nineteenth Century.* Athens: Ohio University Press, 1976.

Wilentz, Sean. *New York City and the Rise of the American Working Class, 1788–1850.* New York: Oxford University Press, 1984.

Williams, John Alexander. *West Virginia: A Bicentennial History.* New York: Norton, 1976.

Yates, Michael. *Labor Law Handbook.* Boston: South End Press, 1987.

Will Watson *worked as a laborer in the Chicago-area steel mills for a decade before attending college. He currently teaches English and American studies at the University of Southern Mississippi at Gulf Coast.*

Words of Fire for Our Generation: Contemporary Working-Class Poets on the Triangle Fire

Karen Kovacik

In the early years of this century, the Gibson Girl blouse (or shirtwaist), accompanied by a long skirt, was considered a staple of the stylish woman's wardrobe—and the Triangle Shirtwaist Company, located in the Asch Building just off Washington Square in the heart of New York's garment district, was one of the largest manufacturers of such blouses in the city. A glance at the billowy shirtwaists on sale in the department stores offered little indication of the material conditions under which they were produced. Gas jets burned day and night in huge loft rooms full of sewing machines. During the most lucrative seasons, workers were expected to be at their machines fourteen hours a day, seven days a week. Despite their long hours, shop employees rarely took home more than $6.00 a week, and they were fined for damaged goods and sewing machine repairs. Such miserable conditions inspired a walkout by the "waistmakers" at Triangle in 1909. Ultimately twenty thousand workers from all over the city joined the strike—the largest labor uprising of American women at that time—because of energetic organizing efforts that targeted women from different ethnic and religious groups and because cross-class alliances like the Women's Trade Union League helped bail out strikers from jail and protested police brutality toward picketers. In the end, the strikers earned some concessions. However, they did not manage to win improvements in the safety or sanitary conditions of their shops, and they still had to purchase their own sewing machines. Worse still, not all employers signed the union contract. Many, including the Triangle Shirtwaist Company, refused to allow a closed shop and continued their business as usual.

A little over a year after the strike was settled, on March 25, 1911, a fire broke out on the eighth floor of the Triangle factory. It was 4:45 P.M., the end of the workday, with some five hundred workers still in the building. Feeding on flammable fabric scraps and sewing machine oil, the fire was soon burning out of control. The Triangle Company had never had a fire drill, and on the ninth floor, site of the largest operation, the stairwell doors were locked from the outside so that management could better control the workers and keep out union organizers. The fire department ladders reached only to the sixth floor. Although the fire was brought under control in eighteen minutes, 146 workers, mostly immigrant women, lost their lives. Twelve different ethnic groups were represented among the dead, though most were Russian Jews and Italians. Many died by jumping from the windows, the force of their impact so great that they tore through the firemen's nets and crashed through the glass grating of the sidewalks. Others, afraid to jump and unable to find a safe exit, burned to death.

In the mid-1980s—a decade dominated by the antilabor policies of Reaganism—several women poets from working-class backgrounds sought to rekindle a spark of communal memory by writing poems about the infamous Triangle fire.[1] This essay examines the work of two poets, Chris Llewellyn and Mary Fell—their distinct yet complementary strategies for depicting the impact of the fire on the working-class communities of the Lower East Side and their recognition of the multiple, often contradictory, roles of the historian-poet as archivist, activist, and artist. An important context for receiving the poems, I maintain, is understanding the unmistakable parallels between the decade of the Triangle fire and our own.

Chris Llewellyn, a self-described "labor poet" from a factory town in northwestern Ohio, devoted an entire volume to the tragedy. Her book, *Fragments from the Fire,* includes many dramatic monologues in the voices of garment workers and people sympathetic to them, as well as a six-page collage poem that illustrates the fire's impact on the community of the Lower East Side. The portraits and voices create a vivid, worker-centered account of the fire. In complicated ways, Llewellyn demonstrates how racism, sexism, and classism are deeply woven into the fabric of this country, dating back to the founding of the republic. Many of her poems focus on the ironies of historiography and the importance of writing history from a range of subject positions—such as the monologue spoken by a black elevator man who notes that trendy Washington Square, near the Triangle factory, was formerly a potters' field and that George Washington once sold a slave "for a bolt of cloth."

Mary Fell, a poet from Worcester, Massachusetts, uses motifs of smoldering and fire to represent working-class lives in her book *The Persistence of Memory.* In addition to seven poems about the Triangle fire, Fell includes poems in the voices of Joan of Arc, the wife of a coal miner, a child prostitute, and a rag seller—voices, as reviewer William Logan remarked, "of women rendered mute by history" (13). Fell became interested in the Triangle fire when reading labor history, particularly Leon Stein's account of the fire and its aftermath. Like Llewellyn, Fell presents the workers' experience from the inside out. Yet unlike the other poet, Fell prefers to create a compelling poetic texture through the juxtaposition of dissimilar images—some lyrical, some grotesque—rather than through the construction of dramatic narratives. "All those ironies and all those images were just lying there waiting to be discovered," Fell remarked.[2] In "Asch Building," she juxtaposes the image of two lovers kissing farewell on a ninth-floor window ledge with "two faceless ones. . ./folded neatly over the steam pipes/like dropped rags." In "Among the Dead," the speaker observes "a pair of shoes . . . [and] in them/two blistered feet." These careful pairings of survival and death, beauty and fear, suggest the chaos at Triangle during and after the tragedy. During the seven-poem suite on the fire, the poet's sequences of image pairs build in intensity, thus dramatizing her deepening immersion in that historical moment and in a worker-centered politics. The culmination of this engagement occurs in "Industrialist's Dream," a monologue in which a garment-shop owner offers grotesquely ironic images of the "ideal" worker.

Despite differences in tone and sensibility, Llewellyn and Fell both write about the fire and its milieu to evoke solidarity with the garment workers, to indict the capitalist class for its ruthless pursuit of profit, to make analogies between that earlier historical moment and our own, and to raise provocative questions about the role of poetry in the social transactions that create "history." Both poets employ religious and sewing motifs as well as exposé testimony to inspire empathy with the women workers and outrage at the industrialists. Finally, Llewellyn and Fell offer poems that self-reflexively explore the compelling and complex relation of the historian-poet to her subjects.

Invoking Holy Revolution

Blessed art Thou, O Lord our God, King of the universe, who createst the light of the fire.

Blessed art Thou, O Lord our God, King of the universe, who didst make a distinction between holy and profane, between light and darkness, between Israel and the heathen, between the seventh day and the six working days. . . .

—Blessing for the Light, Havdallah prayer

Both Mary Fell and Chris Llewellyn use Jewish and Christian discourse and ritual to emphasize the contrast between the secular, profit-driven milieu of New York's garment district and the devout, community-based customs of the immigrant women who worked in the factories. There seem to be at least two reasons for the poets' frequent use of religious imagery and language. First, evidence shows that turn-of-the-century activists of the Lower East Side often incorporated such references in their speeches. According to former union organizer Sidney Jonas, Jewish socialists were fond of making references to the Book of Isaiah, "with its warnings to the rich and haughty and its prophecies of judgment and cleansing" (Orleck 27). Housewives organizing rent strikes and meat boycotts during the first decade of the century frequently mentioned Isaiah in their speeches (27). Second, the Triangle fire occurred on what for many workers was the Sabbath—a week before the feasts of Passover and Easter. Factory managers often did not allow time off for religious observances, especially during the lucrative spring season. In her reminiscences about the Triangle shop, garment worker and union organizer Pauline Newman recalled a sign on the elevator: "If you don't come in on Sunday, you needn't come in on Monday." Indeed, there was no day of rest for the Triangle workers—neither Saturday nor Sunday.

Fell and Llewellyn open their books with references to rituals of the Havdallah, or Great Divide, that mark the transition from the Sabbath to the rest of the week. In addition, Llewellyn prefaces each of the five sections of her book with epigraphs pertaining to fire, ashes, and justice, taken from the Psalms, the Book of Isaiah, and John. In this way, as reviewer Michelle M. Tokarczyk suggested, the poet herself acts "as prophet, alerting the nation to its terrible wrongs" (12). The epigraphs work intertextually with other poems, especially "Sacristan," in which a young Catholic priest prepares sermons with biblical allusions to fire to honor the "Triangle martyrs." In all these instances, Fell and Llewellyn invoke Jewish and Christian sacred texts and rituals as a way of establishing a moral authority over a secular capitalist system that treats workers without human compassion or dignity.

Mary Fell's "Havdallah" functions as a revolutionary prayer that mourns the loss of the traditional, ritualized divide between rest and labor. The shape of the poem, in three seven-line stanzas, recalls the creation of the world in Genesis, with its injunction against work on the seventh day. The first stanza of Fell's poem echoes traditional Havdallah prayers:

> *This is the great divide*
> *by which God split*
> *the world:*

> *on the Sabbath side*
> *he granted rest,*
> *eternal toiling*
> *on the workday side. (3)*

The short lines slow the pace of our reading and encourage us to emphasize such end words as *divide, split, rest,* and *toiling*—underscoring the holiness of the great divide between rest and toil. The second stanza swerves leftward with a pun on *revolution*: "But even one/revolution of the world/is an empty promise/where bosses/where bills to pay/respect no heavenly bargains." The tone here is sharper, angrier, that of a modern-day prophet frustrated with the bosses unenlightened by any revolution, be it of the sun or of labor organizing to fight capital. The very word *bosses* implies a solidarity with the powerless and suggests also the "great divide" between labor and management.

The remainder of the poem transforms a common ritual for ending the Sabbath—the lighting of a dish of wine—into an incendiary prayer for social change:

> *Until each day is ours*
>
> *let us pour*
> *darkness in a dish*
> *and set it on fire,*
> *bless those who labor*
> *as we pray, praise God*
> *his holy name,*
> *strike for the rest.*

The Triangle fire started near the end of the Sabbath. In contrast to that uncontrolled and unwanted burning, the fire in the dish represents a petition for greater control, greater autonomy from the bosses who force family members to "labor/as we pray." It is the kindling of a spark of outrage, the striking of a match that stands in for a different kind of strike, which is as necessary and as important as offering praise to God. Fell politicizes the traditional Havdallah prayer by explicitly rewriting it to include mention of the overworked factory employees and to call for human as well as divine intervention in the struggle for social change.

Chris Llewellyn's "The Great Divide" echoes the themes and motifs of the Havdallah prayers alluded to in Fell's poem but refers more pointedly to the Lower East Side and the Triangle factory itself. In her poem, images of the Havdallah rituals enacted in neighborhood tenements are interspersed with depictions of workers laboring on the shop floor, unable to mark the conclusion of the Sabbath. "The Great Divide" opens with an image of the neighborhood:

> *Henry Street, Cherry Street, Hester Street:*
> *the new world turns toward old Jerusalem.*
> *Sunrays stream on the bearded father-singers*
> *standing beside a hundred rag-stuffed windows. (3)*

Henry, Cherry, and Hester Streets each have vivid connotations of Jewish inhabitants of the Lower East Side. Henry was the site of a famous settlement house founded by nurse Lillian Wald, which provided some measure of relief—health care, food, and support of strikers—to the area's indigent. In Irving Howe's description, Hester is both familiar and exotic, the quintessential "pushcart territory [where you could buy] shawls, bananas, oilcloth, garlic, trousers, ill-favored fish, ready-to-wear-spectacles. You could relax in the noise of familiars, enjoy a tournament of bargains, with every ritual of haggling, maneuver of voice" (257). Cherry was one of the poorest streets in the district and thus was frequently home to workers in the ill-paying garment trades. According to the 1905 census, a three- or four-room apartment on Cherry Street contained 5.6 inhabitants on the average, and most households were headed by a blue-collar worker. Not surprisingly, the *New York Times'* roll of the dead lists several victims from Cherry Street.[3] Llewellyn's description of the area, though compressed, manages to convey a sense of the old-world rituals persisting in the new, as the "bearded father-singers" prepare to bid farewell to the Sabbath. They are attuned to the natural order of daylight and sunset in a way that the garment workers in dim lofts are not.

    "The Great Divide" features four quatrains, each followed by a one-line antiphonal statement. The quatrains establish that sense of contrast between old and new, profane and holy, whereas the one-line statements echo actual prayers or sentiments, such as "Chant the 'Havdallah,' chant 'The Great Divide.'" In quatrain 2, the speaker refers again to the bearded father-singers, the Hassidim, who "praise the Almighty for creating us a Sabbath/that cuts one day away from the fabric of the week." But she quickly switches to an image of a different kind of Singer, the machine that revolutionized the garment trade and increased the already hectic pace of work: "Bent over Singers, their backs to factory windows,/women and children stitch into sunset." The third quatrain incorporates Pauline Newman's reminiscence about the elevator sign regarding Sunday and Monday work, although Llewellyn alters the notice to include Saturday in the prohibition, thereby making it pertain to Jews and Christians alike and to make the warning more ominous: "If you don't show up on Saturday or Sunday,/you're already been fired when it's Monday."[4] The final quatrain, by contrast, offers a lyrical image of the lighting of the ritual flame that marks the end of the Sabbath: "Each [of the fathers] strikes a sulphur-tip match, touches/the surface of the small wine lake." The intimacy and beauty of the gesture, the sound echoes of *s, ch,* and *k,* nonetheless have to be read as a quiet foreshadowing of the impending factory fire, something that the image in the final antiphonal line hints at even more strongly: "Light in the windows, dividing up the dark." The way the poem veers from tenement to shop floor and back again makes the reading of that final line deliberately indeterminate: as readers we are both at the windows with the father-singers and their "small wine lakes" and with the women at the Triangle shop, poised on the sills, backlit by fire.[5]

Llewellyn's longest poem, "March 25, 1911," is an overture introducing recurring motifs of the entire book and drawing on varied sources to provide multiple views of the tragedy, lingering longest on a pair of same-sex "sweethearts," garment workers Sophie Salemi and Della Costello. Poised to jump, arms around each other, the Italian Catholic women whisper increasingly desperate and angry novena-like prayers.[6] The poem's title anchors the event to a specific date, and the first stanza, positioned like an epigraph, situates the fire in regard to numerous cycles: season of the year, day of the week, pay period, religious calendars, and time of day:

> *It was Spring. It was Saturday.*
> *Payday. For some it was Sabbath.*
> *Soon it will be Easter. It was*
> *approaching April, nearing Passover.*
> *It was close to closing time. (4)*

Each of those terse initial phrases—"It was Spring," "It was . . . nearing Passover"—serves as a conclusion to at least three of the twenty-six subsequent stanzas as if to imply that ordinary cycles of time and meaning were disturbed by this tragic event.

The religious time-markers, imagery, and language suggest that in not providing adequate fire protection, the profit-hungry industrialists had committed a desecration. In stanza 14, for example, the ninth-floor girls find the door locked and the telephone dead. The force of the fire, "piling red/ribbons . . . backs [the] girls into windows." To them, the room looks like "a smashed altar lamp"; the flames sound like "screaming novenas." "Soon," the stanza concludes laconically, "it

will be Easter." In stanza 17, the trapped girls, already skeletons, stare
permanently at the cloakroom window likened to a "black crucifix."
The destruction of the sacred emblems of crucifix and altar lamp, like
the interruption of liturgical calendars, is a way for the narrator to convey moral outrage at those responsible for the fire.

This sense of indictment becomes even stronger as the fire heats up,
driving the poem's two martyr-heroines, Sophie and Della, out onto
the window ledge. Arms around each other, their backs to the burning building, the young women look out over the city, imagining their
impending death. Llewellyn positions Sophie and Della, neighbors
from Cherry Street and adjacent workers at Triangle, centrally in the
poem. Iconic figures, they represent the importance, both emotion-
ally and politically, of intimate friendships between women at the garment factory. Annelise Orleck, writing about women activists in the
garment industry, observed that the

> majority of New York's garment workers were little more than girls,
> and the relationships they forged with factory friends were . . .
> intense, melodramatic, and deeply loyal. They were teenage confi-
> dantes as well as factory workers, and they relied on shop-floor rap-
> port to soften the hardships of factory life. . . . For young immigrant
> women trying to build lives in a new land, such bonds were powerful
> and lasting. From these shop-floor friendships would soon evolve the
> ties of union sisterhood. (35)

Orleck also acknowledges that certain women, such as Pauline
Newman, former Triangle worker turned union organizer, "captured
the imagination" of garment girls in a more romantic sense. The
friendship of Sophie and Della, as represented in the poem and in
sources about the fire, also bears the hallmarks of romance, of a "love
unto death." In actuality, the young women did die with their arms
wound around each other, and they shared a funeral. In the poem, the
martyr-heroines Sophie and Della refer to each other as "our only
sweethearts" shortly before their death.

Poised on the ledge, Sophie and Della regard the "crazy quilt of
town." They have become a holy alliance—already omniscient, capable of moving backward and forward in time and inhabiting the minds
of others. In stanza 21, they imagine their funeral, their schoolmates
singing in procession a strange and fractured hymn, the words altered
by the pressure of the moment: "O Trinity of Blessed Light/Our Lady
of Perpetual Help/Ave Maria, Ave Maria/Now and at the Hour/of
the Tarantella" (8). For "our death" in the customary "now and at the

hour of our death" that closes the Hail Mary, the girls substitute the "Tarantella," a lively folk dance from southern Italy that was popular at the time. Earlier in the poem, Llewellyn described the sewing machine heads connected by belts as singing the Tarantella to suggest their rapid pace. The dance, with its quickening tempo and intensity representing the frenetic speed of the factory, invades even the equanimity of prayer.

In the poem's final two stanzas, the prayers become more frantic, their language and syntax more fragmented and compressed:

> *Our Bosses of the Locked*
> *Doors of Sweetheart Contracts*
> *who in puffs and tendrils*
> *of silent telephones,*
> *disconnected hoses, barred*
> *shutters, fire escapes*
> *dangling in perpetual no*
> *help on earth in heaven.*
>   It was Spring.
>
> *The Lord is my shepherd*
> *green pastures still*
> *waters anointest heads*
> *with oil overflowing*
> *preparest a table—now*
> *our arms around each other*
> *we thread the needle where*
> *no rich man can go spinning*
> *the earth's axle we are*
> *leaving in light. (9)*

The Lord's Prayer, the ending of a novena, Psalm 23, and the parable of the camel passing through the eye of the needle all collide in this frantic collage-prayer recited at the moment of the women's death.[7] The first three prayers resonate ironically here: all about God's providence—as giver of daily bread, as bestower of perpetual help, as the shepherd who offers rest and comfort and anointing—they are invoked here to indict industrialists Asch, Harris, and Blanck, who failed to provide safe working conditions and collected $445 for every deceased worker from their fire insurance policy. (Before this deadly fire, the owners of Triangle had in fact reported seven other fires at their plants, a further indication of their negligence [Stein 172–73].) The sacred oil, with which the Lord anoints the heads of his faithful, is here contrasted with the barrels of highly flammable sewing machine oil that were stored at the plant. At the same time, the images of green pastures, still waters, and the prepared table do seem comforting for these Catholic women on the verge of death. Unlike their profiteering owners, Sophie and Della can pass easily through the eye of the needle into the Kingdom of Heaven. With this twisted collage of prayers, Llewellyn invokes the traditional Christian comfort of heavenly reward for the weary and lowly of this world while still issuing a protest against "Our Bosses of the Locked/Doors of Sweetheart Contracts."

Llewellyn offers more revolutionary representations of Catholicism in "Sacristan," a dramatic monologue from the point of view of a sexton who has become preoccupied with the Triangle fire.[8] The poem opens with a recital of the sacristan's customary duties, which include maintaining the priest's vestments and the ceremonial equipment for mass. But the sacristan soon steers the conversation toward the factory fire, referring to two martyr-saints who burned to death: Joan of Arc, who died at the stake, and Lawrence, who was roasted on a gridiron. (According to some sources, Lawrence, despite great suffering, managed to joke with his persecutors, "I'm done on this side. You can turn me over now.") Many of the sacristan's duties involve managing fire— trimming the wick of the sanctuary lamp, replacing candles, procuring "fresh charcoal, sandalwood/Incense for the censor." Like the religious Jews in the poem by Fell, the sacristan seems to take comfort in the habits of ritual. Maintaining an attitude of mindfulness even during the routine observances of scrubbing and shining, the sacristan acknowledges a personal connection with the Triangle victims: "I polish and pray/the names of my brother and the other shirtwaist/ Martyrs so these holy ones may intercede for/us on earth." By characterizing the Triangle victims as "martyrs," by essentially including them in the company of such illustrious saints as Lawrence and Joan, the sacristan is also accessing the more politicized rhetoric of union organizers like Leonora O'Reilly, who had led the waistmakers' strike in the preceding year. At an ILGWU rally shortly after the fire, O'Reilly, remarking on the ongoing dangers that faced garment workers in other shops, referred to the Triangle victims as Christlike "martyrs who died that we may live" (Stein 138).

The final labor of the sacristan is to compose a homily "on the example of the beekeeper/who handles her charges yet is not stung." This suggestive analogy, which can be understood in terms of the sacristan's safe, ritualized handling of fire, also comments self-reflexively on Llewellyn's own process and aim of composition. Like Llewellyn in her inclusion of four biblical epigraphs to the text from Isaiah, the Psalms, and John, the sacristan creates a patchwork text by marking "any mention of fire or garments" and collecting those passages in a book. Like Llewellyn, the sacristan draws on a rich liturgical tradition steeped in metaphor and parable to comfort the troubled and to trouble the comfortable.

Despite the stereotype of religion as "the opiate of the masses" derived from the selective quotation of Marx, both Fell and Llewellyn suggest in these poems the socially radical rather than the quiescent potential of religious discourse and ritual. The language and imagery of the Havdallah prayers, the Book of Isaiah, the Psalms, and saints' lives, the ritual in the home and the homily in the pulpit—all become powerful rhetorical means for expressing solidarity with the workers, for indicting a predatory, profit-driven means of production, and for highlighting the clash between religious-communal customs of the old world and the individualism of the new.

Giving Arrogance and Corruption a Form: The Poetics of the Exposé

I cannot see that anyone was responsible for the disaster. It seems to have been an act of the Almighty. . . . I paid great attention to the witnesses while they were on the stand. I think the girls who worked [at Triangle] were not as intelligent as those in other walks of life and were therefore the more susceptible to panic.

—H. Houston Hierst, juror[9]

Shortly after the Triangle fire, angry cartoons appeared on the editorial pages of New York's many newspapers. One, in the *Evening Journal,* featured a dead garment worker lying on the shop floor. Above her is the slogan, mimicking a classified ad, "Operators Wanted: Inquire Ninth Floor." (In actuality, owners Harris and Blanck wasted little time mourning: within a week of the tragedy, they had opened another shop on University Place, where they again came under the suspicion of the fire marshal for having arranged sewing machines in a manner that denied workers access to the fire escape [Stein 204].) Another cartoon, in the Socialist *Call,* depicted a triangle with the words "RENT PROFIT INTEREST" on each of the sides, with a corpulent industrialist and a skeleton clasping hands in partnership over the lifeless body of a garment worker. "This is the real triangle," the caption read (Stein 63). Both Fell and Llewellyn import some of that polemical wit into poems satirizing persons or institutions hostile to the garment workers.

Fell's poem "Industrialist's Dream" offers a grimly ironic view of the ideal worker from the point of view of the bosses:

> *This one's*
> *dependable won't*
> *fall apart*
> *under pressure doesn't*
> *lie down on the job*
> *doesn't leave early*
> *come late*
> *won't join unions*
> *strike*
> *ask for a raise*
> *unlike one hundred*
> *forty six*
> *others I could name*
> *who couldn't*
> *take the heat this one's*
> *still at her machine*
> *and doubtless*
> *of spotless moral*
> *character you*
> *can tell by the bones*
> *pure white*
> *this one*
> *does what she's told*
> *and you don't hear*
> *her complaining. (8–9)*

The short and often negative phrases in lines 1 through 10 read like a satirical job description that prizes the stereotypical feminine "virtues" of docility and passivity. But the poem turns with mention of the "one hundred forty six," who are characterized by the employer not as innocent victims but as troublemakers—in contrast to the one with "pure white" bones.[10]

The grisly image of the loyal skeleton at her machine might strike some readers as overly polemical, yet when it is read in the context of the management practices at Triangle it appears less heavy-handed. The Triangle Shirtwaist Company did everything it could to maximize profits at the expense of the workers' comfort, safety, and job security. Fell has a way of pushing or tweaking images—the striking of the match in "Havdallah," the blistered feet in "Asch Building," the pure, docile worker as skeleton here—to maximize their intensity and irony while not departing altogether from actuality. Fell described "Industrialist's Dream" "as a kind of coming-out in which I stopped standing on the edges [politically]."[11]

Llewellyn prefers to structure her indictment of the system via a dramatic monologue by one of the jurors who acquitted owners Blanck and Harris of first- and second-degree manslaughter charges in a trial that was held several months after the fire. That poem, "Jury of Peers," opens with a roster of the middle-class men who sat on the panel, along with their professions. It becomes clear that H. Houston Hierst, importer; Leo Abraham, real estate; Victor Steinman, shirts; and Anton Scheuerman, cigars, are peers not of the dead workers but of the industrialists. The rest of the poem is an edited version of the statement by Hierst that functions as an epigraph to this section. Llewellyn has Hierst saying all those things—the fire was an "act of God," the "girls" were "less intelligent"—not once but several times, each time more garbled and less convincing than the last:

> *I've listened to the witnesses*
> *and my conscience is clear.*
> *Harris and Blanck are pretty*
> *good managers. We've reached*
> *the decision that the type*
> *of girl you have at Triangle*
> *is basically less intelligent.*
> *Hell, excuse me, Your Honor,*
>
> *But most of em can't even read*
> *or speak English—and the way*
> *they live! They're lots*
> *less intelligent than the*
> *type of female you find*
> *in other walks of life. I mean*
> *that kinda worker is more—*
> *well—susceptible to panic.*
> *Emotional females can't*
>
> *Keep a clear head they*
> *panicked and jumped my*
> *conscience is clearly*
> *Act of Almighty*
> *God they jumped*
> *conclusion Your*
> *Honor owners*
> *of Triangle*
> *not guilty. (41–42)*

The first stanza replicates Hierst's actual statement almost verbatim, copying even the syntax that favors declarative sentences. In the second stanza, however, Llewellyn intensifies the sexism and the classism of the original, using the sort of xenophobic language that is not uncommon in debates today by anti-immigration polemicists and English-only proponents. The repetitiveness and the self-interruptions of the speaker cause us to question his own intelligence as well as his integrity. By the third stanza, coherence breaks down altogether, resulting in some ironic compressions. The many awkward enjambments suggest a speaker gasping for breath and uncertain of his next remarks. As Hierst is complaining that the women couldn't "keep a clear head," we have to question the clarity of his own thoughts. Like the women on the ledge, he also seems to be panicking. Read alone, the line "God they jumped" conveys astonished horror, and "jumped/ conclusion" is a compressed editorial comment by Llewellyn about the kind of justice that was served. The runover lines "Your/Honor owners/of Triangle/not guilty" suggest the collusion between the legal system and the capitalists. In this sense, judge and jury and industrialists all are peers.

As a counterpoint to poems in the voices of workers, these poetic exposés serve to remind us of the united front between government and industry that hindered any advancement of workers' causes. The industrialists discriminated against workers who belonged to unions or tried to organize one. City police loyal to employers harassed, beat up, and arrested strikers. Triangle owners Max Blanck and Isaac Harris were acquitted of all malfeasance by a jury of their peers.

"Where are the words of fire for my generation?":
Fell and Llewellyn on the Poetics of Cultural Memory

> *I made sackcloth also my garment;*
> *and I became a proverb to them.*

—Psalm 69:11

Both Fell and Llewellyn conclude their poetic sequences about the Triangle fire with poems that explore the conflicting aims and methods of the historian-poet. These final poems raise important questions about poetry's multiple guises—as Aristotelian mirror, as revolutionary call, as catalyst for social change, as conduit of cultural memory. To what extent, for example, should poets insert themselves into their reinventions of historical actuality? When should they edit or depart

from their source materials? What aesthetic criteria should they adopt
when writing about an event that has considerable potential for pathos
or melodrama? What responsibilities do poets have to be historically
"accurate"? How are literary representations of historical events useful? These poems clearly side with the workers over the industrialists:
can the poets be charged with writing "didactic" or "polemical" verse?
Implicitly, and sometimes explicitly, Fell and Llewellyn argue for a
socially engaged poetry, but one still demanding, as Llewellyn put it,
a certain "knowledge of poetry and technical skill" (interview 5).

Fell's approach—dreamlike, lyrical, and imagistic—reimagines the
funeral cortege for the dead workers and then seamlessly segues to the
present in which the poet is guided by the tragic muse-figure of the
nameless dead:

Cortege

A cold rain comforts the sky.
Everything ash-colored under clouds.
I take my place in the crowd,

move without will as the procession moves,
a gray wave breaking against the street.
Up ahead, one hundred and forty seven

coffins float, wreckage of lives. I follow
the box without a name. In it
whose hand encloses whose heart? Whose mouth

presses the air toward a scream?
She is no one, the one I claim
as sister. When the familiar is tagged

and taken away, she remains.
I do not mourn her. I mourn no one.
I do not praise her. No one

is left to praise. Seventy years after
her death, I walk in March rain behind her.
She travels before me into the dark. (12)

In this concluding poem, which pays tribute to the anonymous
worker(s) who died in the fire, Fell positions herself in an unobtrusive
role, as a member of the "gray wave" of mourners "breaking against the
street." The poem revolves around tropes of plurality and anonymity.

Coffin 147 does indeed contain "no one"—the remains are nameless and thus probably belong to more than one person—and the poet-speaker, herself unnamed, claims the unfamiliar "as sister." With these gestures, Fell seems to be reaching for commonalities among working-class women from different historical moments. Her adopted sister, like a guide to the underworld, shows her the way "into the dark"; that sister is also a kind of muse and a stand-in for each unacknowledged worker "whose mouth/presses the air toward a scream."

Llewellyn's "Sear," meanwhile, is a self-reflexive account of her process of composing the book—planting quotations, adding, revising, "arranging line-breaks, versification," consulting source materials. She raises matters of aesthetics and artistic aim without resolving them. In stanza 2, she first quotes Frances Perkins, an eyewitness to the fire who later became Franklin Roosevelt's secretary of labor: "I felt I must sear it/not only on my mind but on my heart/forever" and then an anonymous mother: "When will it be/safe to earn our bread?" (68). Llewellyn emphasizes "Their words." "Yet some call that schmaltz, soap-opera-/Sentiment, Victorian melodrama." Many of her poems do contain elements of pathos or melodrama—the very notion of young women plunging out of windows to their death can be seen as sensational—yet how much is too much?

Llewellyn also questions her own stake in the Triangle project. In "Sear," she offers images of being haunted by the fire: "Riding/the subway, smoke fizzes in my ears and/in my room, electric heater coils glow." Despite, or perhaps *because* of that level of engagement, she wonders how "To write about *them*/ yet not interfere, although I'm told/a poet's task is to create a little world." The poetry workshop cliché about creating "a little world" nonetheless presses the important issues of how, when, and to what extent poets should consciously manipulate their archival materials. Interestingly, Llewellyn refuses to resolve the ethical, political, and aesthetic quandaries that she raises about writing "historical" poetry. Instead, she simply exposes the seams between effacement and engagement, direct quotation and poetic reimagination. A self-described labor poet, Llewellyn clearly reveals a loyalty to her garment-worker subjects but, at the same time, expresses uncertainty as to the extent she should involve herself in their stories and function as an advocate on their behalf. The issue of rhetorical positioning is complicated by the formal elements and aesthetic criteria, both enabling and restrictive, that the poet brings to her subject matter. By holding in suspension all these issues without resolving them, Llewellyn involves readers in the messiness—and also the urgency—of writing about historical actuality.

The Triangle Poems as Examples of Working-Class Literary Production

Like it or not, the foregrounded working-class "I" is never isolated, but crowded from within with other voices. At the core of working-class literature is the realization that the struggle cannot and should not be a singular struggle.

—Janet Zandy, "The Complexities and Contradictions of
Working-Class Women's Writings"

Recent books reporting on the scene of contemporary poetry in the United States—Dana Gioia's *Can Poetry Matter?*, Mary Kinzie's *The Cure of Poetry in an Age of Prose,* and Vernon Shetley's *After the Death of Poetry*—suggest a preoccupation with the genre's relevance, marginality, and durability. Indeed, images abound of the poet laboring in isolation, of the lyric poem as a monologic, elitist genre, and of the intended audience for poetry being exclusively other poets and academics. Yet the work of Fell and Llewellyn—part of a large body of contemporary poetry by women of the working classes—challenges those conventional notions. As the preceding epigraph from Janet Zandy asserts, these poets believe in a multivocal, engaged poetry committed to the people and history and ways of using language that a middle-class publishing establishment has too often deemed unliterary. In her important essay "Writing with Class," Valerie Miner includes a statement by the working-class writer Stan Weir, on the anguish of those exclusions: "I once read . . . about a Spanish prisoner who said that one of the worst tortures was not having a mirror. After a while she began to think she had become deformed. That's what happens to labor. There is no mirror in the media about what we do" (29). Clearly, the poems of Llewellyn and Fell offer much-needed mirrors of working people's struggles.

Both poets evoke the earlier waistmakers' strike and the fire itself as examples of class struggle across ethnic and religious lines. Fell and Llewellyn themselves cross such lines to give voice to particularities of struggles outside their immediate historical moment and ethnic/religious groups. Llewellyn's favoring of the dramatic monologue is something she shares with earlier generations of progressive writers.[12] One of the benefits of the monologue is that by offering an idiosyncratic representation of one speaker's experience, it avoids the overly general polemics of the placard while still having some claim to representation. Cary Nelson, the foremost historian of American labor poetry, contends that such monologues become "representative cultural texts, examples of workers' experience that have at once the conditional authenticity of confession and the generality of types" (106). The complex representations of worker-subjects that potentially occur in the monologue can forge dynamic connections between literature and lived experience.

Fell's more image-centered poetics dramatizes another way for the historian-poet to engage with lives and struggles beyond her own. Her "working-class I" is indeed "crowded from within with other voices" and with images, too. The tropes of plurality and anonymity that she employs in a poem like "Cortege"—in which the poet-speaker merges with her nameless foremothers in the funeral parade for the dead women—are particularly moving and compelling. As Nelson stated, poems offering "images of working-class suffering, discontent, and resistance certainly promote more awareness of the material consequences of class difference. Abstractions about democracy and justice are thereby articulated to specific social and economic disparities" (167–68). Yet in a literary establishment dominated by middle-class values, poetry like Fell's will not always be credited for its aesthetics of "relationality" (Zandy, *Liberating Memory*, 8). Indeed, one reviewer of Fell's book, *The Persistence of Memory*, wrote: "Her finest poems are those which relate to the struggles of others, using concrete images. She describes her own life in somewhat superficial generalities" (Ratner 723). For that reviewer, poetry that does not foreground the self is a noteworthy aberration.

In an interview, Chris Llewellyn explained the relevance of the fire to readers today:

> Since about 1980 we've gone through another big wave in immigration. And again you have a lot of women who don't know English, have come from places where women's lives and women's work are regarded as somewhat cheap, and they don't understand things like overtime or minimum wage. . . . So feminists need to pay attention to history because it's repeating itself. (5)

Indeed, in the 1980s, a number of social and economic conditions conspired to return sweatshop garment production to the United States: an American president whose domestic policies favored unfettered corporate expansion at the expense of labor rights; the growing availability of cheap immigrant labor, particularly from Asia and Latin America; increasing labor costs in Asia due to rising wages and stronger currencies; and "the decision of American manufacturers to shift their production orders back to the U.S. as a cost-cutting measure" (Petras 92–93). According to sociologist Elizabeth McLean Petras, who made a case study of the sweatshops in Philadelphia, the new shops—located mainly in eastern seaboard cities and in California—closely resemble their turn-of-the-century predecessors. Late-twentieth-century sweatshop owners, like their forefathers Harris and Blanck, also pay by the piece, resulting in illegally low wages. They target newly arrived immigrant women, some of whom labor for years as indentured servants to pay for their passage to this country, working long hours without overtime pay. To lower overhead costs in order to compete with exploitative garment manufacturers abroad, the shop owners locate their operations in cramped, old, unsafe buildings. In Philadelphia, Petras uncovered sweatshops in aging factory lofts, Asian restaurants, garages, basements, and apartments. The safety and working conditions in these "modern" shops, due in part to Reagan-era staff reductions of the Occupational Safety and Health Administration (OSHA) and the Wage and Hour Division, are eerily similar to those at Triangle in 1911 (Petras 105).[13]

Until the labor conditions that gave rise to Triangle are permanently eradicated in this country and abroad, the poems of Chris Llewellyn and Mary Fell will be important cultural touchstones of rage and sorrow that can inspire readers, as Mother Jones famously said, "to [mourn] the dead and fight like hell for the living."[14]

NOTES

1. Working-class poets Julia Stein, Safiya Henderson-Holmes, and Carol Tarlen have also written poems about the fire.
2. Phone conversation with the author, March 24, 1996.
3. "Death List Is 141, Only 86 Identified" March 27, 1911: A-2.
4. Howe, in *World of Our Fathers*, notes that some garment-shop owners did allow religious Jews to keep the Sabbath—one of the factors that attracted Eastern European Jews to the needle trades. Howe also notes the incipient class struggle between German and Russian or Polish Jews: "Of the 241 garment factories in New York City in 1885, 234 were owned by Jews, or more than 97 percent, and of these the great majority were unquestionably German Jews" (82).
5. After the tragedy, a number of rabbis were among those demanding an unbiased investigation of the circumstances of the fire. The *New York Times*, March 26, 1911, reported, for example, that "Rabbi Stephen Wise declared that he was willing to take no man's word—especially no official's word—about what the facts of the shirtwaist fire were. . . . [He said,] 'If this thing was avoidable I want to see those responsible punished. If it was due to some corrupt failure to enforce the law, I want to see that determined. And I do not trust public officials to determine it for us'" ("Doors Were Locked" A-2).
6. Whereas Llewellyn focuses on same-sex "sweethearts," Fell and Robert Pinsky portray the heterosexual romance of a man kissing a woman on

the ledge before they both jumped, a story that was publicized by UPI reporter Bill Shepherd, an eyewitness to the tragedy.

7. Josephine Casey, an organizer for the ILGWU, also composed "picket prayers" during a strike of corset makers outside a factory in Kalamazoo, Michigan, in 1912. The workers would get down on their knees and say, "Oh God, Our Father, Who are generous. . . . Our employer who had plenty denied our request. He has misused the law to help him crush us. . . . Thou Who didst save Noah and his family, may it please Thee to save the girls now on strike from the wicked city of Sodom. Oh, help us to get a living wage. . . . Grant that we may win the strike . . . so that we may not need to cry often, "Lord, deliver us from temptation" (Wertheimer 317).

8. Llewellyn was working as a secretary for the progressive not-for-profit group Catholics for a Free Choice when her manuscript was selected for the Walt Whitman Award.

9. Quoted in Wertheimer, 314–15.

10. In actuality, many of the workers who started the strike were quickly laid off by the Triangle bosses. According to the *New York Times,* most of the workforce before the strike was Jewish. "But after the strike ended [the] company, [District Attorney] Whitman was informed, refused to hire back any of these employees, preferring instead to hire Italians, Irish, and Americans" ("Quick Grand Jury" 2).

11. Phone conversation with the author, March 24, 1996.

12. In *Repression and Recovery,* literary historian Cary Nelson includes examples of "worker's correspondence" poems produced by such leftist writers as Mike Gold and Tillie Olsen. Culled from actual workers' letters that appeared in labor publications, the poems functioned somewhat like dramatic monologues. Writes Nelson: "Given line breaks and stanzaic form, these workers' letters gain symbolic cultural force, a literary status they would not have on their own, and potential longterm visibility" (106). An example of such a letter-poem is Tillie Olsen's "I Want You Women Up North to Know."

13. As an example of the strain on OSHA inspectors, given the magnitude of the sweatshop problem, sociologist Todd Gitlin writes that in New York City alone, "[the] state's apparel task force inspects 1,300 shops a year with its 20 inspectors. Close to half have both labor and safety violations and thus can be considered sweatshops. Roughly one-third have blocked aisles or bolted doors" (M5).

In a 1983 report, a New York City investigator described the "typical" garment sweatshop as follows:

> Room appears to be about 20 × 30'. Rear door is closed tight and cannot be opened. Front entrance (and apparently the exit) is narrow and partially blocked by garment racks. Floors were littered with piles of garments. There is only one small window with bars. . . .

. . . There is no back door, but there are two side doors, one of which is blocked by a table, and the other one is hard to open. . . . All windows are permanently barred. The shop has a time clock, but there are only four time cards, in spite of the 20 workers on the premises. The time cards have only a first name, and none have been punched. (Leichter 26–27)

As consumers, we can put pressure on retailers who sell clothing produced in sweatshops through lobbying efforts and boycotts. For up-to-date information about sweatshop production and distribution, contact any of the following: Stop Sweatshops: A Partnership for Responsibility, c/o UNITE, 815 16th St. NW, Washington, DC 20006, tel. (202) 347-7417, e-mail: gcough@uniteunion.org; No Sweat, U.S. Department of Labor, Washington, DC 20210, internet: http: //www.dol.gov/dol/opa/public/nosweat/gcover.htm; La Mujer Obrera Program, P.O. Box 3975, El Paso, TX 79923, tel. (915) 533-9710; fax (915) 544-3730. The UNITE organizers in your community will apprise you of current direct-action campaigns against sweatshops.

14. I'd like to thank Jeredith Merrin, Andrea Lunsford, Marlene Longenecker, and Mary Malloy for offering helpful suggestions on earlier drafts of this essay, and Eric Swank for locating a wealth of information on late-twentieth-century sweatshops in the United States.

Bibliography

"Death List Is 141; Only 86 Identified." *New York Times*, March 27, 1911, A-2.

"Doors Were Locked, Say Rescued Girls." *New York Times*, March 27, 1911, A-2.

Fell, Mary. *The Persistence of Memory*. New York: Random House, 1984.

———. Personal interview, March 24, 1996.

Gioia, Dana. *Can Poetry Matter?: Essays on Poetry and Culture*. St. Paul: Graywolf, 1992.

Gitlin, Todd. "Made in U.S.A. Label Is No Guarantee." *Los Angeles Times*, April 14, 1996, M-5.

Howe, Irving. *World of Our Fathers*. New York: Harcourt Brace Jovanovich, 1976.

Kinzie, Mary. *The Cure of Poetry in an Age of Prose: Moral Essays on the Poet's Calling.* Chicago: University of Chicago Press, 1993.

Leichter, Franz S. "Investigation into the Garment Industry in New York City." Albany: New York State Department of Labor, 1983. Mimeographed.

Llewellyn, Chris. *Fragments from the Fire*. New York: Viking/Penguin, 1987.

———. Interview with Michelle M. Tokarczyk. In *Belles Lettres*, January/February 1988, 5.

Logan, William. "The Persistence of Memory." *New York Times Book Review*, August 26, 1984, 13.

Miner, Valerie. "Writing with Class." In her *Rumours from the Cauldron*. Ann Arbor: University of Michigan Press, 1992.

Nelson, Cary. *Repression and Recovery in Modern American Poetry and the Politics of Cultural Memory, 1910–1945*. Madison: University of Wisconsin Press, 1989.

Orleck, Annelise. *Common Sense and a Little Fire: Women and Working-Class Politics in the United States, 1900–1965*. Chapel Hill: University of North Carolina Press, 1995.

Petras, Elizabeth McLean. "The Shirt on Your Back: Immigrant Workers and the Reorganization of the Garment Industry." *Social Justice* 19 (1992): 76–114.

"Quick Grand Jury Fire Investigation." *New York Times,* March 26, 1911, A2.

Ratner, Rochelle. Review of *The Persistence of Memory. Library Journal,* April 1, 1984, 723.

Shetley, Vernon. *After the Death of Poetry: Poet and Audience in Contemporary America.* Durham, NC: Duke University Press, 1994.

Stein, Leon. *The Triangle Fire.* Philadelphia: Lipincott, 1962.

Tokarczyk, Michelle M. "Of Epic Proportions." *Belles Lettres,* September/ October 1987, 12.

Wertheimer, Barbara Mayer. *We Were There: The Story of Working Women in America.* New York: Pantheon Books, 1977.

Zandy, Janet. "The Complexities and Contradictions of Working-Class Women's Writings." *Radical Teacher* 46 (1995): 5–8.

———. *Liberating Memory: Our Work and Our Working-Class Consciousness.* New Brunswick, NJ: Rutgers University Press, 1995.

———. "'Women Have Always Sewed': The Production of Clothing and the Work of Women." *Women's Studies Quarterly* 23, nos. 1 & 2 (1995): 162–68.

Karen Kovacik *teaches creative writing at Indiana University–Purdue University of Indianapolis. Her dissertation is entitled "'Poetry Should Ride the Bus': American Women Working-Class Poets and the Rhetorics of Community."*

Beyond False Promises: K. B. Gilden's *Between the Hills and the Sea* and the Rethinking of Working-Class Culture, Consciousness, and Activism

Tim Libretti

Restoring Dialectics in Theory, Activism, and Culture

In this essay, I will provide the cultural perspective and grounding for theorizing a deeper, more genuine, more historical concept of class and class consciousness to guide the contemporary working-class activism around a more comprehensive sense of working-class issues. By deeper, more genuine, and more historical, I mean based on a theorization of the dialectical interrelations among race, class, gender, sexuality, and nation. What I hope to contribute in this essay is a theoretical and cultural orientation that brings us back to the point of production (and reproduction), that is, the location of labor where race, gender, and sexuality are produced as an integral part of the mode of production.

In providing this cultural orientation to refocus our critical efforts on the point of production in thinking about a class consciousness comprising the complex interactions of race, class, and gender, I will look at Katya and Bert Gilden's 1971 novel *Between the Hills and the Sea*, which focuses on sexual relations on the factory floor, homophobia, tensions of intraclass relations, and problems of developing class consciousness and maintaining activist energies as it charts the deradicalization of labor unions during the cold war. Although the novel concentrates primarily on sexual and gender conflicts in the working class in the turbulent post–World War II period when men returned from the war expecting to return to jobs occupied by women during the war, the novel also provides a paradigm for thinking about the intersection and production of race, class, gender, sexuality, and nation as a totality connected to the mode of production and their "fusion" into a comprehensive class consciousness. Indeed, because it was written in the 1960s, the novel's focus on the work process and the factory floor in treating issues of sexuality and gender can be read as a direct response to the burgeoning feminist movement that essentially ignored the concerns of working-class women. The novel also complements Georg Lukacs's theoretical approach to class consciousness, as the Gildens self-consciously developed a literary methodology grounded in Lukacs's theories of realism and typicality, although their creative practice also outdistances his critical tenets.

In addition, the collaborative writing method of the wife and husband Katya and Bert Gilden to some extent informs the prose itself with the very sexual dynamic they are representing and provides an imaginative "fusion" of these identities. Indeed, in speaking about their first novel, *Hurry Sundown* (1964), a best-seller and civil rights classic about black and white farmers in the South resisting corporate agribusiness, Katya asserts that the novel is "a real fusion of both our points of view and richer than either of us could have made it alone" (*Life Magazine,* February 5, 1965, 45). This attempt to fuse identities into a coherent novelistic class consciousness is the hallmark of their literary careers, as Katya Gilden, up to her death in 1989, had been working in collaboration with the Black Panther Lonnie McLucas (who had been wrongly imprisoned on murder charges) on his life story. The Gildens had been active in feminist, antiracist, and labor movements from the 1930s to the 1980s (Bert died in the late 1960s), and their literary efforts are extraordinary examples of committed writing that attempt to enact this very fusion of race, class, and gender and to develop a novelistic class consciousness of the racial patriarchal capitalist system.

A False Farewell to the Working Class

The Gildens wrote their novel *Between the Hills and the Sea* (1971) in the late 1960s, an age in which, according to Stanley Aronowitz, "the glow of consumer society" had worn thin and "workers turned their attention to the labor process, which by then had become almost entirely rationalized and devoid of craft"(*Politics,* 227). But the novel turns back to the 1950s to portray the deradicalization of trade unions and the decreasing importance of the work process itself in trade union politics, which focused on increasing wages instead of abolishing labor exploitation. The Gildens reassert work as a unique class experience potentially constitutive of an oppositional culture, consciousness, and political perspective and identity. Indeed, in response to reviews describing the novel as being about "the blue-collar middle class," Katya Gilden wrote in a letter,

> Now it's the whole point of this novel that the working class has NOT become middle class. That no matter what their income or political

opinion, nothing has essentially changed for them. They own neither the machinery they work nor the materials they work on nor the
plant they work in. They are exactly where they always were. (October
21, 1971)

Just as Marx insists that the capitalist mode of production is not just
the production of things but at the same time is the production of
social relations and of ideas about those relations, a lived experience
or ideology of those relations, so the Gildens represent the workplace
of post–World War II, cold war America as the site of ideological production. The factory floor is an ideological battleground fraught with
the sexual conflict generated by the reinstitution of a gendered division of labor after the war when men returned to the workplace and
with the class conflict carried out in the workers' resistance to speed
up and the increasing rationalization of production. In short, they
resisted the increased subordination of human activities and abilities
to the abstract quantitative principle of accumulating capital. Self-identified "novelist[s] of the world of work," the Gildens bring work to the
center of their representational agenda, creating a new radical
sociopolitical epistemology in a cold war setting that magnifies gender
conflict in the workplace where class consciousness is shaped, exploring work as both exploitation and creative human activity, and representing work as producing culture and class consciousness and as a
creative or libidinally invested activity capable of transforming society
and social consciousness.

In representing this world of work in hopes of transforming it and
demonstrating its transformative potential, the Gildens themselves are
developing a new literary or aesthetic mode of production by reinvig-
orating the proletarian literary form. In the unpublished "Notes on
Problems of the Contemporary Novel," Katya Gilden observes:

> The bourgeois novel rarely refers to the working life of its characters.
> Their "real life" takes place outside of work if they work at all. . . . In
> the post-1945 period the American critic so resoundingly repudiated
> the "proletarian novel" of the 1930s that it has remained to this day
> more or less tabu. To our intelligentsia the working class is not cen-
> tral but peripheral in the operation of society and the worker is
> regarded, if at all, as lumpen drifter, ethnic boor or, sentimentally,
> as the ineffable "little guy" of no great dimension, density or conse-
> quence. (Note 3)

In narrating the work process in *Between the Hills and the Sea,* the
Gildens deconstruct the division between mental and manual labor

that defines capitalist production. Although Katya Gilden insists at the outset of her "Notes on Problems of the Contemporary Novel" in distinguishing between "the worker and the intellectual's mode of operation," stating that "the worker deals physically and mentally with a reality outside himself" while "the intellectual deals primarily with materials of the mind, to the point sometimes where he can come to believe that reality exists only as he perceives and moulds it," she is fundamentally against the "dominant aesthetic direction of the past several decades" that "has been intellectual and inward in orientation"(1). Furthermore, the Gildens' own aesthetic focus on work highlights the common roots of artistic and material production and demonstrates the possibility of destroying the opposition between capitalist material production and free, creative labor.

The Sensitive Plant: Engendering Class Consciousness in Literary Form

That garden sweet, that lady fair,
And all sweet shapes and odours there,
In truth have never passed away:
'Tis we, 'tis ours, are changed; not they.

For love, and beauty, and delight,
There is no death nor change: their might
Exceeds our organs, which endure
No light, being themselves obscure.

—Percy Bysshe Shelley, "The Sensitive Plant," 3.II.130–37

These concluding stanzas of Shelley's poem, Richard Caldwell argues, suggest that "the Garden and the Lady 'have never passed away'; they remain in the hidden reality of unconscious desire and its obscure manifestations. It is consciousness, not these eternal fantasies, which is the agent of change." Although the sensitive plant of the poem's title withers and dies when winter ravages the "undefiled Paradise" it inhabits and the maternal Lady, "an Eve in this Eden," dies, the poet concludes that "death itself must be,/Like all the rest, a mockery" (3.II. 128–29), suggesting that this edenic state, which Caldwell reads through Freud as an "eroticized symbiotic fantasy" (Caldwell 225), can be recovered through a subjective reclamation, a bringing to consciousness of the possibility of returning to or achieving this state.

Writing about the fate of the left and working-class struggles in the 1950s, the Gildens invoke Shelley's poem in their portrayal of the deradicalization of trade unions, entitling the first section of *Between the Hills and the Sea* "The Sensitive Plant." The invocation is apt, because while chronicling trade union deradicalization in the 1950s and describing the conditions that ensured the demise of trade unions, the novel also diagnoses this failure as having to do as much with subjective factors as objective ones. The Khrushchev revelations represented a fall from grace, an expulsion from Eden, for the radical left and working class of the 1950s, when the utopian model society of the Soviet Union under Stalin was unmasked. First published in 1971, the Gildens' novel explores this fall, critiquing for future reference, I believe, the subjective response that failed because the working class inadequately defined itself against cold war intimidation and could not achieve a genuine class consciousness.

The sensitive plant in the novel refers literally to the *mimosa pudica*, the potted plant the workers give as a present to a fellow worker. With the pun on *plant* referring to both the flower and the factory, the plant also symbolizes both the tenuous, fragile, and potentially volatile work relationships that threaten to break down at any moment and the equally delicate class consciousness of the workers that is so difficult to maintain and to arouse to revolutionary action—as the character Mariuchi says when all want to touch the plant, "You do this too often, it won't react." The difficulty of revolutionary activity, the novel suggests through this symbol, is primarily subjective. Given that the workers are basically responsible for social production, the possibility of their taking control of the means of production is always present, and so it is only a matter of the working class's discovering its power. Just as the garden and the lady in Shelley's poem have not passed away, the novel suggests, neither has the hope or possibility of a society directed by producers themselves. The Gildens reconstruct a version of the 1950s as "unsilent," countering the repressive historical discourse that urges us to forget that then, as Aronowitz reminds us, "ordinary people persisted in the effort to protect the measure of control over their work or their homes which they had won in previous decades" (*False Promises*, 325).

Treating the work experience in the factory as central to the production of the workers' consciousness, the Gildens' novel also represents how the very alienating effects of the capitalist organization of production against which the workers rebel also prevent them from fully understanding the source of their oppression in the labor process itself. The novel diagnoses the cause of this "subjective" failure of the working-class movement at the point of production to be rooted in the labor process itself, particularly in the sexual division of labor that divided rather unified the working class in the 1950s and precluded the development of a revolutionary class consciousness. The promises of the edenic conclusion to working-class struggle were false, the novel dramatizes, because of the working class's failure to acknowledge and rectify the gendered division within itself and to achieve the necessary androgynous class consciousness for a successful political movement. *Between the Hills and the Sea,* I argue, attempts to construct this androgynous consciousness both positively and negatively: positively through the predominant romantic androgynous image in the novel of the sensitive plant and negatively by charting the subjective failure of the protagonist, Mish Lunin, as representative of the failure of a heavily masculine and homosocial union movement.

As the novel depicts it, the failure of the 1950s was a failure of the working class to develop a subjectivity or class consciousness to comprehend its own objective existence at that historical moment. It is through a novel like *Between the Hills and the Sea* that we can perhaps best understand the political and cultural struggle to develop a revolutionary form of class consciousness, as reflected in the Gildens' own struggle to create a literary form to express the radical content of a sexually divided working class.

The collaborative mode of literary production, given the gender dynamics of Katya's and Bert's collaboration, seems particularly well suited to treating this moment in history when the resistance of women workers to male-dominated unions trying to reclaim jobs for men after World War II became apparent. Male anxiety over women's roles in production after the war, such labor historians as Ruth Milkman and Nancy Gabin point out, sometimes resulted in the domination of men's gender interest over their class interest.[1] Thus the social constructions of gender that underwrote and ratified the sexual division of labor undermined the objective interests of working-class men and women. The Gildens diagnose this division in *Between the Hills and the Sea,* I contend, and posit the need for an androgynous form of class consciousness to deconstruct divisive and hierarchizing gender ideologies.

In *Between the Hills and the Sea,* the Gildens are working toward exactly such a form. Indeed, scenes in the novel demonstrate that an objective, totalizing comprehension of society requires a combination, reconciliation, or fusion of "male" and "female" perspectives. In one particularly telling scene, Mish remembers his wedding day when Priscilla's mother pointed out to the couple a pair of purple finches, an allegory for this necessity for androgyny:

They watched the birds with her a moment. Flying from perch to
perch in search of food or a nesting spot or whatever. The male, rosy-
feathered, landed on the side-yard fence and the female, white-
flecked brown, right behind him. He pointing one direction, she
pointing diametrically opposite, commanding between them a full-
circle perspective on food, security, the next move. (219)

The sensitive plant itself, furthermore, is described in sexually ambiguous terms indicating a combination of male and female anatomy.
When Mariuchi caresses the plant, for example,

sensuously emitting from the palps of her fingers a siren song. The
leaflets responded, folding up, erectile, a closure of liplets, under
the movement of her fingertips, their movement centripetally
engendering movement downward, a flutter of movement down the
green sprays on both sides converging in the swollen base of the
stalk. (65)

Helen Yglesias, writing in a 1990 review of the reprint, feels that both
of the Gildens' novels "are governed by a masculine sensibility, a loss
of vision," even though Katya told her "her aim was to be 'gender neu-
tral'" (Yglesias 46). I think, however, that *Between the Hills and the Sea* is
informed by a feminist sensibility that approximates androgyny, as evidenced in these passages. The novel attempts to comprehend a
moment in the history of working-class struggle problematized by a
complex gender dynamic.

In his study of the erotics of male collaborative writing, Wayne
Koestenbaum finds it a useful method to "enter the mind of the writer
who keenly feels lack or disenfranchisement, and seeks out a partner
to attain power and completion" (2). In a male-female relationship,
we might assume that the female would feel more disenfranchised,
and in the case of K. B. Gilden, this seems to be the case, particularly
given Katya's statement in an interview with Paul Buhle that because
of her blindness in her relationship with Bert, "he lived, and I lived
through him [because she was legally blind]" (Buhle). Katya, however,
seems to have found a means of empowerment and enfranchisement
in the novel, as she relates in *Between the Hills and the Sea* the failure of
Mish's "typical" (in the Lukacsian sense) masculine revolutionary class
consciousness while perhaps unwittingly constructing through a het-
eroglot form, to use Bakhtin's language, an androgynous class consciousness that more adequately comprehends the tensions and
divisions of the 1950s working class.

Between the Hills and the Sea demonstrates both the insufficiency of the typical male revolutionary consciousness and, in its own form, a formal comprehension, if only retrospective, of the objective and radical possibilities and working-class content of the 1950s.

The Art of Work, the Work of Art: Manual Labor and the Production of Culture and Knowledge

Between the Hills and the Sea responds to the conditions of the 1950s in terms of not only its gender dynamics but also its cultural dynamics. In *False Promises: The Shaping of American Working Class Consciousness,* Aronowitz writes,

> If the working class is to make a break with the past, this break cannot result from its militancy alone, or simply from the ability of the ideological left to capture a large working class constituency for its ideas. It will arise out of new conditions, rooted equally in new social relations and in the development of a conscious opposition culture generated by the workers themselves. This culture is hereby defined as the matrix of language, art, and political sensibility that constitutes the world outlook for an entire class. (15)

Between the Hills and the Sea functions as a novelistic handbook for the formulation of a working-class culture specific to and organized against a consumption-based society dominated by mass culture. Through their dramatic representations of the workplace and the production process, the Gildens demonstrate the possibility of deriving a culture from the work process and relationships themselves that, though popular, achieves what Herbert Marcuse calls the artistic alienation of "high" culture. Appropriating Shelley's poetry, for example, and adapting "The Sensitive Plant" to the shop floor to gloss the work experience both exalts labor and legitimates working-class culture against the backdrop of an increasingly mass culture–dominated society. This appeal to a romantic sensibility and the use of romantic techniques and topoi, such as the sublime, are crucial to the Gildens' conception of a resistance or opposition culture at this time.

Linking traditionally "high" cultural forms with factory life both designates work as the social center of cultural creativity and knowledge and redefines, against what Harry Braverman terms the degradation of labor in the twentieth century,[2] the traditional conception of the capitalist division of labor in terms of mental and material production.[3] The Gildens counter this ideology of the degradation of labor in their

detailed narrations of the work process itself. Describing the character Don Pinette's job of materials handler, for example, they write,

> Whoever in personnel had placed Don Pinette in Materials Handling
> ought to be sent back to whatever School of Business Administration
> had graduated him. The job was one of the lowest in the plant, low-
> est of the low, unskilled labor, no experience called for. Calling only
> for a Back. So the man hired a Back.
>
> Only to become an effective Materials Handler, the Back had to
> have a memory as long as an elephant's, the punctuality of a stop
> watch, alertness, initiative, judgment.
>
> He had to know his department as an Indian knows the forests,
> as a plowman knows the fields, as a mariner knows the waters. He
> had to figure out an itinerary adaptable to all possible contingencies
> if he wasn't to run himself ragged. He had to figure out the psy-
> chology of those he worked with if he wasn't to be pulled apart. (39)

Not only can the worker not be reduced to a Back, but he or she must
also be a genius, whereas the person from management, because of
his detachment from the work process, is incompetent and lacks the
knowledge necessary to manage the plant. The Gildens relocate the
worker/intellectual as central to the existence of society and marginalize the putative intellectual on the periphery, reversing the tendency of the bourgeois intellectual and novelist that Katya Gilden
outlined in the passage quoted earlier from her "Notes on Problems
of the Contemporary Novel." Indeed, as she told Paul Buhle,
although intellectuals commonly locate themselves in the center, the
worker actually occupies this position, for even though the worker has
been marginalized, the worker makes "every goddamned thing we
use" (Buhle).

Lukacs's theory of typicality is useful here to an analysis of *Between
the Hills and the Sea* to see how the text attempts not only to comprehend but also to diagnose this particular historical moment in the
1950s and thus formulate or construct a revolutionary consciousness
for this and possibly future moments.[4] In *History and Class Consciousness*,
Lukacs argues that if we view consciousness in terms of its relation to
the concrete social totality, we can determine or infer the thoughts and
feelings that people would have if they could understand their situation and the interests that arise from or apply to their position in the
social whole. We can impute these thoughts and feelings appropriate
to a consciousness or subject position in the social totality, he argues,
because these positions are finite—they are types.[5]

This notion of the type also informs Lukacs's literary studies, particularly his *Studies in European Realism,* in which he exalts realism, the central and defining category of which he identifies as the type. What makes a character a type for Lukacs is that "in it all the humanly and socially essential determinants are present in their highest level of development, in the ultimate unfolding of the possibilities latent in them, in extreme presentation of the extremes, rendering concrete the peaks and limits of men and epochs" (*Studies,* 6). Lukacs's literary and dialectical studies, however, still need to be reconciled in some way, for in *History and Class Consciousness,* types refer to specific class positions, whereas elsewhere for Lukacs the type refers to all of a particular society and epoch. In *History and Class Consciousness,* only the proletarian type embraces the objective reality of the concrete social totality, as Lukacs writes that "the fate of the worker becomes the fate of society as a whole" and that "as the bourgeoisie has the intellectual, organizational, and every other advantage, the superiority of the proletariat must lie exclusively in its ability to see society from the centre as a coherent whole" (68). The Gildens' method, in any case, seems to be directed toward depicting this proletarian type, as they similarly locate knowledge as deriving from the work experience, as rooted in the productive process.

The reason that the Gildens, following Lukacs, conceive the proletariat as occupying this central position is because of the objectivity of its participation in production. This objectivity rests on the assumption underlying Marxist theory that the labor process determines the totality of human life and gives society its basic pattern. Thus workers in the midst of this process have a privileged perspective in that they know the interrelationship of tools and equipment. This enables them to see the outside world not as a collection of separate and unrelated objects but, rather, as a totality of relationships of mutually interdependent and interacting parts. Theoretically, workers can understand social reality as a process whose reification the outside world has frozen for a middle-class perspective—which sees commodities as finished products—but which will be dissolved. This "dereification," achieved through one's work experience, is the strategic effect of the Gilden's narrative of the work process. The narrative is basically a production of knowledge, the hypothetical construction of an objective perspective locating the production of consciousness in the labor process.

As readers, we are initiated into this process and schooled in this knowledge much as Don Pinette, the new Materials Handler, is initiated into the process by Mish. Facing "the overwhelming presence of the machinery" as Mish leads him through the assembly process, Don begins to wonder and even understand: "All this machinery in here just to make them little doojiggers? All these things turning and screwing around just to put a little bitty hole through? It was a beginning. Beginning to make a dent" (41, 44). By this point in the novel, the reader has already read detailed technical narrations of work that bring to the consciousness of the uninitiated the complexity of the productive process and the wealth and depth of technical knowledge necessary to produce and reproduce the world we live in. When we first enter the factory, for example, Mish is busy at work:

> He was tearing down the first machine, his eyes on the blueprint he had taped on the wall beside him. A continent of lines specifying the dimensions and contour of the new contact screw by the ten-thousandth of an inch, the areas where it was to be slotted, threaded, chamfered, cut out of what grade and finish of stock. His mind occupied with the selection of parts required. His hands already in it, geared to dismounting and installing the sequence of precision tools that fed and formed, slid and revolved: each in its turn to be loosened and then tightened with nuts, clamps, set screws, dowel pins, bolts; to be cushioned with bushings, held with chucks, adjusted for distance and angle, timed, tested. (23)

In this sense, the narrative is dereifying. We never really see descriptions of finished objects that as readers we can passively consume. Rather, we are continually swept up in the narrative of and as process, in the continuous and highly technical and esoteric motions of production. Indeed, Katya Gilden tells Buhle that she eschewed a naturalist technique for the novel in favor of a technique that would allow for "a mobile narrative with a compelling drive." She aimed for and succeeded in creating an "organic dramatic action" that privileged "action over detail" and included "no detail for its own sake" (Buhle). The novel's narrative itself, with its emphasis on motion and fluidity, in this sense mirrors or grows out of the rationalized work process itself, which in the novel is characterized by a constant call for and insistence on motion: "At mercury injection, women . . . with a continuous movement of the arm . . . shook each button" and "women at the electrical activation machine . . . paced around the machine in tempo with its mobile, electrically charged track, sliding buttons between little knobs"(47).

Out of the world of work, from the theoretically inclusive perspective of production, the novel attempts to construct a consciousness that comprehends the objective situation in the 1950s and through which the reader, too, will discover the revolutionary possibilities of that historical moment. Indeed, as Michael Buroway paraphrases Marx, "Any work context involves an economic dimension (production of things), a political dimension (production of social relations), and an ideological dimension (production of an experience of those relations)" (39). Because class consciousness is, in E. P. Thompson's words, the way that the class experience is "handled in cultural terms: embodied in traditions, value-systems, ideas, and institutional forms" (10), we can understand *Between the Hills and the Sea* as intervening in the cultural processes that formulate class consciousness and as narrating a literary class consciousness designed to highlight the possibilities for workers at the point of production not only to produce our material world but also to reinvent our cultural and ideological world in a way that transforms exploitation into creative human action for the free development of all.

In short, the Gildens construct in the novel a proletarian type or typical consciousness for the 1950s. This typical consciousness represented in the novel, however, is not located, as in Lukacs's theory, in one particular character, even though Mish's consciousness seems to dominate the novel. Mish's consciousness, however—marked by what in *Theory of the Novel* Lukacs refers to as romantic disillusionment—is just one perspective in the larger novelistic consciousness. Instead of narrowly focusing on Mish's subjective failure and obsession with the edenic past when workers were unified and class conscious, we need to see the novel as a "hetero- as well as polyglot consciousness." As Bakhtin writes,

the novel can be defined as a diversity of social speech types (sometimes even diversity of languages) and a diversity of individual voices artistically organized. The internal stratification of any single national language into social dialects, characteristic group behavior, professional jargons, generic languages, languages of generations and age groups, tendentious languages, languages of authorities . . . —this internal stratification in every language at any given moment of its historical existence is the indispensable prerequisite for the novel as a genre. The novel orchestrates all its themes, the totality of the world of objects and ideas depicted and expressed in it, by means of the social diversity of speech types and by the differing individual voices that flourish under such conditions. Authorial speech, the speeches of narrators, inserted genres, the speech of characters are merely those fundamental compositional unities with whose help heteroglossia can enter the novel; each of them permits a multiplicity of social voices and a wide variety of their links and interrelationships (always more or less dialogized). (271–72)

Indeed, to limit our understanding of the novel to Mish's type of consciousness is to appropriate Lukacs's category of the type, even of the proletarian type, wholesale and simplistically without using it in the complexity it allows for. We need to consider what the "humanly and socially essential determinants" are that would be present in a type. Class, for example, must be understood as composed of different genders and diverse races. In *Between the Hills and the Sea,* gender functions as one of these "humanly and socially essential determinants" that complicates class identity and creates in the novel's class consciousness "its dispersion into the rivulets and droplets of social heteroglossia, its dialogization" (Bakhtin 273).

The Gender of Production, the Production of Gender: Work, Sex, and the Prospects for a Liberated Labor

Viewing the novel itself as a constructed consciousness of the 1950s, which is more extensive than Mish's consciousness, we can open the working class to a study of its internal gender dynamics and perhaps can find some insights into the novel's collaborative production. The collaboration itself may have fostered this "dialogization" or "social heteroglossia" in the novel. According to Koestenbaum, "Collaborative texts, like quilted texts, make the reader vulnerable to heterogeneity and indeterminacy, and by obscuring who wrote what, they prevent the reader from limiting the text's sense"(8). Although we do know that Katya Gilden did the actual writing of the novel, even though it was conceptualized in detail by both (interview, June 10, 1992), we cannot know what content might have worked its way into the writing through Katya's own sensibility and experience of social reality. Koestenbaum rejects the term *heteroglossia* because he "would have found praise of heteroglossia tedious because the prefix 'hetero' suggests this theory's sexual preference" (8), but the term, precisely because of this prefix, applies to both the collaborative mode of literary production and the androgynous consciousness the novel constructs in its attempt to comprehend the content of the working-class struggle of the 1950s.

The Gildens, then, not only bring work from the periphery to the center of social experience in the novel, but they also deal with gender relations in relations internal to the working class. Indeed, after World War II, the defeminization[6] of basic industry and its concomitant effect of reinforcing prewar or traditional gender roles created conflict between working-class men and women. George Lipsitz points out that "within thirty days of the end of the war, 675,000 women lost their jobs—more than double the rate of joblessness of male war workers" (157). Ruth Milkman suggests that the reason for this trend "was the operation of union-instituted seniority systems, and their manipulation by male unionists, to exclude women and to favor returning male veterans in postwar employment" (*Gender,* 132).

The problem, however, was not so much the disemployment of women but the return to the prewar sexual divisions of labor that relied on obviously inaccurate—because disproved during the war—gender constructions. Although Milkman and Gabin point to key women's postwar labor movements among autoworkers and electrical workers (United Vacuum in the novel was based on a real GE plant), Lipsitz recounts an incident that occurred in the Gildens' hometown of Bridgeport, Connecticut, which illustrates the contradictory roles assigned to women at different moments. After being fired after the war, twenty-four women picketed the Lindstrom Tool and Toy Company, and "although they sought reinstatement to jobs they held during the war, the company now contended that such work was too physically-demanding for women to perform" (Lipsitz 161). Traditional social constructions of gender roles were sustained throughout the 1950s, and the National Manpower Council wrote in 1957 that Americans

> continue to have severe reservations about married women with small children working outside the home. They have also been disposed to view with disfavor the competition which women offer men, especially heads of families, when jobs are scarce . . . both men and women take it for granted that the male is the family breadwinner and that he has a superior claim to available work, particularly over the woman who does not have to support herself. (Lipsitz 163)

The message is clear from this historical evidence of social attitudes that the sphere of production was perceived as a masculine arena that the surge or invasion of women workers threatened during the war. *Between the Hills and the Sea* registers this deep-seated male anxiety over the gender of production with remarkable clarity. While initiating Don Pinette into the work process, Mish reflects on the difficulties that Don will have with women workers because he is the only male in his department in a position subordinate to the women and he is the lowest-classified male, but he still earns a higher wage than any of the women. "Toward Don," Mish thinks, "the women would employ every means at their disposal to compensate for the discrimination, the petty tyrannies, and the patronizing witticisms, the denial of advancement they endured at the hands of masculine authority" (53). Nonetheless, despite the privileges male workers enjoy in the factory, Mish feels marginalized in his role in production, reminding him of something he once saw in Italy during the war:

> Once in Italy during the war, in the mountain country south of Naples, he had glimpsed from a distance a massive surface being borne aloft. It was surrounded by a swarm of people as it proceeded down the road. As he neared them he saw that it was an enormous circular table top supported underneath by a stout pedestal of a woman. She carried it square on her head, no hands. A dozen men buzzed around her, all set to set the table top straight up if it should tip.
>
> The tableau had made a profound impression on him. It colored his view of the women here on the floor. All of them on production while the men, high-placed and low, buzzed about, auxiliary to them. (53)

The gender of production, once culturally coded as masculine, comes to be perceived by the marginalized male workers as predominantly female.

But if the gender of production is female, the production of gender in the factory still duplicates oppressive gender roles. As Marx writes, "The worker produces capital and capital produces him. Thus he produces himself, and man as a worker, as a commodity, is the product of the whole process" (137). Thus, at the same time that the women in the novel "gender" production, they also produce what constitutes gender and thus construct themselves in a certain gender role. As Cynthia Cockburn noted, "While people are working, they are not just producing goods and services for their employer and a pay packet for themselves. They are also producing culture" (83). While the women workers regard themselves as workers who control production, creating the possibility of class consciousness, they simultaneously participate in producing the very gender roles that create in them such a strong sense of injustice and that also impede the achievement of class consciousness.

The novel dramatizes this social production of sexuality, as production becomes the sublimated site of sexual energy. We see this in the novel's representation of sexuality as dehumanized and harnessed by dehumanizing conditions of production. The human has to compete with the machine for sexual primacy and potency. Don Pinette, for example, exudes a thick sexual presence, issuing "a scent of grass . . . out of the pores, the hair follicles, the sweat and seminal glands:

the kind of scent that sends feelers out to the female," but he must vie with the machinery for the women's attention:

> Against UV's equipment he posed his equipment, attempting to rouse the girls out of their enmeshment with inorganic matter into enmeshment with him, nature boy. He strode among them, an intrusive spirit, an escapee from the burgeoning spring day outside, demanding response.
>
> Offering gifts of himself in which the women couldn't be less interested. (42)

Don's work, in fact, is finally emasculating, as "all the strength of his muscular body drained down through his thumbs into a minuscule pressure" (63).

Furthermore, the women are more interested in production, particularly the production of sexuality, than Don is. The novel clearly depicts this process in one scene in which the character Leora travels down the assembly line, allegorizing the process by which the worker through production becomes both a worker and a sexualized woman. After Don has been spurned, "All eyes converged, not upon Don, but in the direction of final assembly. Surreptitiously they followed Leora as she wove in and out, vanished behind and emerged from, pursuing her progress to the ultimate assembly line. What would happen when she reached there?" (42). And later: "Mari's eyes were hard on her work and all over the floor at once, on Luckner the time-study man stepping out from around the turntable to consult with the Dirksen group, on Leora circling about mercury injection toward final assembly" (45). Leora is essentially being assembled as she walks through the various stages on the line, and Mari's vision is able to comprehend the totality of this process, linking male supervision and the rationalization of production with the exploitation and sexualization of the woman worker.

One might understand the novel as representing in this chapter what Marcuse refers to as "a scientific management of libido" in which "sex is integrated into work and public relations and is thus made more susceptible to controlled satisfaction" (Marcuse, *One-Dimensional Man*, 75). Indeed, in the representation of the rationalized assembly-line production, human desire is what motivates or fuels production:

> Through a compartmentalization of processes, part of an ingenious scheme to elicit from the human units en route the utmost efficiency,

the component elements were moved swiftly from work station to work station until they were united in the desired object: the electrical wall switch, one-way, two-way, up to four-way. (35)

Beyond this conflation of labor and desire, or sublimation of desire into labor, the novel represents almost every facet of the labor process as saturated with human sexuality. Mish, for example, remembers once showing some of the equipment to his brother-in-law's wife, Gail, who viewed the pieces in sexual terms: "It was all sculpture to her. The ivory toggle—'Why it's a tower, a phallic symbol.' . . . The ceramic belted button—'What a lovely navel'" (36–37). Ironically, after remembering this scene, Mish lives it all over again with Don Pinette:

> With every procedure he defined, they went through the same fandango. To "make out" meant only one thing to Don: what a fella does with girls. To "put out," ditto: what a girl does with fellas. The distinction between the male contact, threaded on the outside, and the female contact, tapped on the inside, could be identified for him only one way. "The male is the one that fits into the female. Get it?" (37)

Nonetheless, throughout the factory, for seemingly all the workers, the aspects of work can be identified in only one way. Even Mish later refers to a piece of equipment as having "tits" (60).

Although in some sense this eroticization of production is linked with the scientific management of the libido, it also contains the possibility of liberation and a nonrepressive sublimation that would allow a nonalienating libidinalization of the work process: in Marcuse's words, "the transformation of sexuality into Eros, and its extension to lasting libidinal work relations," "the transformation of labor into pleasure" (199). The novel thus demonstrates or brings to consciousness the utopian and cultural possibilities immanent even in work relations as they are. As Aronowitz stated, "The fundamental condition for [opposition culture's] emergence must be located among the sinews of society—not outside it" (*False Promises*, 15).

Between the Hills and the Sea affirms humankind's species-being by collapsing the categories of labor and desire and thus reveals the cultural possibilities latent "among the sinews of society." Paula Rabinowitz defines these two poles of labor and desire in the context of the 1930s' women's working-class literature:

> The body of the working-class man of the 1930s—and to an extent its text—is hungry, an empty space once filled by its labor; the body

of the working-class woman, as well as her text, is pregnant with desire for "children," for "butterfat" to feed them, and, most significantly, for "history" to change the world for them. (3)

For the Gildens, however, both men and women labor, and this labor is constitutive of their desire, just as labor—productive life—constitutes for Marx people's life activity and species being. Even though workers are alienated from their work in the novel, they still achieve some satisfaction of desire through labor, as in the following passage: "The components flowed ever more rapidly from hand to hand, the women hating the materials they handled, wrestling with them and yet intoxicated by a kind of exhilaration, the triumph of skill over substance" (59).

Also, as we have seen, the assembly process itself, as the Gildens describe it and as the workers perceive it, fitting the male inside the female, mirrors the consummation of heterosexual intercourse. This very act of labor achieves, if only allegorically, the sexual fusion that the novel suggests is necessary for an androgynous class consciousness. The historical conditions that bring men and women together in the sphere of production, as opposed to maintaining separate productive and reproductive spheres, allow and, in fact, demand this fusion. Indeed, as it is described, the sensitive plant symbolizes the blend of male and female workers that make gendering production one way or the other both impossible and, in terms of organization and praxis, impractical and ineffective. From the first page, in fact, Mish is trying to achieve this fusion but fails. He dreams that he is unable to overcome the sexual alienation, "in a strange house with a strange woman," just as at work his anxieties about female productivity prevent him from achieving with others the collective consciousness necessary to overcome their alienation of labor:

> He awoke to the clangor of concert music in a strange house with a strange woman, straining against the backside, long-curved and full-limbed, sheathed in night clothes and swathed in sheet. Plastered against Priscilla's back, he held her clasped in his crotch as if all was unsolvable between them could be solved by fusion of the flesh, as if in a passion of possession he could by some epoxy, magic, gelid, agglutinate, close the gap. (11)

It was precisely this fusion that Mish experienced with Priscilla during the strike in which they first met: "It was Eden. The bread they broke together was stale cheese danish. The vibration of disturbance between them became palpable as a charged field. Polarized, magnetized, in every particle of themselves compelled to fusion, they leaned toward each other and talked" (146). Their marriage became symbiotic with the union, as "the strike was their courtship. The union was the substance of their marriage" (143).

This desire for sexual fusion and an androgynous class consciousness perhaps fuels the collaborative production as well. Koestenbaum argues that "men who collaborate engage in a metaphorical sexual intercourse" and that collaboration itself signifies that a writer has "a longing for replenishment and union"(9). One can easily imagine a man and woman who collaborate to be engaging in a metaphorical intercourse as well, and the very writing of a novel that charts the downfall of unions seems aimed at helping us understand this fall from grace and replenishing the labor movement and working-class cultural production.

The heterosexist nature of the narrative that underwrites the linkage, even conflation, of sexual and class relations problematizes the novel as a model for a liberating class consciousness that includes and incorporates a resistance to homophobia. The Gildens nonetheless offer valuable paradigms for theorizing this fusion and understanding of sexuality, race, and gender as elements operating within and sustaining the racial patriarchal system. Their representation and treatment of these issues in the content of the workplace and productive relations recommends their work as a valuable contribution to a radical working-class culture.

NOTES

1. For an in-depth sociology of these issues, see the works of Gabin and Milkman cited in the Bibliography.
2. For a discussion of the degradation of labor, see Harry Braverman's *Labor and Monopoly Capital,* particularly 70–85.
3. Marx writes in *The German Ideology:* "Division of labor only becomes truly such from the moment when a division of material and mental labor appears." See *The Marx-Engels Reader,* edited by Robert Tucker (New York: Norton, 1972), 159.
4. In a letter to Otto Brandstadter dated August 8, 1973, Katya wrote that Lukacs "unlocked for us the problem of developing a literary method that would integrate individual and social dimensions of experience" and declared his socialist realism as "never properly understood."
5. For a discussion of economic types, see Lukacs's essay entitled "Class Consciousness," in *History and Class Consciousness.*
6. This term is from Ruth Milkman's *Gender at Work.*

Bibliography

Aronowitz, Stanley. *False Promises: The Shaping of American Working Class Consciousness.* Durham, NC: Duke University Press, 1973.

———. *The Politics of Identity: Class, Culture, Social Movements.* New York: Routledge, 1992.

Bakhtin, Mikhail. *The Dialogic Imagination,* edited by Michael Holquist and translated by Caryl Emerson and Michael Holquist. Austin: University of Texas Press, 1981.

Braverman, Harry. *Labor and Monopoly Capital: The Degradation of Work in the Twentieth Century.* New York: Monthly Review Press, 1974.

Buhle, Paul. Interview with Katya Gilden, July 1976.

Buroway, Michael. *The Politics of Production.* London: Verso, 1985.

Caldwell, Richard S. "'The Sensitive Plant' as Original Fantasy." *Studies in Romanticism* 15, no. 2 (spring 1996): 221–52.

Cockburn, Cynthia. *Machinery of Dominance: Women, Men, and Technical Know-How.* London: Pluto Press, 1985.

Gabin, Nancy. "'They Have Placed a Penalty on Womanhood': The Protest Actions of Women Auto Workers in Detroit-Area Locals, 1945–1947." *Feminist Studies* 8, no. 2 (summer 1982): 373–98.

Gilden, K. B. *Between the Hills and the Sea.* Ithaca, NY: Cornell University ILR Press, 1989.

Gilden, Katya. "Notes on Problems of the Contemporary Novel." Unpublished (personal copy).

———. Letter dated October 21, 1971 (personal copy).

———. Letter to Otto Brandstadter dated August 8, 1973 (personal copy).

Koestenbaum, Wayne. *Double Talk: The Erotics of Male Literary Collaboration.* New York: Routledge, 1989.

Libretti, Timothy. Interview with Jairus Gilden, June 10, 1992.

Lipsitz, George. *Class and Culture in Cold War America: A "Rainbow at Midnight."* New York: Praeger, 1981.

Lukacs, Georg. *History and Class Consciousness,* translated by Rodney Livingstone. Cambridge, MA: MIT Press, 1971.

———. *Studies in European Realism.* New York: Grosset & Dunlap, 1964.

Marcuse, Herbert. *Eros and Civilization: A Philosophical Inquiry into Freud.* Boston: Beacon Press, 1966.

———. *One-Dimensional Man: Studies in the Ideology of Advanced Industrial Society.* Boston: Beacon Press, 1968.

Marx, Karl. *Early Writings,* edited by Tom Bottomore. New York: McGraw-Hill, 1963.

Milkman, Ruth. *Gender at Work: The Dynamics of Job Segregation by Sex During World War II.* Urbana: University of Illinois Press, 1987.

———. "Redefining 'Women's Work': The Sexual Division of Labor in the Auto Industry During World War II." *Feminist Studies* 8, no. 2 (summer 1982): 336–71.

Rabinowitz, Paula. *Labor and Desire: Women's Revolutionary Fiction in Depression America.* Chapel Hill: University of North Carolina Press, 1991.

Thompson, E. P. *The Making of the English Working Class.* New York: Vintage Books, 1963.

Yglesias, Helen. "Chronicle of the Class Wars." *Women's Review of Books,* July 1990, 46.

Tim Libretti *is an assistant professor of English and women's studies at Northeastern Illinois University in Chicago. He has published widely on U.S. Third World, and proletarian literatures and issues related to Marxism, cultural studies, working-class studies, and race and ethnicity theory.*

Teaching Labor History Through Song

Pat Wynne

Sam runs into the classroom. He's so excited he can hardly talk. "I just wrote this lyric in my head," he says. "I didn't have a pencil." He recites it to us. The song is about his job as a bellman at a San Francisco hotel and the bosses he has to deal with. Sam, a shop steward with the Hotel and Restaurant Worker's Union, Local 2, never wrote a song in his life before this class, and now he can't stop.

I teach a course in labor song and labor history at San Francisco City College and Laney College in Oakland, California. In the course, my intention is twofold: first, to expose my students to labor songs and the events that inspired them and, second, to help the students write songs based on their own experiences and thereby create their own labor culture.

In my classes, hummable, sing-along songs pour out of Sam and students like him. The joy of creation, the excavation and expression of life stories and memories: these are the rewards of popular movement culture. By contrast, mass culture inhibits creativity and self-expression.

Let's define some terms. By movement culture, I mean the songs, stories, poems, plays, and graphic art that are produced by people involved in social change. Movement culture is the internal life of any political movement—be it abolitionist, populist, labor, socialist, civil rights, environmental, women's, gay and lesbian, communist old left, or new left. It offers hope and vision for an alternative social system.

Movement culture is an *alternative* and a challenge to received culture. It reaches back to residual values and meanings that were created by *real people* of the past. It represents human experiences, aspirations, and achievements that the dominant culture neglects, undervalues, opposes, represses, or cannot even recognize—experiences such as the culture and history of working people and the labor movement.

The Frankfurt school (Marcuse, Adorno, Fromm, Horkheimer, Lukacs, and others) contrasted art with mass culture. They regarded art as a utopian protest against reality, which provides a source of hope and an inspiration to struggle for social change. They defined mass culture as an accommodation to this reality, which has the effect of rendering its consumers impotent and their imaginations barren.

Mass or dominant culture is a selective tradition. The ruling elites use their version of the past to ratify the present and indicate directions for the future. The vulnerability of dominant culture is that the real record can be recovered through institutions that preserve alternative visions. For the labor movement, those institutions include labor archives, labor studies departments in colleges and universities, working-class studies centers, and the Labor Heritage Foundation in Washington, D.C.

Residue formed in the past is still active in the cultural process as an element of the present. Although it is not verified by the dominant culture, it is still alive and practiced by the people. To take a simple example, when was the last time you heard "Solidarity Forever" or "Union Maid" sung on the radio or TV? Yet we know these songs.

The old left movement culture challenged the dominant culture by promoting traditional, rural folk music and topical song, in opposition to what they saw as a corrupt and mindless popular culture. Robbie Lieberman wrote a wonderful book on this topic called *My Song Is My Weapon* (University of Illinois Press, 1989). By coincidence, Robbie's father, folksinger Ernie Lieberman, was my camp counselor when I was a child, and he gave me an alternative to mass culture by teaching me to love movement songs.

According to Lee Haring, quoted in Robbie's book, mass culture "does not want to preserve [art]; it wants to use and use up and throw away . . . [and] then go on to something else" (239–40).

Horkheimer and Adorno, members of the Frankfurt school, argued that the trouble with mass culture is that it is not truly popular. It is foisted on people, rather than created by them, and serves the interest of domination and potentially of totalitarianism (and certainly, we might add, the interests of the record companies that profit). Horkheimer and Adorno go on to assert that in the United States, conformist behavior was instilled by the dissemination of mass culture rather than by the use of terror.

In teaching labor history through song, my aim is therefore to oppose mass culture in the most fundamental way: by empowering working people. In class, we recover the residual values of the past by learning about real people—our unsung heroes and heroines—and then singing about them!

My basic perspective is summed up in one of my songs (written with Bernard Gilbert):

Labor History (by Pat Wynne)

> *Chorus: They never taught us any Labor History*
> *It's a mystery how we survived*
> *We know all about the captains of industry*
> *But it's the unions that helped keep us alive (2 times).*

1. Who needs Washington and the cherry tree
   He could not tell a lie
   But they tell us lies about who does the work
   and who gets the gravy and why.

   Forget about the Boston Massacre
   And that stuff about the tea
   Remember the Hay Market Massacre and the fire
   in the shirtwaist factory.
   Chorus

2. They spend a lot of time on Old Swamp Fox
   And those endless battle sites
   Just tell me how we got the eight hour day
   And who fought for worker's rights.

   Everybody knows the oil baron's names
   But the hist'ry books don't write
   About miners injured on the job or killed
   trying to win a strike.
   Chorus

3. They taught us all the May Pole Dance
   And sent us out to play
   They give us what they call Labor Day
   But it isn't on the first of May.

   Sure is hard to work a job, takin' knocks
   from the company
   But if you fight back with your union
   You'll be makin' Labor History!
   Chorus

Now that I've outlined a little theory, I'd like to describe what actually happens in the classroom. We start each class with stretching and breathing exercises and a vocal warm-up. These help relax people at the end of their workday and to invigorate them. Also, by learning basic vocal techniques, students become more effective singers and chanters. They discover how to articulate more clearly and to be louder on the picket line, without hurting their vocal cords. In this participatory democracy, it gives them the tools to lift their voices together in song or protest.

I begin teaching the history of working people in our hemisphere at the beginning, with native people. To honor the native peoples on our continent, I present the Seneca canoe song, in the Seneca language. Ray Fadden at the Six Nation Museum in Onchiota, New York, summarized the meaning of the song for me: "Watch your actions. The creator sees everything." He says that Seneca sing this song because it makes them feel good. I imagine them in their canoes, singing together as they fish or transport necessities and allowing the song to ease the work.

Then I jump forward to the mid-1800s, a time of technological transition and disruption. The next song is about skilled shoemakers who could no longer earn a living because factory-made shoes were sold so much more cheaply.

Peg and Awl (Traditional)

1. In the years of eighteen and one, Peg and awl. *(2 times)*
   In the years of eighteen and one, pegging shoes was all I done
   Hand me down my pegs, my pegs, my pegs, My awl.

2. In the days of eighteen and two, Peg and awl. *(2 times)*
   In the days of eighteen and two, Pegging shoes was all I'd do,
   Hand me down my pegs, my pegs, my pegs, my awl.

3. In the days of eighteen and three, peg and awl. *(2 times)*
   In the days of eighteen and three, Pegging shoes was all you'd see,
   Hand me down my pegs, my pegs, my pegs, my awl.

4. In the days of eighteen and four, peg and awl. *(2 times)*
   In the days of eighteen and four, I said I'd peg them shoes no more,
   Throw away my pegs, my pegs, my pegs, my awl.

5. They've invented a new machine, peg and awl. *(2 times)*
   They've invented a new machine—purtiest thing
      you've ever seen.
   Throw away my pegs, my pegs, my pegs, my awl.

6. Makes one hundred pairs to my one, Peg and awl. *(2 times)*
   Makes one hundred pairs to my one, Pegging shoes
      it ain't no fun
   Throw away my pegs, my pegs, my pegs, my awl.

The song evokes a resonance and a visceral emotional connection with the shoemakers that a prose narrative couldn't achieve. Music is a right-brain learning experience, although the words draw on left-brain skills. Combine the two with that emotional upwelling, and you have an extremely effective learning tool.

We continue with songs about the experiences of farmers, buffalo skinners, slaves, and mill workers.

Cotton Mill Girls (Traditional)

1. I've worked in the cotton mill all my life,
   And I ain't got nothin' but a Barlow knife,
   It's a hard times cotton mill girls, It's hard times everywhere.
   Chorus: It's hard times, cotton mill girls, (3 times)
   It's hard times everywhere.

2. In nineteen fifteen we heard it said,
   "Move to cotton country and get ahead,"
   But it's hard times, cotton mill girls,
   It's hard times everywhere.

3. Us kids worked twelve hours a day
   For fourteen cents of measly pay.
   It's hard times, cotton mill girls,
   It's hard times everywhere.

4. When I die don't bury me at all
   Just hang me up on the spinning room wall
   Pickle my bones in alkyhol-
   It's hard times everywhere.
   Chorus

"Cotton Mill Girls" has the lively beat of an old-fashioned hoedown. I teach the high-voice students a soprano descant, which creates a two-part harmony, and we really start to enjoy ourselves. This is usually one of the songs we perform in our concluding concert.

Turning to songs about immigrant labor and organizing drives, we remember May 1, 1886, when half a million workers across the country laid down their tools and vowed not to pick them up until they had won the eight-hour day. It was America's first general strike. Ironically, we are one of the few countries in the world that does not celebrate May Day.

Eight Hour Day Song (Anonymous)

We mean to make things over
We are tired of work for naught.

With but ne'er enough to live upon
And not an hour for thought.

We want to feel the sunshine
We want to smell the flowers
We are sure that God has willed it
And we mean to have eight hours.
We're summoning out forces
From the shipyard, shop and mill,

Eight hours for work, eight hours for rest
Eight hours for what we will.
Eight hours for work! Eight hours for rest!
Eight hours for what we will.

When we sing this song, I remind my students of the events on Saturday, May 1, in Chicago, when a peaceful march for the eight-hour day by eighty thousand workers and their families ended in a police riot that left four men dead. At a protest meeting the next Monday evening, in Haymarket Square, a bomb exploded, killing fifteen people. Local strike leaders—anarchosyndicalists—were arrested and tried for conspiracy; seven men were sentenced to hang. The Haymarket massacre and its aftermath brought the eight-hour day movement to a temporary halt. Workers returned to their jobs and their twelve-hour weekday with reduced salaries.

As we know, workers eventually won the eight-hour day. Today, however, when many people have no work or have part-time work, and others are forced to work overtime without extra pay, it seems that we need another eight-hour day movement. (Contemporary composer Charlie King has a song called "Bring Back the Eight Hour Day.")

Although the "Eight Hour Day Song" has its own melody, I prefer to sing the words to the tune of the "British Grenadiers," which is better known. In so doing, I am creating a parody: I am singing a popular tune with other words. The familiar tune helps people sing along more easily. It is a way of co-opting mass culture for our own ends. As I'll describe later, parody is one of the song forms I encourage my class to use when writing their own songs.

I devote a large portion of my classes to the history of working women.

Life Is a Toil (Anonymous, nineteenth century)

1. One day I was walking; I heard a complaining and saw an old woman, the picture of gloom.
   She gazed on the mud on her doorstep (T'was raining), and this was her song as she wielded her broom:

> *Chorus: Oh, life is a toil and love is a trouble*
> *Beauty will fade and riches will flee*
> *Pleasures they dwindle and prices they double,*
> *And nothing is as I would wish it to be.*

Before the 1830s, working women were generally domestics, shop girls, or farm women. Although widows and unmarried women were allowed to own boarding houses, inns, and other businesses, married women did not have that right; they could work only in their husband's businesses. I often think of Agnes Smedley's book *Daughter of the Earth*, set around the turn of the century, in which the only independent woman was a prostitute.

The earliest mill workers were young women and children.

Babies in the Mill (by Dorsey Dixon)

1. I used to be a fact'ry hand when things were movin' slow
   When children worked in cotton mills, each mornin' had to go.
   Every mornin' just at five the whistle blew on time
   To get those babies out of bed at the age of eight or nine.
   Chorus: Get out of bed little sleepy head and get your bite to eat.
   The fact'ry whistle's calling you; there's no more time to sleep.

The first textile mill was Slater's Mill in Rhode Island, built in 1791. There were nine workers, all under twelve years old. They worked fourteen hours a day, six days a week. By 1832, two-fifths of the workers in the textile industry were children. Known as "mill mites," they were worked to death, spending their short lives in the cold, dank air of polluted mills. It wasn't until 1938 that the Fair Labor Standards Act set sixteen as the minimum age for children to work, unless the work did not involve mining or manufacture and did not interfere with health and education.

Since children could not stand up to the rigors of a fourteen-hour day, six days a week, mill owners started a campaign to entice farm girls to the cities, with promises of high wages, more leisure time, and silk dresses.

The Mill Mother's Lament (by Ella Mae Wiggins)

1. We leave our homes in the morning, we kiss our children goodbye,
   While we slave for the bosses, our children scream and cry.

2. And when we drew our money, our grocery bills to pay,
   Not a cent to spend for clothing, not a cent to put away.

3. And on that very evening, our little son will say,
   "I need some shoes, mother and so does sister May."

4. How it grieves the heart of a mother, you everyone must know,
   But we can't buy for our children, our wages are too low.

5. It is our little children, that seem to us so dear,
   But for us, nor them, dear workers, the bosses do not care.

Ella Mae Wiggins lived in the back country of the Smokey Mountains in the 1920s. Of her nine children, four died of whooping cough because she could not afford to buy medicine. Her salary in the cotton mill was $9 per week. When the union came to Gastonia, North Carolina, the workers welcomed it, but the mill owners resisted, with help from the police, the sheriff, and paid thugs. Ella Mae wrote songs in support of the strike. This is the concluding verse of "The Mill Mother's Lament":

6. But understand, all workers, our union they do fear,
   Let's stand together, workers, and have a union here.

Ella Mae was shot in the back by hired thugs on her way to a union rally. The mill owners didn't underestimate the power of song!

Mining was another rich source of songs. In class, we sing songs by Sarah Ogan ("I Am a Girl Of Constant Sorrow"), Jim Garland ("I Don't Want Your Millions, Mister"), Florence Reese ("Which Side Are You On"), and Aunt Molly Jackson ("I Am a Union Woman"), all from Harlan County, Kentucky, where, in the 1920s and 1930s, many workers and their families found themselves negotiating the transition from farming to coal mining.

The women were raised as daughters of miners and then, at fourteen or fifteen, they married miners. Times were desperate and poor. When the unions came to organize the miners, Harlan County became a war zone: "Down in Harlan County there are no Neutrals there," as Florence Reese sang in "Which Side Are You On."

To illustrate the dire deprivation of the miners, Florence's sister-in-law, Aunt Molly Jackson, told this story: "I reached under my arm and I pulled out my pistol and I walked backwards. And I said, 'Martin, if you try to take this grub away from me, if they electrocute me for it, I'll shoot you six times in a minute. I've got to feed some children, they're hungry and they can't wait.'"

I Am a Union Woman (by Aunt Molly Jackson)

1. I am union woman, just as brave as I can be,
   do not like the bosses and the bosses don't like me.
   Chorus: Join the C.I.O.—come join the C.I.O. (2 times)

2. I was raised in old Kentucky
   Old Kentucky born and bred
   But when I joined the union
   They called me a Russian Red.
   Chorus

3. This is the worst time on earth
   That I have ever saw
   To get killed by the gun thugs
   And framed up by the law.
   Chorus

4. When my husband asked the boss for a job
   These are the words he said:
   "Bill Jackson I can't work you, sir;
   Your wife's a Rooshian Red."
   Chorus

5. If you want to join a union
   As strong as one can be
   Join the dear old C.I.O.
   And come along with me.
   Chorus

6. We are many thousand strong
   And I am glad to say
   We are growing stronger
   And stronger every day.
   Chorus

As we've seen in the case of Ella Mae Wiggins, many workers gave their lives to bring in the union. Some lost theirs in the course of an ordinary working day. In my class, we commemorate the women who died in the 1911 Triangle Shirtwaist fire in New York City with two songs, one in Yiddish by Morris Rosenfeld, the poet of the sweatshops, and one in English by Ruth Rubin.

To contrast with the sadness of industrial accident and unnecessary mortality, we also consider the vision of working people, the struggle not only for a wage but also for dignity, for bread and roses.

Bread and Roses (by James Oppenheim)

1. As we go marching, marching, in the beauty of the day
   A million darkened kitchens, a thousand mill lofts gray.
   Are touched with all the radiance that a sudden sun discloses
   For the people hear us singing, "Bread and Roses, bread and roses."

"Bread and Roses" celebrates a union victory in the woolen mills of Lawrence, Massachusetts, in 1912.

Our survey of labor history and culture swings through the Depression, pauses to look at women welders in World War II, and continues to the present, with lyrics about waitresses, Watsonville cannery workers, Dolores Huerta and the United Farm Workers, computer operators, Earth First activist Judi Bari, and many more.

Labor culture is not dead. In San Francisco, the Freedom Song Network keeps it alive, at picket lines and monthly song swaps. In Washington, D.C., every year, the Labor Heritage Foundation hosts the Great Labor Arts Exchange at the leafy campus of the George Meany Center. In northern California, the Western Workers Labor Heritage Festival brings together labor activists and performers to honor the work of Martin Luther King Jr. Up and down the eastern seaboard, the People's Music Network holds conferences twice a year to encourage politically engaged performers and songwriters. Numerous other events across the country keep this tradition alive.

Songwriters in this tradition today include, to name only a few, Si Kahn, Charlie King, Jon Fromer, Joe Glazer, Ann Feeney, John McCutcheon, Tom Juravich, Jose Luis Orozco, Linda Hirschhorn, Julie McCall, Paul McKenna, Bernard Gilbert, myself, and many others. Labor culture is certainly not dead!

In this spirit, I end each class by helping my students write songs and stories. All aspects of their lives—as workers, spouses, parents, artists, students, or SSI clients—are important. Their stories and songs will help inspire others, break down our isolation in this consumer-oriented society, and speak to our common humanity, especially as working people.

I teach them a few easy song forms, using examples from labor history:

1. In *zipper songs,* one line or phrase is replaced to create a new verse; that is, the new phrase is zipped in. For example, if the first verse is *This little light of mine,* I'm gonna let it shine," the next verse might be *We've got the light of freedom,* we're gonna let it shine," and so on.

2. In *call-and-response songs,* which come from the African tradition, the leader sings a line, and the group repeats it. A well-known example, from the 1960s civil rights struggles, is "I'm on My Way."

3. In a simple *blues,* the basic verse consists of three lines spread across twelve measures or bars of music: the first two are identical, and the third wraps up the rhetorical point. For example, from Bessie Smith's "Poor Man's Blues" (1930):

> "Mr Rich Man, Mr Rich Man, open up your heart and mind *(2 times)*
> Give the poor man a chance, help stop these hard, hard times."

This African American form provides a powerful means of writing about personal experience, in the workplace or elsewhere.

4. *Talking blues* and *rap* are spoken forms with a rhythmical musical accompaniment; separated by fifty years, they represent the same tradition and offer the same opportunities for wry, articulate expression.

5. *Parody*, as we've already mentioned, is a way of appropriating, or subverting, elements of mass culture. Some of the most skillful practitioners of parody were the Industrial Workers of the World, the IWW. The IWW was a singing union. In its short life, it made itself the most militant and dramatic organization in the history of American labor. In 1908, J. H. Walsh, an IWW (Wobbly) organizer in Spokane, Washington, perfected the use of parody in organizational activities. He explained the casual origin of Wobbly parodies: "There are so many hundred idle men in this country that many around headquarters have little to do but to study the question, compose poetry and word up songs to old tunes. . . . Among the IWW membership there are a few good singers as well as jawsmiths."

Many of the Wobbly songs were parodies of hymns sung by those other street-corner preachers, the Salvation Army. Here's an example by Joe Hill, the most famous, and perhaps the most prolific, IWW song writer:

The Preacher and the Slave (by Joe Hill) (Tune: "The Sweet Bye and Bye")

Long haired preachers come out every night.
Try to tell you what's wrong and what's right.
But when asked how 'bout something to eat.
They will answer with voices so sweet.
Chorus: You will eat, bye and bye,
In that glorious land above the sky.
Work and pray, live on hay,
You'll get pie in the sky when you die. (That's a lie)

And the starvation army will play,
And they sing and they clap and they pray.
Till they get all your coin on the drum,
Then they tell you when you are on the bum.
Chorus

If you fight hard for children and wife,
Try to get something good in this life,
You're a sinner and bad man, they tell
When you die you will sure go to hell.
Chorus

Workingmen of all countries unite
Side by side we for freedom will fight
When the world and its wealth we have gained
To the grafters we'll sing this refrain.
Chorus: You will eat, bye and bye
When you've learned how to cook and to fry.
Chop some wood, 'will do you good,
And you'll eat in the sweet bye and bye.

Other IWW writers include Richard Brazier, Ralph Chaplin (who wrote "Solidarity Forever"), Laura Payne Emerson, Pat Brennan, Covington Hall, Charles Ashleigh, and T. Bone Slim.

After the students have learned a few songs in these basic forms, I suggest to them that we all write a song together, and we choose a topic by consensus. In one class, we put together a blues about the lack of respect for older workers, called "The Slowing Down Blues." In another, we wrote a rap about various aspects of dehumanization, from the destruction of small farms to speedups and downsizing. Another class wrote "Rock Around the Marriot," a parody of "Rock Around the Clock," about a labor dispute at the local Marriot hotel.

These exercises are meant to whet the students' appetites, to get them started so that they'll go home and write their own songs. And write they do!

As a culminating experience, we put the songs together and create a low-key performance for labor studies faculty, students, and friends. I create simple harmonies and call-and-response arrangements for the songs. Most students have never sung in public before, but they give it all they've got. One man brought his clarinet, long gathering dust in his closet, to improvise an instrumental break for a blues he had written.

Here's a sampling of lyrics by some of my students:

We're on the Union Side (by Sam Zeher) (Tune: "Down by the Riverside")

1. Well we're marching on the picket line
   We're on the union side *(3 times)*
   We're marching on the picket line
   We're on the union side *(2 times)*
   Don't be a scab, don't cross our line *(2 times)*
   We're on the union side.
   Don't be a scab, don't cross our line *(2 times)*
   We're on the union side.

3. The boss man tried to cut our pay
   We're on the union side *(3 times)*

That's why we're on the line today
We're on the union side *(2 times)*
The bosses' greed is such a shame *(2 times)*
We're on the union side
The bosses' greed is such a shame *(2 times)*
We're on the union side.

They Control Us *(by Jason Justice)* *(Tune: "De Colores")*

2. They control us, they control us as wage slaves who're working to
    make bosses richer
    They control us, they control us and tell us that wages are low due to
    profits
    They control us, they control us and tell us how lucky we are to be there
    But someday we'll rise up and resist their orders and refuse to work
    here and there
    And someday we'll rise up and take back our work place and workers
    will make the job fair.

Out of My Way *(by Janita Thurman)* *(Tune: "When the Saints Go Marching In")*

1. Out of my way, hear what I say,
    I'm a working woman of today;
    I've paid my dues, I have my rights,
    I won't give up without a fight.

2. So now you say, you'll cut my pay
    Well I refuse to work that way;
    I've paid my dues, I have my rights,
    I won't give up without a fight.

Working the Grill Blues *(by James Conway)*

1. The kitchen's goin' faster, speeds up every day
    The kitchen's going faster, speeds up every day
    It's double time, out in our restaurant—I burned myself two times today.

2. Young folks cook it faster, they're more docile and cheaper than me.
    Young folks cook it faster, they're more docile and cheaper than me.
    But when it's done, it's just a mess and has no quality.

Class War *(a rap by George Johnson)*

3. They're puttin' social programs in the ditch
    So they can steal from the poor and give to the rich
    Every election, it's the same old pitch
    "I'm on your side," then they do the big switch.
    Chorus: It's time to start fighting, stop begging on our knees (2 times)

6. 'Cause it ain't about gettin' a better health plan
   It ain't about learning to say yes to the man
   It ain't about gettin' all you can
   It's all about the dignity of woman and man.
   Chorus

Techno-Life of Hell *(by Class at Women's Labor Summer Institute, San Francisco State University, 1996) (Tune: "Amazing Grace")*

1. Amazing screen and keys I pound
   My wrists and eyes detest
   I once could read and write and think
   Now I'm stiff, blind and depressed.

2. Bill Gates is not a saint to me
   Steve Jobs can rot in hell
   Who would have guessed these technogeeks
   Have made my life a hell.

3. Amazing Boss, you led me here
   Your fortune I provided
   But now through years as I break down
   I find myself down siz–ed.

4. Amazing hands, how dear you are
   I now need surgery
   It may not help, but what's my choice?
   Loss of movement has taken over me.

5. A dead end job, awaits for me
   Seduced by technology
   They say it's the future, but I don't agree
   They can kiss my ass, virtually!

Rock Around the Marriot *(Hotel) (by Labor Song Class at San Francisco City College, 1996) (Tune: "Rock Around the Clock")*

Introduction: 1, 2, 3 o'clock 4 o'clock rock!
5, 6, 7 o'clock 8 o'clock rock!
9, 10, 11 o'clock 12 o'clock rock!
We're gonna rock around the Marriot!

1. We used to feel demoralized
   But now we're getting organized.
   Chorus: We're gonna rock around the block tonight
   We won our recognition fight
   We're gonna rock, we're gonna rock around the Marriot!

2. The first five years our jobs were rough
   Without the union the boss was tough
   Chorus

5. We're gonna rock the Marriot all night
   We'll rock right thru' the contract fight
   Chorus

7. Maid, cook, waiter and bellhop
   We all win with a union shop
   Chorus

8. Local 2 knows what to do
   Dignity for me and you.
   Chorus

Each week when the class ends, at 10:00 P.M. after an eight-hour workday and three hours with me, the students go home feeling energized. One man said that the class felt as good to him as going out with his buddies for a few beers; I considered this a supreme compliment.

I can't help but think how revitalized workers would feel if they could create songs about their own lives—songs they could use on picket lines or to pep one another up at meetings or simply to ease the work they do and the burdens they carry. The students' self-excavation in class also clarifies the aspects of their lives that must change for the better and reminds them that they are stronger and more likely to effect change if they band together in unions. By writing songs, they empower each other and keep labor culture alive. To paraphrase Pete Seeger, "Every successful political movement is a singing movement!"

NOTE
"I Am a Union Woman" by Aunt Molly Jackson is reprinted by permission of Storm King Music Inc. Copyright 1966 (renewed) by Storm King Music Inc. All rights reserved.

Pat Wynne *is a writer, musician, voice teacher, performer, and cultural activist. She teaches at San Francisco City College and Laney College in Oakland, California, in the labor studies department. She belongs to the Freedom Song Network, a group of singers that keeps the labor song tradition alive in the San Francisco Bay Area. She also performs in a two-woman show called "Working Women's Stories and Songs" and a one-woman performance piece entitled "Days of a Red Diaper Daughter," based on a memoir that appears in Janet Zandy's anthology* Liberating Memory.

You, with the Stars in Your Eyes

At the Playgal Club, us go-go girls
didn't have a dressing room and had to use
the Ladies Room each night to pin on our
sequins and fringe and hairpieces
and take our 5-minute smoke-and-pee breaks,
Spike, our Simon Legree boss timing us, with a
stopwatch, and if we stayed longer than 6 minutes
he kicked on the Ladies Room door, yelled inside,
ironically rhyming, "Hey! Get your ass down the ramp,
you little tramp!"

During our first break, the guys' wives and dates
frowned at our tarantula eyelashes,
scorned our French bikinis still outlawed
on California state beaches, letting us know
that they were the real ladies in the Ladies Room,
sometimes one of them asking,
"How can you do such a thing?"
But then, during our second break,
after they'd had a few beers, they'd ask
what kind of eyelash glue or hairspray we used,
how did we learn to do the Pony, Jerk,
and Mashed Potato so good, and sometimes say,
"You're so lucky to work here."

Oh yeah, oh sure, we'd say, cynic hearts beating
beneath the push-up bras, our feet and hamstrings
aching, our hair and bikinis reeking
of beer, smoke and sweat, but yet,
deep down inside, just for a moment,
we were flattered into feeling like a movie star,
a homecoming queen, Gracie Slick, or Cher,
these drunken, blurry-eyed women
who led ordinary lives as housewives and secretaries
giving us the only sincere compliment of the night,
or week, until Spike kicked open the Ladies Room door again
and yelled inside,
"Hey!"

—*Joan Jobe Smith*

Jehovah Jukebox

The blue collar guys thought us
go-go girls were damned lucky
to work in a beerbar instead of
a hellhole like they did, we got
to do all the things they wanted to
do all day while they pushed and pulled
steel, we got to talk, smoke, shoot pool,
or drink a beer anytime we wanted to, plus
we got to listen to the jukebox all day long
for free.

Never mind that we'd never get vacation pay,
sick leave, overtime, or old age pensions,
that beer made us fat, the bar's darkness
and smoke making it another kind of hellhole,
and that the jukebox was as earbusting
and mindnumbing as their Jupiter machinery.

Never mind that instead of a crazy,
never-can-be-pleased supervisor
threatening lay-off, we had our own
nemesis reminder of our inferiority
and mortality: the Pastor Mick Jagger
fomenting foreboding every day
from the polycolored plastic jukebox pulpit
as he told us stupid girls, us honky-tonk
women under His thumb, having nineteen nervous
breakdowns, the ways of the angry-handed
God-of-the-day, and screamed at us
that we couldn't get no satisfaction,
or what we want, and what a drag it was
getting oh-
old.

—Joan Jobe Smith

Joan Jobe Smith *worked as a go-go dancer during the early 1970s before receiving her master of fine arts degree from the University of California, Irvine. She recently won the Chiron Poetry Prize for* Love Birds, *a collaboration with her husband, poet Fred Voss. In 1998, England's The Poetry Business published her fourteenth collection,* The Pow Wow Café.

On Language: An Essay

Merrihelen Ponce

As a writer of the Mexican American/Chicano experience, I write predominantly in English. *El íngles* was my first written language; to this day I express myself best in that idiom. Although much of this is due to acculturation and, by extension, to a school system that strove to "Americanize" children of Mexican immigrants (like my parents), my fetish with proper English was also drilled into me at home.

My older siblings, especially my sisters, spoke good English, taking care to enunciate each word and to speak without an "accent." Often, they corrected me. Learning a new word was not difficult; I was made to repeat a word over and over until it sounded right. Rarely did I consult a dictionary, terrified of the many rules in the English language.

Few folks in our town owned books, let alone a bookcase. Whether or not they read at all, I never knew. Their first priority as immigrants to this country was not to learn English but to provide for their families. Most got by with a minimum of *el íngles*. In fact, few of my friends read anything other than the comic books sold in town or exchanged for candy.

The books bought by my older sister from the Book-of-the-Month Club were in English, as were those I devoured at school and at the public library, where each summer I read in alphabetical order. Early on I realized that a command of English could open up new, exciting worlds and take me away from the mundane to far, distant lands.

Writing well in English was a challenge. Our teachers stressed the importance of spelling correctly. Although kind, they loomed over us as we struggled with words like *science*, which I felt should be spelled *cyans*. Few of my classmates wrote legibly; fewer still spelled correctly; we learned to keep erasers handy. We were scared stiff of dictionaries, knew next to nothing about phonics, and less about vowels. Mostly we took a chance, hoping the teacher would recognize the scribbles smeared across the paper. Our grades suffered, as did our self-esteem.

For native speakers of Spanish, reading aloud in class was traumatic; words in English did not look like they sounded. A slip of the tongue proved embarrassing. Those who pronounced the word *sheep* as "cheep" were considered backward, even dumb. Our obsolete textbooks—(ours was a poor school)—were chock full of long, difficult-to-pronounce English words, none of which were reader friendly. At times, our inability to articulate *en ingles* was misconstrued and thought to indicate a lack of intelligence. In some cases, it was a reason to hold us back a grade.

Although English was the language of authority, it was also the one in which we absorbed knowledge. All school rules were printed in English, as were the report cards we took home to our mostly illiterate parents. Our school principal, teachers, and the public health nurse praised—or scolded—*en ingles.*

At catechism we learned about sin and damnation from booklets approved by the archdiocese, written not in Latin but in standard English. We confessed our transgressions to our Spanish-speaking priest in hushed tones—in English—while attempting to disguise our voices. We asked for absolution and then, feeling lighter of heart, bolted out the door. And although our pastor chanted in Latin, he condemned the sins of the flesh in precise English.

Without some knowledge of *el ingles,* it was difficult for our parents to function. Bus routes were printed in English, and so were the utility bills paid in cash. Few *mexicanos* trusted in banks; checks were what rich (white) folks used. More important, some proficiency in English was necessary to decipher street signs, labels on medicines, and the instruction booklets that came with a new appliance.

Many of my friends were embarrassed by a parent's lack of English and preferred not to have them around at school assemblies. *Pobrecitos.* Our poor parents—who worked hard to ensure a better life for their children—were rarely told of school functions, only those at Christmas. Everyone knew the words to "Jingle Bells."

English was the language of money. And unless one patronized only *la tienda de Don Jesus,* English was the language of sales clerks, cashiers, and bank tellers. When returning coke bottles to the store, we calculated our earnings in pennies, dimes, and nickels. When sent to the store by our parents—and told we could keep the change—we added and subtracted with speed. *En ingles.* We thought in dollars.

English was the language of business and commerce. Only those of us who spoke English well (without an accent) would be hired to clerk in department stores or as telephone operators. The rest could expect to spend their working lives as mechanics, waitresses, or laborers. To be a secretary and wear white gloves and tailored suits (once my ambition), a girl had to have good writing skills, know shorthand, and, in addition to speaking good English, be familiar with the "business English" taught in high school and secretarial schools.

Still, English was the language of fun! When playing in the street, most game rules were explained in English, but we coached one another in Spanish: *menso, tírele 'pa aca, córrele!* And yet, English was the language in which my friends and I communicated our deepest, secret thoughts: who liked whom, which boy was cute. At night I pondered the right meaning of a word and then scribbled it in my diary.

Language was not a complicated thing in our home. In our family, everyone spoke both Spanish and English. We easily went from one to the other, often in the same conversation. It was acceptable—and practical—to mix and match, to make up words. We communicated with our parents in mediocre Spanish and with one another in English peppered with Spanish.

When I was growing up, *el español* was not given too much importance. In fact, the Spanish language was secondary to English and, like a poor relation, thrust to the back of our collective minds. No one thought to teach us Spanish grammar or how to enunciate words correctly. I never learned to memorize the Spanish alphabet or to spell correctly. To this day I have problems with certain words.

Since few of our parents were literate, fewer still realized the importance of being bilingual. At school we were told, "Speak English, only English. You're not in Mexico now." Clearly, it was more important to have a good grasp of English than to retain our mother tongue. At one time my siblings and I attended "Saturday school" where we learned to recite in Spanish.

Spanglish (which had not yet been identified as such) was the language in which we communicated with our peers. For the most part we spoke in English, but now and then—as though obliged to remember our Mexicanness—we threw in some Spanish, not the Castilian taught in high school, but a hybrid of sorts. Our language evolved from necessity.

To most kids, it was important to know the latest slang (and cuss words) in both languages. It was also crucial not to get caught using them. Often we made up words on the spot; some were quite original. A favorite was *mentolato* (from Mentholatum, the ointment mothers rubbed on sick kids). *Esta mentolato,* we screeched, implying a kid was mentally deranged.

Whereas my friends parroted their older siblings by using words like *hep to the jive, cool,* and *all reet, tweet,* I preferred the language of *pachucos* (later identified as *caló*). It was different and often funny, providing one did not get caught spewing off. My favorite sayings were: *órale, chingón, simón! ontablas que no te habia vidrios.*

My knowledge of written Spanish was picked up by osmosis and from *La Opinión* (my father's favorite newspaper), but also from reading aloud the letters sent from Mexico to Doña Luisa, our adopted grand-mother. By the time I was five or so and an ardent churchgoer, I was able to discern, from the Catholic liturgy, the relationship of Latin to Spanish.

Spanish was the language that I associated with love, romance, Mexico's María Félix (a femme fatale without peer), and Jorge Negrete, who sang love songs in Spanish while atop a horse. Although rock and roll (then called rhythm and blues) was what teenagers danced to, the most romantic ballads were *en español;* Los Panchos was a favorite group. Unlike Mexican singers who screeched, Los Panchos sang in soft, muted tones. "Nochesita," "Perdida," "Los Dos." Often, their Spanish voices lulled me to sleep.

When translating a work from English to Spanish—I search my *Simon & Schuster International Dictionary* for the right context, *el contexto* in which to use a word. When stumped, I pore over all my dictionaries (I have five) until satisfied with a word choice. Often I change it again.

My first major translations (from English to Spanish) were "Cuando ívamos a la nuez" and "Los piojos" (part of *Hoyt Street: An Autobiography*) for the June 1984 issue of *Fem: Revista cultural feminista* (Mexico City) which focused on Chicana writers. I reread *los cuentos* and then compared them with the original manuscript. The only major changes were of misspelled words. To date I have translated and published numerous works in *Fem,* among them "Holy Week," "Los tisicos," and "El mes de mayo."

When writing my novel *The Wedding*—it describes a 1950s blue-collar wedding in a California barrio—language did become a problem. I wanted it to reflect the language and thought patterns of post–World War II Mexican Americans, most of whom spoke more Spanish than English. Because the characters were of the working class, it would have been historically inaccurate for them to use standard English, let alone formal English. I had to invent a language based on the vernacular I grew up with: a blend of working-class Spanglish mixed with caló.

Words have power. I may argue that my work is not political, but more and more I see the power of the pen and how literature serves to contradict, illuminate, and refute negative stereotypes of Mexican Americans/Chicanos. When writing "Los piojos" (the yearly lice inspections of Mexican American kids in grammar school), I knew I was making a political statement about racism and shame. I felt uneasy at portraying the Anglo teachers at Pacoima Elementary as racist—most were sensitive to Mexican American culture—but I wrote that piece not for myself but for my schoolmates who felt the sting of criticism more often than I did.

If we are judged by our use of language, then I want to be among the best. I love to try out new words in my writing and in everyday conversation. I'll try a new word for a week and then file it away in my head. For a time I used—and overused—words like *pedantic, pedestrian, perspicacious, and perfidy,* then went to *sophomoric, sententious, and salacious.* One friend teased: "You must be in the s's now." That Christmas she gave me *The Superior Person's Guide to English,* which lists words I never even heard of.

As an academic, I am expected to write scientifically, using language devoid of slang and clichés, unlike that found in fiction. Although this is not usually a problem, if I'm not careful, my narrator can sound like a social scientist.

At the moment, I write fiction to take a break from footnotes, bibliographic entries, and essays, but it might never see print. Once I pick a theme, my imagination goes wild; my hands fly over the keyboard . . . out pop words and more words. *Soy escritora.*

Merrihelen *(also know as Mary Helen)* **Ponce** *has a doctorate in American studies from the University of New Mexico. Her dissertation is entitled "The Life and Works of Fabiola Cabeza de Baca, a New Mexican Hispanic Woman Writer: A Contextual Biography." She is the author of* Taking Control *(1987),* The Wedding *(1989), and* Hoyt Street: An Autobiography *(1993). She currently resides in Sunland, California, where she is working on biographies of Mexican women writers.*

The Silent Psychology

A Presentation at the 1995 Youngstown Working-Class Studies Conference

Barbara Jensen

I am one of that breed of placeless professionals who comes from a background in which no one I knew was a professional. Unlike most of these "strangers in paradise," no one ever pushed me to "get ahead," nor was I eager to leave the class I was in. Everyone I knew and cared about was working class until I was in my midteens. We did not see ourselves as deprived. We knew by the time we got to junior and senior high school that there were kids who were different from us. They dressed differently, they talked differently, and the teachers treated them differently. They floated through teeming hordes of us in the congested, action-packed hallways as if we didn't exist. To us, they were the phantoms. I loved my place among our tribe of working-class kids. I earned special respect by demonstrating courage (I mouthed off fearlessly to teachers and spent entertaining afternoons in detention hall with the other wise guys), humor (those comments to teachers were actually pretty funny), and unflinching loyalty. We saw those cashmere kids as the deprived ones: they didn't seem to be having any fun. They obeyed the teachers. We thought they were pathetic; they just weren't cool. They thought school was about what happened in the classrooms; we knew it was about what happened in the hallways. They just didn't seem to get it.

I am from an extended family of more than a hundred people that is still wholly working class; I am the only one with a college degree. The tract houses of our neighborhood were created specifically for the working class, and everyone who lived there was. It never occurred to me to want to be middle class. I think having such an unadulterated blue-collar childhood gave me a particular vantage point that informs the writing of this essay. I stumbled more than set a course out of the working class over a period of many years and various adventures, and the passage has never really been complete. At twenty-six, when I decided to go to college so I could get a job I liked, it was to the surprise of my peers and family. My family discouraged these eggheaded pursuits and said I should get "a nice civil service job" if I wanted to make something of myself. After I got my first degree, people had a variety of reactions. They ranged from mocking and resentful ("you'd think with your education, you could operate an electric can opener") to awkward ("that's different") to impressed. But they were impressed in an weird way, as though they didn't know me, as though I wasn't me anymore. Most poignantly, some were ashamed of themselves in my presence. Chatting with family members at one of our many reunions, they said things to me like, "Oh me? I'm just at the machine shop still." I had never heard them talk like that before—to someone else it would be (proudly), "Yep, still at the machine shop. Just got another raise. Yep. Doin' good."

Richard Sennett and Jonathan Cobb's book, *The Hidden Injuries of Class* eloquently described the kind of double bind our society puts working-class people in by making them choose between remaining loyal and connected to the people close to them or "getting ahead" through achievements. It is one of the ways our society ensures that there is actually someone to build the buildings that architects design; to lay the pavements that civil engineers sweep across paper; to pour and fire and box and sell the fine china that more privileged people get to buy. He calls it "fraternity versus ability," and indeed it is.

But the bind is more than double: it is quadrupled and quintupled and on and on until it is a mesh of psychological knots. The complexity of this psychological trap leaves working-class people gnawing off their own souls to escape the pain. It issues most profoundly from the fact that beneath layers of betrayal and confusion, there is a whole fabric of life that is quite different from the cloth out of which the middle class is cut. The greatest bind is not simply that one must choose between "being somebody" or remaining part of the community that constitutes psychological "home." It is the fact that crossing classes occludes all that went before it. There are knots upon knots in our society to bind the working-class psyche. But as we wind our way through them, we will find buried treasure at the center, treasure lost to those who leave. Spun out in slender threads that weave through the various compromises that cloak and dampen the spirits of working-class people is a vital, soulful kind of center. To describe only the wounds of these people is to obliterate them. Then again, to ignore the knots is to be unable to imagine what is obscured.

Now we must move from visual to auditory metaphor because what is invisible externally to those on the outside is experienced internally as a silence. We must strain to hear silences inside silences, a cacophony of silences, all the white space and ground beneath the middle- and upper-class figures that fill up the picture that society paints.

Compounding the silence of societal invisibility is classism, which promises that whatever is visible of working-class life will be regarded with contempt or pity. Classism is silence. It decides what will pass as "good taste," equates education with intelligence. While racism invents scientifically unsound "races" and discriminates against people who "belong" to the wrong ones, classism—curiously—discriminates against the "wrong" classes while simultaneously erasing the reality of class. The ideological silence of class—the cherished myth that we all are one big middle class and that anyone can be president—is a sturdy psychological armor in the body politic. Working-class people become simply people who have bad taste or are not intelligent or are not ambitious. This socially imposed self-consciousness makes it hard for working-class people to see their own culture, to hear their own voices. Societal (read middle-class) contempt for "rednecks" and "working stiffs" seeds and nurtures the awful personal silence of shame. All this contributes to the stifling silence of political manipulation. Politicians condescendingly "speak for" and deceive the people who work on the other side of the economic and political tracks. Economic injustice, felt deep inside as resignation, creates a silencing of spirit. Such people know they are being used by others and know, too, there is nothing they can do to stop it. "Nobody said life was fair," my father always said.

Silence is broken by the act of speech. But who shall do this speaking? By definition, professionals voice their own class biases. That is, they are the only ones whose job it is to do the voicing—writing, teaching, researching, publishing, radio, television, journalism, filmmaking—these all are professional jobs and as such require one to be a member of that class. Maybe this is why classism remains the quietest of the "isms," for by definition, there is no representative of this group to do the speaking. When working-class people enter the professional middle class, they pass through psychological portals into a world already wholly defined and created by the middle and upper classes. It is a world and worldview that they have to internalize before they can join it, a culture, really, that is fundamentally different and that replaces the assumptions of their own. Some people stay awake through all this and speak, but the very act of attempting to explicate working-class experience requires using a middle-class style of communication, which recreates middle-class culture more than anything else.

Even all this is not enough to explain the silence. The last knot we will tug at here leads us into the substance within the silence. The kind of communication available to working-class people, the patterns of speech and gestures that are specifically working class, are built on meaningful silences, on shared implicit shades of meaning. No vehicle is provided, or allowed, for universal understanding. It is an intimate language for members only.

Some definitions are in order before I continue. By *working class,* I mean all people who work with things for a living, not just the industrial working class. When I say middle and upper classes, I mean people who hold professional jobs, who work with symbols rather than things. I want to make four points in this essay: that the inner life of the working class is shrouded in silence, as we have seen; that a cultural divide can be drawn between the working class and the poor, on one hand, and the middle and upper classes on the other; that beneath that shroud, working-class culture has a psychology and an integrity of its own. Finally, I will look at how strange and psychologically complicated all this makes the crossing of classes. I will explore the act of communication to illustrate cultural differences, and I will explore cultural differences to illustrate psychology. As a psychologist, I suspect that to understand working-class people, we need to redefine psychology apart from its primary preoccupation with intrapsychic and individual experience. We need not ignore the internal, intrapsychic realm, for it is one place where we find the intricate and dissonant psychological weave that is the essence of working-class psychology. But I believe that to study working-class psychology only in the context of individuals or families, as psychologists usually do, is to miss the point. I think maybe we need to invent a kind of "cultural psychology."

In his 1978 article "A Semiotic Approach to the Suitability of Psychotherapy," James Meltzer recognized that something was amiss when "lower-class people" entered a psychotherapy in which language was the primary tool. In an attempt to help working-class people better fit into what is, arguably, a middle-class experience, he hopped fields to sociology and found Basil Bernstein's work on linguistic codes ("Linguistic Codes," "Social Class") to be helpful. Bernstein set up separate groups of middle and working-class people, matched for IQ, and asked them to discuss their views of capital punishment so he could study the patterns of their speech. Although all the subjects used the same language, the two groups used different linguistic codes; that is, they used the language in fundamentally different ways to achieve different ends. Whereas Meltzer used this information to inform psychotherapists, we can use it to understand better the psychological (and cultural) differences among the classes.

Bernstein described two linguistic codes: the "elaborated code" found in the middle-class group and the "restricted code" found in the working-class group. An elaborated linguistic code has a much larger lexicon (word choices) and an array of structural options (choices of how to put words together) that create speech that is specific. This code commands the speaker to be precise and to differentiate one idea from another. It is a universal language that speaks to a very general audience. Meltzer used as an example the response from people when asked where chewing gum is usually purchased. The middle-class person's reply was, "At a cashier's counter or in a grocery store," whereas the working-class people said, "At the National" or "From Tony" (Strauss and Schatzman as cited in Meltzer). Bernstein noted that to be performed well, an elaborated code generally requires formal education. He specified that the act of speech differentiates the speaker from the listener.

It seems to me that speech is thus both medium and message of a middle- and upper-class culture that encourages people to be individuals. It assigns the greatest value to those who stand out most clearly, to those who are "outstanding," as demonstrated in Bernstein's research. He found that the middle-class group frequently used the phrase "I think" but that the other group rarely did. It is a phrase indicating differentiation, separating the speaker from the listener and inviting an opposing "I think" from the other. I also would contend that it is a signal of a culture that prizes individuality as well as competition among individuals to force the "best and brightest" to rise to the top.

By contrast, the restricted code used by the working-class group is implicit rather than explicit. Lexicon and structure are much more restricted. Body language, vocal tone, pace, and variations in volume are used to communicate more than actual word content. The use of "buzzwords" brought nods of understanding. Whereas the gestures and nuances are understood by people in the same group, someone else would not understand half of the communication. Bernstein noticed that language was actually operating differently in this group, that it was being used to "signal social position," to connect people, rather than to differentiate them from one another. We can see that using a group's own signs and symbols reaffirms both membership in the group and the group itself. The working-class person is not ignorantly assuming that the interviewer knows where "the National" is or who "Tony" is (as some might suppose); rather, their linguistic code is designed for members, not outsiders. Its purpose is to connect people from within and to keep outsiders out. A differentiated kind of speech creates distance between people; it would undermine the intimacy of this group. The demonstration of this in Bernstein's study was the "sympathetic circularity" tags he found only in the working-class group.

People ended sentences with something that would connect them again to the others, that would invite agreement—"wouldn't he?" "you know?" or "isn't it?"—and the others would nod. Again, the communication signals its culture as well, a culture based on the need to belong. Although Bernstein later abandoned specific linguistic indicators of the code, I find his initial indices to be useful, as they reflect a culture based on human connection, community, and cooperation.

Meltzer understood that these codes indicated fundamental differences in communication and could have extrapolated that to culture, as Bernstein later did. What is difficult to understand from a middle- or upper-class perspective, however, is that both of these codes and cultures have "restrictions" and benefits for the people in them. Whereas middle-class culture allows people to "self-actualize" their abilities, to develop intellectually and artistically, to "become" in a very individual sense, working-class culture allows other things. What is viewed from a middle-class point of view as a kind of mindless herd mentality is experienced in a working-class community as intimacy, belonging, and loyalty. From a working-class perspective, we can see the middle class's severely restricted body language. Can you imagine a news anchor who speaks with great feeling and facial expression and uses his hands? Working-class people perceive most middle-class people as talking heads. They don't fully trust people who show no expression or emotion. Why is it that middle-class people don't trust people who do? Whose experience is the more "restricted"? Can we really presume the superiority of a culture based on individuality, when its members flock to therapy and to support groups out of loneliness, its philosophers wear thin the themes of "ultimate aloneness" and "alienation," and its young adults (college students), have one of the highest suicide rates?

Bernstein and Meltzer each initially described the restricted aspects of working-class communication and, by implication, culture, in accomplishing a middle-class task (succeeding in education, discussing intellectual ideas, or talking to a therapist). In a middle-class context, it is easy to see working-class subjects as unfortunate and deprived, and of course, in that setting they are often at a disadvantage. But what is true of this kind of communication, of this culture, when it is in its own element? What is it like to not have to achieve success to become a person of worth? What is it like to be valued primarily for how well you can connect to other people, by how loyal and generous you are? What is it like to feel part of others, to have your idiosyncrasies accepted and regarded fondly but to not be an "individual"? Carol Gilligan talked about why women develop an ethic of responsiveness to the needs of others, as opposed to the ethic of fairness that men develop based on their individuality. American Indian literature portrays a community in which the Western preoccupation with individuality seems odd and unnatural (Momaday, *House* and *Ancient Child*; Turner). I suggest that working-class people, of any gender or ethnicity, experience a tribal kind of connection with others in which caring for people is primary.

But if working-class life can be described as a culture, then it is a colonized culture. The effects of the conquerors are everywhere evident in the working class, and the cognitive dissonance that results from being torn between opposing cultural expectations is profound. Still, as with any culture boxed inside another one, we can see the many noncorresponding faces of working-class life peeking from behind the ill-fitting facade of the dominant culture. If you were raised in it, you can see the whole thing if you try. If you were not, it is almost impossible for an insider to explain it by the act of expository speech alone.

Bernstein said that the purest form of a restricted code is found among tribal people, and I have said that I think working-class culture—and by extension, the psychology of the people in it—is a tribal kind of experience. I would say "community oriented," but that is not enough to describe the way people feel part of one another. They have the kind of loyalty and responsiveness that means people do not stop to think before they share whatever is needed among them. It is not that working-class people cannot distinguish between self and others. Instead, that dichotomy is significant only when the two conflict. Most of the time, "self and other" is a false dichotomy. People live responding to and including one another, cooperating in a way that makes everyone feel accepted and requires no achievement to belong. You belong just by the way you talk and where you live and who your family is—just by the way everyone is woven together. It seems to me that working-class people develop a kind of extraphysical identity. It makes for a more spontaneous kind of living. People may have projects or goals, but the fabric of life and identity is not bound up in achieving these goals to prove or to become themselves. They just are. People come out of their houses and see their neighbors and get to talking. It might go on a very long time, despite whatever initial plan they may have had. Eventually the two neighbors will say what they came outside to do, paint the boat, weed the garden, and then maybe they will do their tasks together. Summer comes and there are no camps or lessons the kids have or get to go to. They just gravitate toward the kids they like and "hang with" them. They wander around the neighborhood, into the swamps and abandoned buildings, sneaking into strange places their parents wouldn't want them to go. They have many adventures. This kind of living in the "here and now" is something middle-class people undergo years of therapy to "achieve." This kind of unselfconscious dance of intimacy is something no number of marathon therapy retreats can create.

It is not surprising that another characteristic of working-class psychology and community is personal authenticity and congruence, to put it in middle-class terms. I would say that it is a genuineness, that people are "real." The MMPI (Minnesota Multiphasic Personality Inventory), a highly reliable and valid personality inventory, shows that working-class people have low "K" scales. The K scale is a validity scale that measures a "sophisticated" ability to "fake good," to make yourself look better than you feel. It goes up as people acquire more education. Psychologists are told not to be alarmed if it is high among "educated" people, but it may be considered a sign of pathology if it is high among working-class people. This is not as classist as it seems. It is true. Working people are not trained to work so hard at looking good. Part of their tribalness is sharing hardship, and there is plenty to be had. It's not so much that people verbalize their difficulties as that they truly share them with one another. People live and work very close together, and they know when a family is fighting or when a kid runs away, when someone is ill or has died. They show up with casseroles ("hot dish" in Minnesota), they mow the lawn, they do your dishes. They say with a look what words cannot say. Not only "I understand" but "we are in this together." Because they are. The recipient accepts without shame, knowing that she or he will offer the same at some other time.

I see this openness and honesty in my working-class students. I teach at a university that has a high percentage of working-class students, and we try to make both process and content meaningful to them. In an effort to reduce the class bias of higher education, I give two assignments for the quarter. One is a traditionally middle-class assignment, a term paper, with references. The other is more amenable to different cultural styles, a journal. I encourage people to use their own language style, and I do not correct spelling or grammar. What I find is fairly consistent: the middle-class students excel at writing papers, and the working-class students excel at writing journals. I ask my students to apply some aspect of their weekly journal to their personal lives. The working-class students are remarkably candid and personal compared with the middle-class students. They are proud of what they have survived. It may be harder for them to understand the theory involved, but their ability to synthesize theoretical material into a personal context is remarkable.

I like the way working-class people think. Like women of any class, they have been taught that thinking is not their domain. Consequently, they have not been rigidly trained in how to do it ("objective," critical, "rigorous" thinking); they have not been trained to create distance between themselves and their ideas. When they do explore ideas, they are passionate about what they think, and their thinking is often fresh, vital, and informed by personal experience. Working-class culture also has these properties, I believe, beneath layers of shame and silence. I like the way working-class students learn. They take in pieces of information and see how it matches what is inside them, using personal experience as method and measure. Rarely lost in arid intellectualism, they learn without losing touch with their bodies, without losing their "common sense." This may be less true when colleges labor to take all this away from them.

Music education is a good example of both the costs and the benefits of being from working-class culture. I grew up musically inclined, and I begged for a piano and lessons we could not afford. Although in school I tested very high for musical ability, I never received any formal music training (unless you count the uncannily irritating plastic flutophones we all received in the fourth grade). My big brother taught himself how to play the guitar, and we sang at family reunions. Later, with help from others, I taught myself how to play the guitar. It was a revelation to me when I finally took piano lessons as an adult and learned more about formal music. But what separates me now from my fellow musicians is the amount of feeling, fun, and improvisation I am capable of. I still wish the intellectual aspects of music came more easily to me, as they probably would have if I had been taught them earlier in life. But I would never trade the vitality and feeling I got from learning by ear, from people who just hang out and play music for fun, disconnected from any achievement except the task at hand, comparing myself with no one, performing only if I felt like it for people who saw me, and my music, as their own. The people I sang for were more likely to join in singing than to evaluate my performance. The "restriction" of intuitive musical vocabulary imposed on my middle-class counterparts by learning through rote and recital is clear. I learned to play music, not recite it.

Play is one of the benefits of living in a working-class culture. It is ironic because of the backbreaking (literally), mind-numbing work that people have to do. Nonetheless, play is really play. When working-class guys go fishing, they loll around the lake, they hang out, they talk, they wait for "the big one." When middle-class guys play golf, they do some of the same, but they also try very hard to achieve a better game, to improve their skill. When working-class people go bowling, they try to improve their game, but they bowl in leagues (always a group thing), and an eternity goes by before their turn comes up again. Again, they spend most of their time hanging out and visiting, and when they score, they score for the team. When middle-class people play racquetball, it is nonstop competition and concentration on the game. Middle-class people tend to play very hard because they have to keep competing and achieving. I don't think this seems much like leisure to working-class people. It is not hard to extrapolate what this says about the psychology of the people involved. Working-class people just live and accept what life brings their way. Sometimes this is the powerlessness of resignation, but at other times, it is a graceful acceptance of the worst and that we can't control it all. Again, middle-class people purchase psychotherapy and flock to twelve-step groups to try to understand this, to be able to "achieve" this kind of ability to accept life's difficulties and move on.

But I do not want to deny the psychological pain, which is so plentiful for people in the working class. That, too, is too close to the way we are supposed to swallow our oppression and the presumption that we really do not exist. I have tried, because it is so rarely done, to illuminate the positive differences in working-class culture and psychology. Still, there is no denying the demoralizing effects of all the silences I discussed earlier. There is no denying the devastating effect that the world of work has on working-class people and their inner lives. Year after year of dangerous, repetitive, and exhausting work wears out the soul as well as the body. Just as stimulating work that engages one's intelligence and creativity has an uplifting, "self-actualizing" effect on people, so work that consistently denies these qualities has a deadening or self-destructive effect. This encroaching psychological weight is experienced as a numbing, a depth of exhaustion, an increasing passivity of the spirit. Perhaps this is why working-class culture is at its most vital among teenagers.

Lillian Rubin, in *Worlds of Pain,* and Richard Sennett and Jonathan Cobb have spoken eloquently on the injuries of the working class. I turn now to my fourth point, one piece of that "world of pain" that Rubin did not cover, the crossing of classes. As a graduate student writing a thesis on social class and psychology, I plowed through small mountains of obtusely written and myopic journal articles until I found a gem by Geraldine K. Piorkowski. Her dry little article, "Survivor Guilt in a University Setting," left me in tears. At last, someone explained what was happening to me. At last, I found a writer who did not denigrate her working-class subjects or erase their life experiences.

Although Piorkowski did not describe the kind of cultural and psychological strain that I have described here, nor did she comment on the contrasting psychological particulars of the different classes, she saw clearly that her "lower-class" counseling students were going through a profoundly different college experience than were their middle-class counterparts. She found common complaints of depression, difficulty concentrating, preoccupation with family and friends "back home," and sudden dives in academic performance. They just stopped being able to race up the class ladder as they had before. I can't help thinking it was as if these students had suddenly realized that the dive they were making into the murky waters of higher education would forever obscure the shore they had left. It was as if the psychic cord between them and their people had stretched as far as it could and they just snapped back to someplace where they could still see that shore.

Piorkowski saw similarities between these working-class college students and Robert Lifton's description of the survivors of the Hiroshima tragedy. Working-class students seemed to have replaced the query "Why did I live when they died?" of Lifton's survivors with "Why should I succeed when they failed?" The promise of a work life offering greater control, creativity, intelligence, income, and status makes the injuries and indignities of the working class stand out even more boldly. I have indicated that as the years of hard labor and uncertainty wear on in a working-class life, there is a gradual silencing of dreams and the will to dream them, and I suggest that this is the same fear of spiritual or psychic death that Piorkowski sensed in the families and friends of her troubled students. As Sennett and Cobb stated, it is when someone "makes it" in the middle-class sense that their people are suddenly held against that standard and found lacking. Superiority and shame then replace solidarity.

Piorkowski found Lifton's "survivor guilt" to be at root of these students' academic derailments and also of the "psychic numbing" shared by Lifton's survivors. Lifton also found a common "distrust of nurturance" and "struggles to formulate meaning" in what had suddenly become a meaningless world. I have found all these things in "upwardly" mobile people in my teaching and clinical work. I have found them in myself. I have suggested some of the psychological qualities in working-class life that are not replaced in middle-class communities. It is difficult for anyone to move from one group identification to another. How much more difficult will it be when belonging is so closely intertwined with identity? What is it like to know the new group will never accept you in the way you were once accepted, because it is not in its nature to do so? We must add to this confusion the fact that the "upwardly mobile" person's new identification, the professional middle class, has an implicit contempt for what little it knows about where that person came from. In a classist society, eager-to-be-accepted, budding professionals gladly internalize it all: heck, no, I'm not one of "them," entangling themselves again in knots and silences. No mere trip away from home is this journey. Crossing classes means redrawing one's internal map so dramatically that the outer and inner landmarks will never again match up in a way that could lead one home for a visit.

Being cut off from one's history means that one is cut off from oneself as well as from one's people. Object relations theory has shown that the foundations of the psyche, the basement of the house of personality, if you will, is built with images internalized from early childhood. These early identifications are experienced as basic, as identity, as "the real me." This is one of the reasons that people who have been treated badly as children have so many problem feelings and behaviors as adults. An internalized negative sense of self can result in dissociation: the cutting off of internal connection with the parts inside that hurt or feel unacceptable. Clinical psychologists are familiar with the effects of serious dissociation: the memory losses, the placelessness, the frantic search for a sense of identity, the distrust of nurturance. What are the psychological costs of cultural dissociation? African Americans have spoken about this regarding ethnicity; women have spoken about it regarding gender. We can only guess what it means to cross classes, what kind of loneliness is involved in a transition in which there is no one to even hint that something is lost, something is wrong. Nothing quite fits, and nobody in the new place can explain what has happened to you.

So the challenge stands before those of us who have crossed classes to remember everything we are supposed to forget. We propose to study with words what is known through glance and gesture. We have glimpsed at the strata of silences. We have seen differences in worldview fundamental enough to constitute a cultural divide between the classes. We have mined a bit of the buried treasure of working-class sensibility, and we have imagined the psychological violence involved in ravaging that culture within ourselves to assume a middle-class lifestyle. In psychology, we favor the notions of insight and integration. So now we gather up all the scraps of memory and insight that we can find and weave them together into a bridge—I imagine one of those high, swinging kind through mountains—over the cultural chasm of class. Writing this essay has been part of that integration for me. Carl Jung described a client's recurring dream in which he fell off a mountain. The man was a highly successful businessman from humble origins. Jung told him he needed to slow his headlong rush into the upper middle class, to try to integrate rather than dissociate his history. The man did not and actually died within a year or so by falling off a mountain during a skiing trip. When I was finishing graduate school, I dreamed that I was walking on the high ledge of a skyscraper. I dreamed over and over that I was looking for a new pair of shoes; often I was hoping for a red pair of shoes. Perhaps I wanted to keep the vitality and passion of the class I come from as I walked into a new life. Perhaps, like Dorothy in Oz, I wanted to know I would have a way back home. I wrote my thesis on class and psychology, hoping to bridge, hoping for shoes that could walk into both my new and my old life.

As I prepared this essay for the working-class studies conference where I originally presented it, I sacrificed badly needed writing time to drive across Minnesota to an important family reunion. I knew no one would ever understand my needing to work on an essay like this. As it was, I had to talk my Aunt Lu into changing the reunion from the weekend of the conference. "Well, you can't make people come," she said, irritated. "Brent ain't coming neither. He's got a fishing trip." I tried to explain it just wasn't the same as a fishing trip, wondering if that was really true. What finally convinced her to change the date was the fact that I had already paid for my plane ticket. I keep traipsing back and forth, trying to balance on that improbable swinging bridge that connects my worlds. I present this essay here in hopes that there might be some neighbors hanging around out there to help me work on it.

Works Cited

Bernstein, Basil A. "Linguistic Codes, Hesitation Phenomena, and Intelligence." *Language and Speech* 5 (1962): 31–46.

———. *Class, Codes, and Control.* Vol. 1. London: Routledge, 1971.

———. "Social Class and Psychotherapy." *British Journal of Sociology* 15 (1964): 54–64.

———. *The Structuring of Pedagogic Discourse—Class, Codes, and Control.* Vol. 4. London: Routledge, 1990.

Gilligan, Carol. *In a Different Voice.* Cambridge, MA: Harvard University Press, 1982.

Lifton, Robert J. *Death in Life.* New York: Random House, 1967.

Meltzer, James D. "A Semiotic Approach to Suitability for Psychotherapy." *Psychiatry* 41 (1978): 360–75.

Momaday, N. Scott. *House Made of Dawn.* New York: Harper & Row, 1968.

———. *The Ancient Child.* New York: Harper & Row, 1990.

Piorkowski, Geraldine K. "Survivor Guilt in the University Setting." *Personnel and Guidance Journal* 61 (1983): 620–22.

Rubin, Lillian B. *Worlds of Pain: Life in the Working Class Family.* New York: Basic Books, 1976.

Sennett, Richard, and Jonathan Cobb. *The Hidden Injuries of Class.* New York: Vintage Books, 1973.

Strauss, Leonard, and Anselm Schatzman. "Social Class and Modes of Communication." American Journal of Sociology 60 (1954): 329–38.

Turner, Fredrick W. *The Portable North American Indian Reader.* New York: Penguin Books, 1980.

Barbara Jensen *is a psychologist in private practice in Minneapolis and teaches community psychology and the psychology of women at Metropolitan State University. She also does counseling, consulting, and training in primary and secondary school settings, and she frequently goes to family reunions.*

Writing with and Against the Master's Language: Lessons in Critical Literacy from Working-Class Women

Jane Greer

The study of working-class issues has recently boomed, with most scholarship on working-class writing focusing on those worker-writers who have sought to make their voices heard in literary or academic circles. Texts such as Tillie Olsen's *Yonnondio*, Rebecca Harding Davis's *Life in the Iron Mills*, Sandra Cisneros's *The House on Mango Street*, and Dorothy Allison's *Bastard out of Carolina* are becoming part of an emerging canon of working-class literature.[1] There also are exciting anthologies such as Janet Zandy's *Calling Home* and *Liberating Memory*, in which members of the working class express their experiences in poems, essays, and photographs. Equally provocative is the scholarship on working-class students in the classroom. Karyn Hollis researched the Bryn Mawr Summer School for Women Workers; Julia M. Allen explored the People's College of Fort Scott, Kansas; bell hooks theorized about the role of class in the classroom; and James Thomas Zebroski wrote about his own experiences "passing" as an academic and the strategies he uses as a university professor to reach working-class students who may be experiencing the same dislocations he experienced.

These all are important contributions to the emerging field of working-class studies, but little research has been done on the writing working-class women actually do on the job, as secretaries who schedule appointments and take phone messages, as custodial workers who empty trash cans and mop floors, as assembly-line workers who help produce everything from computer-processing chips to the food on grocery store shelves.[2] How do working-class women, who often work in unsafe, unreliable, oppressive, and exhausting jobs, negotiate the linguistic border between the written languages they are comfortable with outside the workplace and the written languages of those in power in the workplace? How can we understand and perhaps even validate the workplace silences of women at the bottom of the corporate caste system? Under what conditions can working-class women learn not merely to reproduce the potentially repressive language of their workplace masters but also to reconstitute and reclaim that language so that it no longer marginalizes them?

This essay will try to answer these questions and extend our knowledge about working-class women's writing in the workplace. I present two contrasting scenes of workplace writing: the factory floor of a subsidiary of a major U.S. automotive manufacturer and a midwestern regional marketing office for the employee benefits division of an insurance and financial services corporation. Although I took these two scenes of writing from particular and local workplace contexts and my reconstructions of them are, no doubt, idiosyncratic and partial, I believe that these scenes also reflect experiences that others may share. As Jacqueline Jones Royster noted, "individual stories placed one against another against another build credibility and offer . . . a litany of evidence from which a call for transformation in theory and practice may rightfully begin" (30). My hope is that my stories can serve as the opening call in such a litany of evidence.

Writing from the Factory Floor: Communal Ties and the Creation of Internally Persuasive Discourse

Scene 1 unfolds on the factory floor of a subsidiary of a major U.S. automotive manufacturer. I gained access to the manufacturing plant through a research partnership undertaken by Ohio State University (OSU), the automotive manufacturer, and the United Auto Workers (UAW). Because they faced an uncertain future owing to increased competition from foreign automakers and a generally sluggish domestic economy in the late 1980s and early 1990s, the managers and union representatives at the subsidiary's plant wanted to move away from the antagonism that typically characterized their interactions. Instead, they wanted to move toward a more cooperative, egalitarian working relationship in the hope that by working together they could save the plant and their jobs. A number of research projects intended to smooth this change in corporate culture received funding from OSU, the UAW, and the automobile manufacturer, including Professor Kitty Locker's proposal for a yearlong study of how the written documents at the plant might facilitate (or undermine) changes in the plant's corporate culture. I was fortunate to join Professor Locker's project as her graduate research assistant and to create my own, smaller, research project on the writing of the factory women.

Making up roughly 20 percent of the fifteen-hundred-member union workforce, the women were vital to the plant and led lives as complex as the door locks they helped assemble. In reading more than

650 plant documents, including both management and union newsletters; employee complaint and suggestion forms; training manuals; and anonymous, underground "hate" mail directed at management, I learned about Annette Scott, who was selected to attend a twelve-hour training workshop at the UAW's educational center so that she could better handle public relations for the union; Evelyn Watring, Clare Zari, and Opal Grater, who served as officers in the union's retiree organization; Rose Ackley, who used the plant's Transition Center resources to enroll in a program to become a paralegal; and Mabel Hawkins, who competed in the plant's annual golf outing.[3] Just as historians of America's working women like Rosalyn Baxandall and Linda Gordon recognized that women's labor does not easily fit into traditional categories of "work" that reflect a patriarchal bias, I saw that the women working in this factory were continuously moving among various subject positions. They existed at the bottom of the plant hierarchy during their shifts, but they occupied leadership positions in the union (though typically in "feminine" areas like public relations or the women's committee); they worked eight hours at physically exhausting jobs and then attended college classes at night and on weekends; they held working-class jobs but participated in country club sports like golf. Because of the apparent complexity and richness of the working lives of these factory workers, I wanted to study not just what was written about these women in plant documents but also how they chose to write themselves into the factory's discourses.

Although the women working on the factory floor at this plant were actually required to do very little writing on the job, they often voluntarily contributed articles to various departmental and company newsletters and the union newsletter. These articles ranged from human interest stories about the accomplishments of coworkers to occasional UAW committee reports. I now will discuss some of the personal profiles they published in company newsletters. Although such "feature" or human interest stories appeared in the weekly company-wide newsletter and in the monthly union publication, *News and Views,* I will focus on the personal information stories appearing in the *Door Lock Newsline,* a newsletter initiated by Jim Kreider, superintendent of business unit 3 and distributed to the several hundred employees making door locks. In explaining his motives for starting the *Door Lock Newsline,* Kreider explained that he wanted to give his employees the "facts" about the business unit's performance and its future: "I wanted to communicate information. If anything, these people out there [on the factory floor] needed information. Heck, I knew they needed information." Kreider's article in the first issue of the *Door Lock Newsline* is typical of his contributions. In this article, Kreider promises that the *Newsline*

> will tell you what is going on in our business. If the news is good, we will tell you about it here. If the news is not so good, we will still let you know in black and white. . . . The only way to know what each of us has to do to assure our future, is to have the facts and the facts are what you're going to get here.

Kreider's priorities were facts and crucial information. But in the thirty-one issues of the *Door Lock Newsline* published during a three-year period, eleven articles appeared offering personal information about the lives of the factory workers.[4] Written by women working on the factory floor, these articles were diverse in subject matter, describing the singing talents of a particular worker on a palletron line, the involvement of a millwright with the American Legion, or the sewing abilities of a coworker.

An article about the singing talents of an employee on a palletron line is representative:

Make a Joyful Noise
by Carla Anderson

> For all new employees from other plants, who haven't yet met the acquaintance of Paula Thomas, you're missing someone special! Everyone else that has worked in the Palletron area on 2nd shift, has at one time or another, met and talked with Paula. Once you met her you won't forget her. It is such a joy to talk with one of the nicest ladies in this plant and Paula has been working here for over 24 years. She presently works on the A-line (Palletrons 5 and 6) and her supervisor is Kathy Schmidt.
>
> Paula's proudest activity in her private life is her work with her church. She has attended St. John Baptist Church at 1145 St. Clair Avenue for the past twenty five years. Not only has she sang with the St. John Gospel choir for twenty two years she is the President and lead vocalist! You can hear Paula sing every Sunday, except the 3rd Sunday, which is reserved for the men's choir and little children's choir.
>
> Another activity very close to her heart is her Sunday School Intermediate class, which she has taught for many years. In fact, Paula started teaching Sunday School at the tender age of 16 while growing up in Alabama. But wait, brothers and sisters, that's not all! She is also treasurer of the church Building Fund for the last ten years and has been the church Announcer for the past twenty years.

> I know that Pastor William Snow must feel really proud to have Paula
> as a church member.
>   Paula always has a kind word for her co-workers here, and believe
> me, we need someone to help lift our spirits! Isn't it nice to know that
> we here at [this plant] have in our midst a co-worker, who does
> indeed, "make a joyful noise!" God bless you, Paula.
>   Say amen, somebody!!

The author of this article first tells us that Paula Thomas works in "the
Palletron area on 2nd shift" and that her supervisor is Kathy Schmidt,
thereby positioning Thomas in the factory's hierarchy. The rest of the
article focuses on what is explicitly designated as Thomas's "private
life," her involvement with her church. Although such information has
little to do with the making of door locks and seems far removed from
Kreider's goal of providing "facts" about the business unit's economic
performance, this information can be read as a complex and provocative fusion of the values necessary for the plant to meet its production
and financial goals (values that the plant's managerial staff felt were
lacking in union members) and the personal commitments of the
female worker. Anderson praises Thomas for her long-standing loyalty
to her church and her willingness to take on added responsibility as a
treasurer of the church building fund. Similarly, in an article about a
millwright's involvement in the American Legion, the writer expresses
her admiration for the millwright's dedication, and in an article about
a woman who paints and stencils on sweatshirts, the writer applauds
the craftsmanship of her coworker.

Writing simultaneously with and against the "master's" language,
these articles seem to function as what Mikhail Bakhtin calls "internally persuasive discourse." In his glossary of Bakhtin's technical
terms, Michael Holquist defines "internally persuasive discourse" as
that which is "akin to retelling a text in one's own words, with one's
own accents, gestures, modifications" (Bakhtin 424). Such internally
persuasive discourse stands in opposition to Bakhtin's notion of
"authoritative discourse," which "is fused with political power—an
institution, a person" (343) and which "binds us, quite independent
of any power it might have to persuade us internally" (342). In these
stories, the women working in the factory challenge the authoritative
discourse of the managers like Kreider who privilege only the "facts"
necessary for the smooth running of the plant. The decision of the
women factory workers to use their personal lives and the lives of their
coworkers as vehicles for asserting their commitment to values (loyalty, teamwork, dedication, craftsmanship) that would help ensure

the plant's survival could easily be read by management as a waste of time, paper, and linguistic resources. Instead, I would suggest that these women workers' "retellings" of such values "in their own accents and with their own gestures" reflect their commitment to the plant and their jobs. Furthermore, I believe that such texts fulfill an important function in cementing the workers' communal bonds and increasing their solidarity. In the final lines of her article, Carla Anderson addresses and affirms the subject of this public document ("God bless you, Paula") and calls for her coworkers to join in the praise ("Say amen, somebody!!"). This final call allows Anderson to reinforce the communal bonds that connect those sharing in the work of the factory.

The noted labor activist and feminist Meridel Le Sueur argues that working-class writers

> need a dynamic and dialectic structure. We not only want to describe the world, we want to change it. Instead of description, narration, removal and objectivity, alienation, we need a structure that includes the thesis, the antithesis, and the synthesis. . . . This structure will help [working-class writers] see life itself dynamically, alive in conflict, changing with inevitable and endless possibilities. (no page number)

These women working on the factory floor have clearly taken Le Sueur's urgings to heart. As complex interweavings of corporate and personal values, newsletter articles like the one by Carla Anderson function as moments in which the women demonstrate a critical literacy and claim for themselves empowered subject positions. As "dynamic and dialectic structures," texts like these personal interest stories allow for multiple solidarities and create new vocabularies that do not reduce issues of power and inequality in the workplace to a single script. Through these texts, the female factory workers seem to have synthesized their own subjectivities with the material conditions of their jobs in ways that point toward "inevitable and endless possibilities" for workplace relations between union and management. These factory women have found ways to write both with and against the "master's" language.

The Silence of an Administrative Assistant

Scene 2 unfolds in the midwestern regional marketing office of the employee benefits division of a major insurance and financial services corporation. The texts produced by Jackie, a female service representative working in this office, sharply contrast with the texts of the women factory workers. Having worked myself as a benefits manager for two years in the same office with Jackie, I was quite familiar with her work. As a "pink-collar" worker with no formal education beyond high school, Jackie often drafted routine letters to clients and communicated with the company's home office through memos. A year after I left the office to return to graduate school, Jackie and her boss, Dave, graciously agreed to take part in a research project I was conducting on "real world" discourse communities. For my research, I analyzed a sample of twenty different documents, ten selected by Jackie as representative of her "best" written work and ten selected by Dave as representative of his "best" written work. I then completed discourse-based interviews with Jackie and Dave based on the methodologies outlined by Odell, Goswami, and Herrington.

Jackie's texts indicate that she is not in a position to create the sort of politically powerful, multivocal, and internally persuasive texts that the factory workers use to redefine workplace relationships and claim greater authority for themselves. Instead, the letters and memos she drafted indicate that she had internalized her boss's directives concerning "good" writing and, along with them, had internalized her own subservient status.

First, a bit of background about Jackie's boss, Dave. At the time of my research, Dave had been with the insurance company for twelve years, and at the age of thirty-one, he was one of the company's youngest regional marketing managers. He took great pride in his accomplishments. In describing his writing, Dave lavishly praised the rigorousness of his undergraduate English classes at a prestigious midwestern liberal arts college. He also cited the *Wall Street Journal* and *Fortune* as texts that he read regularly and that influenced his writing style. Throughout my interview with Dave, he often reduced his thoughts on writing to a number of rules or maxims, and he made it clear that he always tried to follow them. Dave was firmly committed to principles of effective writing such as "Letters should never be longer than one page, and paragraphs should be short and to the point"; "Always put the main point in your first paragraph"; and "Extra words just 'thought fatigue' your readers." These sorts of rules are common in most business writing textbooks, and most corporate communicators would agree with them as general guidelines for effective writing. But when we turn to Jackie and the texts she produced, we can begin to see the ways in which such rules, especially when espoused by a powerful manager, can be disabling for subordinate women in the workplace.

At the beginning of my interview with Jackie about her writing, she expressed great anxiety about her texts. She frequently asked me if I thought she sounded "professional." As we discussed a letter she had written to a client explaining a billing error, she noted: "I sound terrible—like such a wimp. I'm entirely too apologetic. These people probably think they can walk all over me" (see figure 1). As I examined this letter, I was mystified by her perception that it was overly apologetic. When I pressed Jackie to be more specific about which sentences were "wimpy," she evaded the question, merely reiterating her concern about how others perceived her.

Like the letter reproduced in figure 1, all the samples of Jackie's writing that I reviewed were models of competence and clarity. They were complete, well organized and easy to understand, and projected a positive image. But Jackie's anxiety about her writing is perhaps easier to understand when we consider how she learned to fulfill her job duties, including handling correspondence. Jackie told me that she learned everything "on the job" and from Dave; she said, "I picked up everything as I went along." Many of the things Jackie picked up were "rules" similar to the kinds of maxims that Dave espoused. She told me, "Dave has taught me never to say 'I'm sorry' in writing." Later in the interview, Jackie added that it was from Dave that she learned the importance of never writing a letter in anger. She also repeated Dave's warning—a warning frequently heard around the office—about "covering your ass" in letters and memos. For Jackie, Dave's "rules" of writing functioned like Bakhtin's "authoritative discourse." They derived their power solely through their association with Dave, and Jackie seemed unaware that such rules might actually come from principles of audience analysis or reflect a commitment to being reader friendly.

Even though the women writing from the factory floor have found ways to write against the conventional discourses that would make them passive participants in industrial production, Jackie seems unable to locate herself outside a disabling belief system in which knowledge, authority, and power are accessible only by writing in the language of her organizational superiors. And the thought of failing to comply with or fulfill her supervisor's criteria for effective written texts leaves Jackie feeling vulnerable. With such anxiety about her writing, Jackie is content to serve as Dave's mouthpiece, never claiming for herself the right to speak in a language she finds internally persuasive, even when she is writing to her workplace peers, that is, service representatives and administrative assistants working in other offices. Because of the anxiety Jackie feels about her writing, it is hard to imagine that she would

Figure 1

Rob Ranier
O'Grady Hastings/Mitchell Financial Services
National Bank Building, Suite 343
Manhattan, KS 66623

RE: Jackson Corporation
G-32,345/98,762

Dear Rob:

I just received word from the home office that Jackson Corporation are paying the wrong rate for the family class. Currently they are paying just the dependent cost ($27.79). This does not include the single coverage or the Life and AD & D charges. The class cost is $43.79. I have attached a copy of the rate card. To get this class cost you would add the employee and dependent cost together (example: $16.00 + $27.79 = $43.79).

A charge due has been generated because of this error, in the amount of $3,767.93. The breakdown of these charges follow:

10–85	$690.38	2–86	$469.20
11–85	579.60	3–86	469.20
12–85	565.80	4–86	483.00
01–86	510.75		

Please notify the contract holder of this billing error and have the back charge submitted as soon as possible. The billing department has given the group a 6-1-86 due date. If the back charges are not paid by that date, a lapse letter will be sent.

If you should have any questions or need additional information please let me know. Thank you in advance for your prompt attention.

Sincerely,

Jackie M. Harris
Service Administrator

cc: Sue Connors - Billing

ever contribute to a company newsletter. As long as Jackie feels dominated by Dave's rules for writing, it is unlikely that she will develop a critical literacy that would allow her to create dynamic and dialectic texts that would do more than merely reproduce the existing power structures that have already left her feeling pained and vulnerable about her communicative abilities.

Of course, many factors are responsible for Jackie's attitude toward her writing that may not have been visible to me, and so I will not generalize on the basis of the limited research I have presented here. I do hope, though, that my work underscores the richness of working-class women's workplace writing. As Janet Zandy remarks in her introduction to *Liberating Memory,* if the emerging field of working-class studies concerns replacing private silences with public sounds, we need to fill the silence that has surrounded the on-the-job writing of working-class women. We need to begin looking beyond the working-class women who have expressed themselves through poetry, essays, novels, and other forms of public discourse that are not aimed at coworkers and bosses. We need to find ways to encourage women like the factory workers I have described in their attempts to reconfigure workplace languages, and we need to listen to the silences of women like Jackie whose voices have been overwritten by the authoritative discourse of those higher up in the corporate caste system. To transform the personal and professional lives of all women, we need to understand the ways in which they can build workplace communities that challenge the hierarchical structures and language practices that can marginalize and isolate working women.

I would like to close with a quotation from Meridel Le Sueur, which I think speaks powerfully about the position of working-class women writing on the job:

> The word, like the plow, the chisel, the needle, the spindle, is a tool. Of all the materials man works with the tool word is perhaps the most social. It is through the word that you speak to others, influence others, tell others what has happened to you.
>
> Everyone must make this tool his or her own. You must not be afraid of this tool simply because you have not had formal training in its use. With practice, like any other tool, it will turn to your hand. (unnumbered page)

NOTES

1. The bibliography in Paul Lauter's "Working-Class Women's Literature: An Introduction to Study," Cheryl Cline's annotated bibliography of autobiographies by American working-class women, and Constance Coiner's brief bibliography at the conclusion of "U.S. Working-Class Women's Fiction: Notes Toward an Overview" are invaluable for this growing canon. For a discussion of teaching the literature of the working class, see Linda Strom's "Reclaiming Our Working-Class Identities: Teaching Working-Class Studies in a Blue-Collar Community."

2. Even in business and professional communication, a field ostensibly concerned with on-the-job writing, there is little about working-class women. The fall 1991 issue of the *Journal of Business and Technical Communication* was a special issue, "Gender and Professional Communication." But the study subjects of the contributors, like Elizabeth Flynn, Mary M. Lay, Diane D. Brunner, and Jo Allen, were female faculty members in midwestern universities, students enrolled in a chemical engineering design course, and professional women working as technical writers. By focusing on women who have earned or aspire to professional and managerial positions, articles such as those in *JBTC*'s special issue present a somewhat distorted vision of gender in the workplace, since women typically constitute less than 5 percent of senior management in the nation's industries, and 62 percent of the individuals earning the minimum wage are women, according to statistics released by the U.S. Labor Department in the spring of 1995.

3. To comply with the confidentiality clause in the original research partnership agreement between the plant, the UAW, and OSU, I am using pseudonyms for both the union members and the managers at the plant.

4. Interestingly, no articles offering personal information about any of the managers appeared in any issues of *Door Lock Newsline*. In interviews, Kreider and the managerial staff of his business unit continually emphasized their desire to minimize the messages they received and to use written communication for only the most essential facts. As I shall explain, the union members, and the women union members in particular, seemed to see written texts as playing a significant role in establishing connections and creating a dialogue in their work community.

Bibliography

Allen, Julia M. "'Dear Comrade': Marian Wharton of the People's College, Fort Scott, Kansas, 1914–1917." *Women's Studies Quarterly* 22, nos. 1 & 2 (spring/summer 1994): 119–33.

Bakhtin, M. M. *The Dialogic Imagination*, edited by Michael Holquist and translated by Caryl Emerson and Michael Holquist. Austin: University of Texas Press, 1981.

Baxandall, Rosalyn, and Linda Gordon, eds. *America's Working Women: A Documentary History, 1600 to the Present*. 2d ed. New York: Norton, 1995.

Cline, Cheryl. "Autobiographies by American Working-Class Women: An

Annotated Bibliography." *Women's Studies Quarterly* 23, nos. 1 & 2 (spring/summer 1995): 121–30.

Coiner, Constance. "U.S. Working-Class Women's Fiction: Notes Toward an Overview." *Women's Studies Quarterly* 23, nos. 1 & 2 (spring/summer 1995): 248–67.

Hollis, Karyn. "Liberating Voices: Autobiographical Writing at the Bryn Mawr Summer School for Women Workers, 1921–1938." *College Composition and Communication* 45 (1994): 31–60.

hooks, bell. *Teaching to Transgress: Education as the Practice of Freedom.* New York: Routledge, 1994.

Lauter, Paul. "Working-Class Women's Literature: An Introduction to Study." *Radical Teacher,* December 1979, 16–26.

Le Sueur, Meridel. *Worker Writers.* Worker Writer Series No. 4. Reprint, Minneapolis: West End Press, 1982.

Odell, Lee, Dixie Goswami, and Anne Herrington. "The Discourse-Based Interview: A Procedure for Exploring the Tacit Knowledge of Writers in Nonacademic Settings." In *Research on Writing,* edited by Peter Mosenthal, Lynne Tamor, and Sean A. Walmsley. New York: Longmans, 1983.

Royster, Jacqueline Jones. "When the First Voice You Hear Is Not Your Own." *College Composition and Communication* 47 (1996): 29–40.

Strom, Linda. "Reclaiming Our Working-Class Identities: Teaching Working-Class Studies in a Blue-Collar Community." *Women's Studies Quarterly* 23, nos. 1 & 2 (spring/summer 1995): 131–41.

Zandy, Janet, ed. *Calling Home: Working-Class Women's Writings.* New Brunswick, NJ: Rutgers University Press, 1990.

———, ed. *Liberating Memory: Our Work and Our Working-Class Consciousness.* New Brunswick, NJ: Rutgers University Press, 1995.

Zebroski, James Thomas. "The English Department and Social Class: Resisting Writing." In *The Right to Literacy,* edited by Andrea A. Lunsford, Helene Moglen, and James Slevin. New York: Modern Language Association, 1990, 81–87.

Jane Greer is an assistant professor in the English department at the University of Missouri at Kansas City and the director of the Greater Kansas City Writing Project. She teaches composition courses and courses on women and literature. Her current research project is a recovery and exploration of the reading practices of working-class women in the 1930s.

Traveling Working Class

Janet Zandy

*"These mills they built the tanks and bombs/That won this country's wars . . .
Here in Youngstown/Here in Youngstown"*
—Bruce Springsteen

Introduction

Wilma Elizabeth McDaniel, a prolific but not widely known working-class poet, was born in 1918, the fourth of eight children of Oklahoma sharecroppers. She and her family left the 100-degree heat and dust bowl barrenness of Oklahoma in the 1930s and migrated with thousands of others to the promised green of California. Ms. McDaniel, who now lives in Tulare, California, does not like to talk about the details of her life, the unremitting poverty and low-wage labor. Instead, she wants her poetry to tell that story. McDaniel and other working-class writers demonstrate how one single life story is inseparable from those of one's neighbors, one's region, and whole communities of working people. This story-poem about Orville Kincaid should be familiar to those who have crossed certain borders and feel ambiguous about leaving other worlds behind:

The Academic Career of Orville Kincaid

*Back in the old neighborhood
some will remember him if
you prod them. The boy who didn't
wear socks until he was past thirteen.
All will remember his love of books,
reading while he stood in line for his
family's welfare butter and flour.*

*But they lose him for his scholarship
years at Oxford University, trying to
erase who he was. Eating watercress
sandwiches
when he really wanted grits and gravy.*

And none of them had read of a man
who walked out of a ten-story window
wearing a velvet robe
with a copy of Yeats in the pocket.

I begin with Orville Kincaid's "academic career" because in its clear
and direct working-class idiom the poem points to two important
themes inherent to working-class studies: (1) the movement of some
working-class people out of familiar places, out of communities, and
into academic enclosures of great promise and great peril and (2)
alternatives to suicide. I speak not just about the tragic suicide of individuals, but of a loss and killing of collective memory and experience.

In "Traveling Working Class" I ask you to imagine a journey that is
both real and metaphoric. We are the descendants of many travelers—
those who gambled on new opportunities, those who were violently
torn from their homes, and those who were displaced by economic
change. The literature and culture we call contemporary and
American brims with tropes of migrations, border crossings, movements, disruptions, dislocations, and unsettled settlings. I use the word
travel to acknowledge a degree of choice that earlier generations may
not have had. But it is hardly a vacation, and it is not an easy journey.
We need space to tag the necessary baggage, to draw a map of the territory, and to imagine alternative places.

Locations and Beginnings I

I'll begin with my present location. For the last twenty-five years I have
lived in Rochester, New York. I didn't plan to live there—planning a
future was not part of my working-class experience; rather, getting by,
working toward a better circumstance, was. How I got there seems less
important to tell than what Rochester represents in terms of our larger
concerns about working-class culture. Like many other medium-size
U.S. cities, Rochester is a double city. It has an inner city, an outer city,
and a ring of suburbs of substantial wealth. It is the corporate headquarters for Kodak and Bausch and Lomb, and it is also a place where
one-third of all city children live in poverty. Class differences are sharp
in Rochester but rarely acknowledged. Rather, the media present the
perspective and well-being of the business class as normative; that is,
what is good for the corporation is good for the average citizen. Last
year (1994), the CEO of Eastman Kodak Company was awarded a
yearly salary of $6 million. I say *awarded* because I cannot imagine work
that would earn that amount of money. The salary and bonuses he

received were an acknowledgment from stockholders and Wall Street that he did a good job of restructuring, reengineering, and refitting the Kodak workforce. In other words, he laid off a lot of workers—seven hundred in the immediate Rochester area and ten thousand worldwide over a span of some years.

I want to pause by describing how Kodak—which has a history of paternalism and is generally less ruthless than many other corporations—went about "pink slipping" or notifying workers of their job status. Workers—in this case, mostly white-collared and college-educated "employees," because the production workers had already been hit by the first wave of cuts—were called into their supervisor's office and given a envelope with a piece of paper and a booklet. Written on the paper was one of three messages: you retain your job; you may transfer to another job; or your job has been eliminated. The booklet was more interesting. Entitled "Coping with Change: How to Manage the Stress of Change," its cover depicts four stressed-out, multicultural workers clinging to a little battered boat named USS *Uncertainty* and bracing to be engulfed by the wave of CHANGE. (CHANGE is spelled out in white foam on the wave.) Imagine just losing your job and being handed this comic book on how to cope with change. It doesn't take a course in Derrida to deconstruct the visual message: Change just happens, like a big wave from out of the blue, and no one is responsible for the wave, so you better learn how to hold on to your own skimpy place in this nearly sinking boat if you want to survive. This cartoon recipe for weathering change could be dismissed as just a bad joke or caricature if it weren't clear that someone somewhere in corporate culture thought that this was a good idea and useful to people faced with the devastation of losing a job they thought was secure. The message is: *you* had better change. And if you lose your place in this increasingly crowded and narrow boat, you had better learn to swim (adapt to change) or expect to be dumped into the drink and sink.

This emphasis on individual coping skills and de-emphasis on corporate responsibility is as American as apple pie and junk piles. It is also a consciousness trap. People are coaxed to individualize, personalize, and internalize economic loss. What the camera lens fails to capture in this cute picture of tidal waves of change and sinking ships are the estates on the shore, safe and secure, whose inhabitants are few but whose wealth is astronomical and growing.

At the very least, working-class studies can "de-individualize" this change and make visible the wealth on the shore, to enable people to understand what is happening to them from a larger, global, workers' perspective. Working-class studies can also claim some space where a mutuality of learning can occur, where tenured academicians can learn something from displaced workers.

Now I want to say something about the place where I teach, the Rochester Institute of Technology. In my institution, most students have little enthusiasm for the liberal arts, as many feel that any course not directly related to acquiring job skills is worthless. Their feelings are understandable. Hammered by expensive tuition, juggling school and part-time jobs, and anticipating student loan payments for most of their adult lives, these students have little space for "economically disengaged learning." One senior engineering student (who works thirty hours a week and comes from a working-class family) told me that his job as an engineer is to eliminate jobs. What happened, I wonder, to the notion of engineers as builders?

But even this student can be reached and can be convinced that all is not well in the corporate culture. All you have to do is ask if he knows anyone who has recently lost a job.

Here's a different perspective, from a senior business major:

> Why do we put money capital ahead of the most important of all assets—human capital? I spent three years at Kodak and saw many flaws of corporate culture. However, [the] most shocking experience came this past summer at the end of my contract. I was [literally] put to work in the dark, [in] photographic paper storage. Some of the guys I worked with spent 30 years there, and I still don't know how. People were like ghosts, the only way to see someone was a small blinking red light, or a red flash light, which they were allowed to use only in certain areas. After three months of this I was getting depressed, I needed some light, sometimes I couldn't even figure out what time it was. Imagine thirty years of hard work in total darkness and then you get a cheap gold watch and "sorry about your health" note, or worse yet, a phony cartoon telling you how to cope with changes.

Isn't it about time these "worker ghosts" were seen? Isn't it about time for working-class studies?

Locations and Beginnings II

Now I want to travel back to another place and another beginning. I am a child in the 1950s, living in the shadow of Manhattan in urban, working-class New Jersey. On Sundays, when my father wasn't working the weekend shift, my family would frequently visit the graves of relatives. Those Sunday cemetery car trips are vivid in my memory,

particularly the visits to my grandmother's grave in the Jewish cemetery. I see myself as a child of six or seven. I see the gray marble, the
ivy, the junipers, the squiggly Hebrew letters carved everywhere. We
visit Anna, my grandmother's grave, say our prayers, and look for
stones to place on top of the tombstone to mark our visit. I feel the isolation of this particular grave because all the other family members
were buried in the Catholic cemetery several miles away. But in my
memory it is not a sad or cheerless place.

I have not revisited that grave in nearly thirty years, at least not physically. But in my mind, I stop there often. It is through the remembrance of those visits that I feel a particular grounding, not so much in
the physical location, but in story and memory, in my grandmother's
hidden-from-history life story. I suspect that most of us have such hidden stories. Anna's life has been haunting me for a long time. I always
tell it briefly, partially, because some of the meaning of the story is the
knowledge that all the strands of the story cannot be gathered up and
told completely. It is the story of a very young woman who was never
taught to read or write, although she was the daughter of a rabbi. She
traveled alone from Europe to America, married out of her religion,
and was consequently declared dead by her Orthodox family. Before
she was sixteen years old, she was a wife, mother, and orphan. Over and
over again, I have tried to imagine her circumstance—ostracized by her
family, without literacy, raising ten children to adulthood through the
Great Depression and two wars, and working all the time—in the daily
battle against dirt in crowded spaces, cooking on a wood stove, scrubbing clothes on a washboard, nursing children, feeding what she called
"poor souls" in the neighborhood. When she died at the age of fifty-
two, she looked eighty by today's standards. Work marked her body, but
it didn't destroy her humanity. She had, to borrow Toni Morrison's language, "the alien's compassion for troubled people" (149).

I tell Anna's story not to elicit a weepy, nostalgic response or a sen-
timentalized reverence for roots. Instead, I tell Anna's story because it
is my inheritance. It is an alternative grounding to the cartoon version
of generational change. I have no letters, no memoirs, no memory
even of her physical touch, but I have her story told and retold by family members. And I am absolutely certain that my work rests on it and
that I could not speak to you without that story in my memory and
consciousness. That story is a gift, but it is also a responsibility. It is a
kind of cultural haunting, a steady pressure to act out of Anna's experience. I carry it with me into the world, draw on its strength. It helps
clarify my thinking. I need this story to do my work in the world. That's
what I mean by memory as agency.

Now I want to think about these two locations and beginnings: There is corporate city, USA, and my grandmother's story. What do these two locations mean for mapping working-class studies and traveling working class? What do they mean for us as cultural workers?

Let's consider our map. Maps are not innocent, as Denis Wood shows in his fine book *The Power of Maps*. Maps pass themselves off as something. The power of the map lies behind the map, in the hands of the mapper. Remember those maps of the world based on power rather than geography? The United States is depicted as huge, dominating the Western Hemisphere and the globe; Africa is tiny; Central America is nearly erased.

Now I want you to consider what a map of the terrain of academic knowledge might look like. What is surveyed and mapped as "knowledge" depends a great deal on the power of the mapmaker. For a long time, the university knowledge map represented almost exclusively the interests of the ruling, white, elite, minuscule minority. Some of that geography has changed, but the terrain is still contested, and despite the efforts of progressive, democratic forces in the academy to redraw that map, the representation is still highly distorted.

I am thinking now of the mapper's hands in corporate city, USA. It seems to me that disembodied corporations are the current mapmakers, defining the territory, telling students what they need to learn to get jobs in the new technological world order so that they can become part of the global "knowledge elite." You might think of it as "schooling for transnationals." Corporate boards and university boards of trustees fold into the same collection of tiny, powerful elites who often unconsciously represent business interests as knowledge and as an all-pervasive reality.

It is clear that on this new corporate/education map, there is no place for my grandmother's story other than as cheap ethnic nostalgia. Nor will there be much space for labor history, workers' culture, or collective perspectives. Stories of the violence of labor struggles have enormous affective power on students, so it's no wonder they are missing from school texts.

When looking at this map, I do not travel with a sense of defeat or despair, but I do have a point of view that's been thrust on me from working at a technical institute where there is no such thing as English majors or history majors, American studies or labor studies, and no mushy liberal confusion about the direction of those in power.

It seems to me that our work is to continue the fight for the power of the map. We need to construct, reconstruct, remember, reinvent, rediscover, reconnect, and struggle for the knowledge that belongs to the majority of people, the working class.

Junctions

I want to speak more specifically about what I mean by "traveling working class." Remember that scene in the movie *Thelma and Louise* when Thelma decides to get away from her husband and take a trip with her girlfriend Louise? She throws this heavy chunky suitcase on her bed and pulls out dresser drawers loaded with stuff. She pauses over her belongings— jewelry, underwear, hair dryer, socks, sweaters—what to pack? The decision is too hard. Momentarily paralyzed with indecision, she gives up and, in one great swoop, empties a whole drawer into her suitcase and greets Louise with enough matching luggage to put Elizabeth Taylor to shame.

I suspect that my tendency to overpack is not unique to me. When you live for so many years as a working-class person with a sense of imminent emergency, you develop an overcautiousness, on one hand, that is the flip side of a lack of confidence in public space, on the other. It is hard to know what you need to know and what you need to have. It took me a while to catch on that it wasn't always necessary to travel with food.

These prosaic working-class habits are not disconnected from our larger concerns about working-class knowledge and the academy. How do we pack? What class do we travel? Whose map do we use? Who stakes out the territory? Or how do we not follow in Orville Kincaid's footsteps?

Those of us who were born into working-class families encounter a juncture in our travels not faced by middle-class and upper-class people. In a myriad of subtle and not so subtle ways, we are told to adjust our language, our behavior, and perhaps our values, to get rid of all this working-class baggage and travel light if we want to "make it" out. We are not expected to ask what the "it" is we are making. And who determines where we are we going. It seems to me that questions of what gets discarded, what gets transported, and who decides are at the heart of our work. For too long because of the pressures of assimilation and the denial of class difference, working-class people who have attended the academy have let others make those choices for them. We have been given the message that workers have no culture, and if they don't possess material goods, then they have nothing. For too long we have been in a double bind: erased as a presence in a class-denying society and simultaneously experiencing acute class prejudice.

There is an alternative way to travel, and I must say that I felt this in my bones long before I knew it in my conscious mind. It was as if the working-class bodies I recognized so well knew something that my academically trained mind couldn't quite grasp. This alternative involved carrying something with me out and into the world. What? It wasn't my personal achievement or the conventional American Dream version of success (which is moribund, anyway). It certainly wasn't being cool and wearing work clothes as a fashion statement. Nor was it rejecting a decent life. I've never met any hardworking people who didn't want an easier material and physical life for their children. But they don't want their lives ignored or forgotten or disrespected; they want the circumstances of their lives understood. And they want people who have a little power to support them and not deny them.

This process of carrying our knowledge of working-class life into the world is reciprocal. As we witness, we draw strength from our own history. Now I shall describe some considerations for equipping ourselves for building working-class studies. The first is the matter of identity.

Often when I speak to students about class, I spend some time on "decloaking," that is, making class visible in Disney-saturated America. I remind them that we all are born into a class identity, even though that identity can be mixed, hybrid, multiple, and fluid. Who writes the college tuition check is a handy class marker. And of course, our individual identities must be seen in relation to other identities, that's what class means. Working-class identity *is* discernible in the context of U.S. capitalism: if you're expected to dispose of it—you're probably working class. But of course, in late capitalism, disposal is not understood as the elimination of all classes and the redistribution of wealth. Rather, you're expected to take your place in a highly individualistic, competitive social Darwinism. The message is: if you want to improve your material conditions—if you want the goods—then be ready to let go of that sticky, adhesive, communal sensibility. Or, to go back to our comic book—if you want to survive on that rickety boat, throw everyone else overboard!

There are alternative travel arrangements, but we have to travel with baggage that may not fit neatly into bourgeois compartments. We begin with the realization that working-class identity is not negation. Class defined in collective terms as shared economic circumstances and shared social and cultural practices in relation to positions of power means more than the absence or presence of things. We live in a country that is fixated on measurement or, rather, mismeasurement. Where are the tools that measure working-class cultural identity? On what grid does collective responsibility fit?

Consider how class identity travels with us from generation to generation. Our material circumstances may differ from our parents', and certainly from our grandparents', but we may still inherit certain values, attitudes, shared histories, uses of language, and even bodily postures that we reconceive, reevaluate, and restore as we move in time. This is what Stephen Jay Gould calls the "arrows" and "cycles" of cultural time—what changes and leaps forward and what circles back and is repeated. Or what Alessandro Portelli describes in oral narratives as "shuttlework," telling the tale in the present but picking up bits and pieces of the past as you go along, going back and forth in time like a shuttle (65).

It seems to me that American literature has a great deal to teach us about traveling working class. Indeed, American literature is replete with tales of travel—characters hit the open road, go down the river, and board trains. Let us briefly consider two autobiographical novels of the same time period: Aniza Yezierska's *Bread Givers* (1925) and Agnes Smedley's *Daughter of Earth* (1929). Their protagonists, Sarah and Marie, respectively, literally board trains to leave behind the chaos, dirt, and economic deprivation of their childhood, but they leave with feelings of great ambivalence about the relationships left behind. Both characters have a longing for knowledge and an exquisite desire and love for beauty. Yezierska's protagonist, like the author herself, seems stuck in undefined space—not quite the Anglo pioneer she aspires to be—but not able to unburden herself from what she sees as the weight of her father and of the generations before him. She lacks a political vision and an alternative paradigm to bourgeois life. Smedley's Marie is also searching for models and a way out of poverty. This novel ends with a packing-up and a leave-taking: Marie leaves with feelings of acute loneliness but also with a certain consciousness, a certain knowledge that she will carry with her from Colorado to New York to China to the world, that she is forever connected to those who die "*not* for the sake of beauty." They die for other reasons: "exhausted by poverty, victims of wealth and power, fighters in a great cause."

Smedley had little use for what she called "salon socialists" and contempt for those from privileged circumstances who blamed poverty on the proletarian's unwillingness to work hard enough. Smedley was able to make a consciousness leap that Yezierska in her idealization of the American Adam could or would not make, that is, seeing her parents' poverty as linked to a much larger international struggle of the oppressed many against the powerful few. In a letter written in 1930, Smedley says, "Always I think that I shall write one more book before I die—just one book in which I shall, many years from now, try to show what the capitalist system, with its imperialist development, has done to the human being—how it has turned him into a wolf" (MacKinnon and MacKinnon 135).

I suggest that out of the dialectics of these two working-class novels, we can discern possibilities for doing our work in the world. It is possible to leave and look back without turning to stone. When traveling working class, we need to pack a critical class consciousness and solidarity that go beyond identity politics.

Our work is not about celebration. It is full of ambiguity and contradiction. It is a bildungsroman with a working-class difference. It is about building on what is already there, about girding and sustaining, not replacing or rejecting working-class identity. Raymond Williams and Tillie Olsen and many others have marked the way. What is new is what is happening in places like Youngstown, Ohio, opportunities to make that space official—to say that within the confines of what we call institutional knowledge, we cannot claim authority if we exclude working-class epistemology. This is more than memory recollected, more than the inheritance of grit and stamina, more even than our own survival. It is the institutionalized relationship between knowledge and justice, and hence this working-class journey.

Now, since we are in charge of our own mapping, we also have to be alert to traps and dead ends. The first one is getting stalled at the junction of reciting class injuries. Stories about class prejudice and ignorance abound. I hear many and tell a few myself. Unnamed class prejudice seems endemic to the academy. Watch how waitresses or cleaners or cabdrivers are treated at academic conferences. Are they even visible? Well, what can be expected in a society with so few positive images of working people and where there are such false dichotomies between physical and intellectual labor. It is important to recognize and name incidents of class prejudice, hatred even, but it is just as important to use those occasions as compost for other projects. In other words, let us not linger too long on the hidden and not so hidden injuries of class. I am not saying that we should not affirm our life experiences, but there is a danger of getting stalled at the personal injury stop and not taking on other issues.

Another trap is language, particularly academic language. I have seen intelligent, good-willed academicians get together to discuss important issues and never get beyond the definition stage. What is class? How do we define it? Who is or isn't working class? These are questions that I think about a great deal, but I suspect there are other ways to answer them than with either a plodding academic approach or an intoxication with highly theoretical language that is not grounded in a lived reality. Class experience is real and not necessarily textual. Any study of working-class culture should certainly include orality and also the nontextual expressions of how the working-class body speaks. How do we bring, for example, the physicality of the working body into the academic classroom? I am arguing for a more complex intellectuality, always conscious of how knowledge is framed and how pervasive bourgeois sensibilities are.

It may be a good thing for us not to feel at home in the academic habitat in order to retain a sense of the strategic importance of our work. It reminds us of how much we don't know. That the whole story is always out of reach. That we, as Tillie Olsen writes, "will never total it all." That we realize, as Raymond Williams puts it, "the most uneventful life would take a library of books to transcribe."

Destinations

Obviously, determining final destinations for working-class studies cannot and should not be the work of any one person. But I want to offer some considerations for our work together. To be sure, the journey is not going to be easy. But it never was.

One of the many complications we face is the absence of a parallel political movement outside the academy to match our work inside it. For example, women's studies as a field might not have found credibility without the street action of the women's liberation movement—which in turn was influenced by the antiwar movement which was influenced by the civil rights movement. But we cannot wait for a grand movement. We have to begin somewhere, perhaps even leading in the building of an international working-class labor movement both inside and outside the academy.

Another daunting aspect of our work is selection and representation. Contrary to bourgeois notions of working-class people's having "no class," we have an abundance of culture: a wealth of writing, much of it now in print; oral, social, industrial, and community histories; and a long legacy of music and visual and folk art. These stories and histories have extraordinary power. With this cultural plenty come hard questions of selection and issues of representation—how to account for the lived experiences of literally millions of people.

How we organize this material, how we think about time, is another consideration. Our selection of working-class materials might be guided by a reciprocal sense of time, of how one moment informs another, how the future and the past are held in the present. This is a dialogue or conversation with other voices around particular historical moments, what I call the "I, they, and we" of working-class voices. We have many narrative and poetic contemporary retellings of specific events in labor history, for example. This is not an appropriation of the past but an internalizing of time to reinform the creative act in the present.

To be sure, it is a great responsibility but also an extraordinary opportunity for cultural workers to define the territory for working-class studies. We have the power of our grandparents' stories—and we know how to use the technology to get them out.

What might working-class studies look like in its many geographic sites and cultural permutations? Briefly, I want to offer a few observations from my own travels, in the form of intersections and interventions. I want to stop traveling for a while, get off the train, and notice some fields of intersection, clearings where meadow and forest meet and various species commingle.

It seems to me that a key but overlooked area for building working-class studies is with children. Perhaps we should develop more programs and contacts with elementary school teachers. So much labor history has been lost. My college seniors had never heard of the Ludlow massacre or the Triangle fire, for example. Perhaps if we start early enough talking about the ongoing class war in American history, a generation of young people might find some things in common with their elders. Certainly we can provide alternatives to civic pablum about Betsy Ross sweetly sewing the flag or George Washington not telling a lie about cutting down the cherry tree. A lot of lies have been told, but they're not really about cherry trees.

Also, the practice here at Youngstown University of moving the classroom into the work site is an important point of intersection. We might consider it a mutual exchange of literacies. Teachers have knowledge about how to form ideas into written and spoken language, and workers have the knowledge of specific labor practices and concerns, particularly safety and health issues, underemployment and unemployment and job scarcity. We also need to listen better, to use oral history and personal narratives in our classes so that we can build into our courses the voices of people whose lives are not located in the university.

Another crucial point of intersection and alliance is with multiculturalism and women's studies. We should structure our academic practices—our courses and our selected texts—so that we can offer models of what I call reciprocal visibility. Our study of class must be informed by differences of race, ethnicity, sexuality, and gender. Class is multicultural. In particular, we need more study and exposure of the relationship between race and class and how the race card is used by the dominant class to deflect worker solidarity. An international capitalist system has hierarchies of humanity. We need to identify those forces that block a collective consciousness. There are many opportunities for informed comparative readings if we focus on work, labor, and jobs in multicultural texts. I also suggest that we take a transnational and postcolonial perspective in our development of working-class studies, especially as we look at what constitutes "home"—the transitory, unpredictable, slippery nature of home. We can get to intersections of gender, race, and class if we begin with home and work.

Next, we need to intersect with the producers of progress and technology. I suggest that we engage in discursive practices (that is, talk) to computer experts, scientists, and engineers. I even would welcome critical alliances. Jeremy Rifkin and others are predicting that these knowledge elites are among the few who will have meaningful work in the near future. We need to establish spaces, places of intersection, for conversations about technology, progress, and work. We need to question the Forrest Gump view of PROGRESS, a big wave of change (as in the Kodak layoff comic) that just happens. We can draw on our scholarship in literature and history to critique commonplace notions of progress (hand every engineer a copy of Kurt Vonnegut's *Player Piano*). Progress is not an engineless train—it is driven by identifiable business and government interests. Progress is inseparable from power relations. It seems to me that who defines and controls "progress," who profits from it, and who is destroyed by it—is at the heart of working-class studies.

I suspect that it might be easier to intersect with engineers and computer scientists about working-class studies than it would be to convince the Modern Language Association to make working-class literature a permanent discussion group. Engineers and computer scientists can be reached not only because many of them are just a generation or two away from their own working-class roots but also because a case can be made that they will miss crucial pieces of knowledge if they don't recognize working-class craft and labor practices. That is, solving technical problems depends on workers' knowledge.[1]

Philosopher Simone Weil went to work in a factory (and risked her health) in order to internalize the physicality of the working body into her mind and consciousness. About technology she wrote, "All technological problems should be viewed within the context of what will bring about the best working conditions. The whole of society should be first constituted so that work does not demean those who perform it" (McLellan).

Finally, we circle back in this journey to the historicity and future of work. The theologian Dorothee Soelle offers this:

> All workers act within a particular society and culture. All have inherited tools, technology, knowledge from past generations of workers. . . . To develop a historical sense of what work has been, to know what our grandparents did and the path they took to their achievements, is the aim of an educational process that puts self-understanding and human worth before capital. Yet this approach to work is almost unheard of in a nation like the United States, which evaluates labor primarily in terms of productivity. . . . Work is communal not only in the space of a given community but also in time, as the shared memory of what we have received from the past that accompanies us into the future. (94–95)

I conclude by extending a wish—it is the same wish that I have for my children, for myself, for all of us—I wish you good work. By that, I mean work that is creative, not destructive; work that is safe (something millions of people cannot take for granted); work in which you are the subject, not the object; work with a sense of history; work that offers fair compensation, autonomy, and space to hone your craft; work that allows you time to develop your humanity—to read, think, listen to music, observe nature, plant gardens; work that makes a clear distinction between human beings and things, that does not turn human beings into things. And finally, work that offers small occasions for big acts, opportunities to give something back and to make a contribution to our common humanity. I cannot think of a better final destination.

NOTES
This essay was originally given as a keynote address at the "Working-Class Lives/Working-Class Studies" conference at Youngstown State University, Youngstown, Ohio, 1995.

1. Eugene Ferguson, a mechanical engineer and historian of technology, concludes his book *Engineering and the Mind's Eye* by arguing that human abilities and limitations need to be designed into systems, not designed out of them.

Works Cited
Ferguson, Eugene. *Engineering and the Mind's Eye*. Cambridge, MA: MIT Press, 1993.

MacKinnon, Janice R., and Stephen R. MacKinnon. *Agnes Smedley: The Life and*

Times of an American Radical. Berkeley and Los Angeles: University of California Press, 1988.

McDaniel, Wilma Elizabeth. "The Academic Career of Orville Kincaid." In *Liberating Memory: Our Work and Our Working-Class Consciousness,* edited by Janet Zandy. New Brunswick, NJ: Rutgers University Press, 1995.

McLellan, David. *Utopian Pessimist: The Life and Thought of Simone Weil.* New York: Poseidon Press, 1990.

Morrison, Toni. *Song of Solomon.* New York: Knopf, 1977.

Portelli, Alessandro. *The Death of Luigi Trastulli and Other Stories.* New York: SUNY Press, 1991.

Smedley, Agnes. *Daughter of Earth.* 1929. Reprint, New York: Feminist Press, 1973.

Soelle, Dorothy. *To Work and to Love.* Philadelphia: Fortress Press, 1988.

Wood, Denis. *The Power of Maps.* New York: Guilford Press, 1992.

Yezierska, Anzia. *Bread Givers.* 1925. Reprint, New York: Persea, 1975.

Janet Zandy is an associate professor of language and literature at the Rochester Institute of Technology. She is the editor of Calling Home: Working-Class Women's Writings *(Rutgers University Press, 1990),* Liberating Memory: Our Work and Our Working-Class Consciousness *(Rutgers University Press, 1995), and an award-winning issue of* Women's Studies Quarterly *on working-class studies (Feminist Press, spring/summer 1995).*

In Memory of Constance Coiner: A "Foremother" of Contemporary Working-Class Studies

Photo by Steve Duarte

Constance Coiner
June 18, 1948–July 17, 1996

From Virginia Coiner Classick, M.S.W., Woodland Hills, CA

My sister, Constance Coiner, and her twelve-year-old daughter, Ana Duarte-Coiner, were killed on TWA Flight 800. Constance's partner and Ana's father, Steve, hugged them good-bye, watched them go onto the plane, and heard the news of the explosion while driving home alone to Binghamton, New York. Our sister Mary and I talked through the night, waiting until the dawn when we could call our mother. "When the phone woke me up," she said, "I knew."

Several days later a reporter called and asked if I had any comments about how TWA was treating families of the victims. I said that I had other things to say about the deaths of Constance and Ana. Although I have never had one word published, I want to say some things about their death, and all violent death.

When initially the crash was thought to be a terrorist act, I was stunned when I heard people proclaim that they were not going to be daunted by this, as if moving ahead with lives unchanged to "show them" was the best way to honor this tragedy. How convenient it is to talk about "those crazy people" or "the cowards," to externalize this into some fringe, isolated, demonized "other," as if there were no connection between this event and the culture in which we all live. To understand this, one only has to listen to talk radio hosts who package the obscenities of intolerance for entertainment or politicians who whip up the masses against "the enemy." There is no mystery for me about why Constance and Ana died. Anyone with any sense of connection to humankind must be profoundly moved by this event to struggle against all those conditions in our society that are the seedbeds for this and all violence. The real mystery is still, as it has been pondered through the ages, how tolerance, compassion, fairness, justice, generosity, and peacemaking can coexist with racism, intolerance, hatred, greed, and indifference to the well-being of the human family.

I have felt devastating grief. It has felt like someone has taken a piece of tin and cut my feelings to ribbons. Each of us in the family has a piece of this grief. But Steve has all of it, and the enormity of his loss is uppermost in the minds of all of us. This is public grief, a *Newsweek*-cover, white-ribbons grief. The extent of our pain is widely acknowledged. Because of the nature of this tragedy, we are given permission to grieve openly. I am mindful of so many people who must so often bear their grief in isolation, among them partners of AIDS victims, or families of loved ones lost to addiction or suicide. This is privileged grief. I am not suggesting that grief can be compared. But we can compare the circumstances in which grief is endured. I grieve in the air-conditioned comfort of my own home. I sleep in a comfortable bed, and if I can't sleep, I am comforted by my partner, Chuck. I have a clear picture of grief without comfort.

I visited a tiny village in El Salvador and talked with a woman whose child was shot out of her arms with U.S.-funded weapons. After this child was killed, and another wounded, she then had to swim across a river to a refugee camp in Honduras. I think of Meridian, Mississippi; of Armenia; of Bosnia; of Baghdad; of Buchenwald. The hardest edges of my grief have been softened by the sounds of voices on my telephone, by flowers delivered at the door, by regular meals, by hot water. Rescue workers and highly sophisticated equipment were brought in to find the survivors. The mothers of the disappeared in El Salvador, Chile, and Nicaragua did not have the FBI coming to the house to get hair from the hairbrushes and fingerprints from the computer to help identify their children. This is a privileged grief. Most grief resulting from violence and hatred is borne in the midst of horror and hardship and most often by people of color or victims of religious persecution. The tip of the finger of my grief can only reach out to touch the edge of those experiences throughout our history. Our commonality is that our grief is the result of violence, and all violence can be prevented.

There are moments when I am overwhelmed by the forces of destruction and the indifference to the human family with which so many people live their lives. And yet I still hold to a vision of peace and justice, so those of us who are left (I think that Constance would chuckle at the double entendre) must redouble our efforts. There is new meaning to the phrase "doing her justice." I believe that at the table of peace, there will be bread and justice and people who are students and dear friends of Constance. I gather strength from that. And for the struggle ahead, I hear that singular voice of Constance yelling from the stands, "You go, homegirl."

Constance and Ana were found together on the ocean floor. Constance always sparkled. She was a magnetic woman, a devoted sister, my dear friend, my most dedicated cheerleader. She usually signed her letters to me "solidarity forever." They leave a space that will never be filled. I will miss both Constance and Ana for the rest of my life.

The struggle continues. For Constance, for Ana, the struggle must continue.

From Karen E. Rowe, professor of English at the University of California, Los Angeles: Remembrance for Constance Coiner and Ana Duarte-Coiner, Memorial Gathering, Pacific Palisades, California, October 6, 1996

Remembrance: May Women's Voices Speak to You Always

For Constance Coiner and Ana Duarte-Coiner

Silence—my friendship with Constance began in silence, or to be more precise, it began with her introducing me to Tillie Olsen's *Silences,* which I quoted once again in commencing an American women writers course much like the one Constance herself would have taught this fall at SUNY, Binghamton. Only this school year, this October afternoon, her voice is the silent one. As Tillie has written, "History and the present are dark with silences. These are not natural silences, that necessary time for renewal, lying fallow, gestation, in the natural cycle of creation. The silences I speak of," she continues, "are unnatural; the unnatural thwarting of what struggles to come into being, but cannot," or the "unnatural thwarting" of the tragedy that carelessly took Constance's and Ana's lives on July 17, 1996. My voice has been almost as silent, struck dumb and speechless, a normal loquaciousness replaced by an inarticulate grief that many of us share. I understand now what I did not understand before, what "stunned into silence" means, what it means to struggle with the injustice of loss, with the guilty belief that it should have been me, not Constance, not Ana, with an inability to comprehend the lost possibilities—and possibility was always what Constance presented to her friends and her students. It would be easier had I known Constance less well because then the words wouldn't sound so clichéd, so banal. But in our hearts and memories, I hope we hear the vibrant human being speaking to us and through us—Constance's tenacious intensity, her lovingness, her political outrage, her rollicking humor, her desire always to listen to the story behind the story of those she met, taught, interviewed, counseled. Silence may be what has defined the beginning and ending of my relationship with Constance, but the in-between was filled with talk, dialogue, gossip, laughter, confessions, confidences shared, and just plain old-fashioned female gab.

Constance and I began our nineteen years of friendship in the spring of 1977, feminist sisters under the skin if not, like Virginia and Mary, sisters by birth and hereditary lifetimes. We both were caught up even then in the academic cycles of commencement that seem to promise such renewal and beckon with hope toward the as-yet-unexplored landscapes of the mind shared with the as-yet-unknown histories of our students. Mary reminded me recently that I had taught her two quarters before Constance, and Heidi Preschler and I have reminisced about the seminar in which she too first met and was moved by Constance. I taught Constance the first course in her graduate career at UCLA, a seminar in the spring of 1977, "Mothers and Daughters in Women's Literature." The "fearful symmetry" is not lost to me as we remember the lives and deaths of Constance and Ana, a mother and daughter duo, dynamic, daring, and dauntless, certainly unlike anything we read about in Adrienne Rich's *Of Woman Born*, in which matrophobia was more prevalent than mother worship. I know that Ana was her mother's delightful "pal," a "red-diaper baby" from the day she was born. When our conversations began to spill over from the classroom chats about Adrienne Rich, Doris Lessing, and Virginia Woolf into the personal confidences about our lives, I cannot now remem-

ber, but husbands, boyfriends, and partners came and went; consciousness groups were formed and disbanded; and somehow in
between Constance designed her own individual Ph.D. in American
Studies with a little help from her faculty and friends, even while she
moved from El Medio to Georgina to Culver City.

I've been reading *Notes from the Shore* by Jennifer Ackerman, given
to me by Geraldine Moyle, whose friendship with Constance and with
me was forged out of those same years in the late 1970s and early
1980s. Ackerman describes a passionate lover of nature, named Bill,
someone I think Constance would have been drawn to as much as she
was to walking in Palisades Park by the ocean or hiking in the Santa
Monica Mountains. Bill, we are told, "sees the world of light and
motion not in a continuum . . . but in frozen frames, a series of discernible stop-watch tableaux" (40–41). My memories of Constance are,
I realized, "frozen frames," "stop-watch tableaux," moments out of time
that keep reappearing in the mind's eye, in words that leap from her
letters, in photographs that capture her outbursts of triumph and pleasure. Ackerman writes about the Atlantic seacoast near Lewes,
Delaware, north of Ocean City, Maryland, and I recall the table in the
dining room in Culver City where Constance and I sat when we discovered that she had been born in, and we both had lived in,
Baltimore, both sharing the faith and ultimately the oppressiveness of
devoutly Lutheran families, her father having gone to the seminary to
become a Lutheran minister. We joked all the time, trying to figure
out how two good "transplanted Lutheran/eastern girls" ended up
working for radical feminist change in the "People's Republic of Santa
Monica." Constance never lost an underlying devotion to serving
humankind, but her faith turned from a prescriptive belief in institutions, governments, and churches to a faith in what individuals and
activist groups could do, what women and students could do, if
empowered and banded together. As a student of the Old Left of the
1930s as much as of the New Left 1960s, Constance's commitment to
social justice made her ultimately into an "in"sider who spoke with an
"out"sider's perspective for the working class, for the ethnic student,
for the returning woman, for the student who lacked privilege—much
like Tillie Olsen, Meridel LeSueur, and Carolyn Forché, about whom
she wrote. In reading some student letters that Stephen Duarte left
with me when he came this August to bring Ana and Constance home,
I heard the voices of her students filled with the same energy, passion,
and penetration that characterized Constance's teaching. Because he
was on a first-name basis with Constance, like all her students, Willis
didn't sign his last name, but he wrote:

She used to say that I was her "talisman of despair." I'd smile, modest, but flattered that someone so intelligent, so charismatic valued me. I couldn't wait for class, to hear her speak, to feel the passion that she felt about teaching, about empowering, about remembering, about revolutionizing. . . . I'm sure you can imagine her trying to learn over seventy names, running up from the board, . . . her eyes that opened and glowed when students critically thought and "got it." She became my talisman, my hope and inspiration that everything will be okay, that my knowledge can be used for something greater, that I have some agency to use. She made me love the study of English. I wanted (and still want) to do what she did—teach, write, speak, move, inspire.

Constance wrote in her New Year's letter from January 5, 1996, that

on the undergraduate level, SUNY-B is the toughest public university to get into in New York state; most of our students come from the NY city area; many of them are eligible for ivies their parents can't afford. These factors result in what is for me a dream student population—generally skilled, serious, and vocal students who are not privileged and have no sense of entitlement.

For those students, Constance's love of teaching kids without privileges or entitlements, whether at Binghamton or in UCLA's freshman summer program, was a perfect match of radical reformer with ripe minds.

Ackerman writes, "I've learned that the way in to a new landscape is to pull at a single thread. Nearly always it will lead to the heart of the tangle" (9). But I find that every thread in my years of friendship with Constance, every "stop-watch tableau" could open up into a woven fabric of remembrances, connections, webs of love and caring, tangles of pain and pleasure. I hear Constance struggling over what it will mean to raise a child—will she have time, how can she steal time, to write a dissertation? I see her unwrapping the hand-knit baby afghan that my mother had made for Ana. I hear Pachelbel's *Canon in D* playing quietly as Ana sleeps and we talk. I listen to her stories of rolling down the freeways of Los Angeles singing labor songs to Ana, those melodies the first lessons for a child who would become a lover of music and a pianist and her first tutorials in leftist politics. I see Constance standing in my office doorway in Rolfe Hall urgently beseeching another letter of recommendation, due date ASAP. We go back and forth, I remember, in conversation and chapter readings about how much can be revealed from oral histories of still-living authors—and I share the moment when her contract from Oxford becomes a reality. I smile reading *Better Red,* hearing the echoes, hearing the greater maturity of critical voice since the dissertation's initially stumbling articulations. I see Constance surrounded by the graduate-division staff accepting her award as an Outstanding Graduate Student of the Year. I remember offering her a party dress to wear, because she didn't have one suitable for the chancellor's dinner for the Distinguished Teaching Award winners. I watched her filled with animation and generosity as she gave all of us on her Ph.D. committee loaves of French bread and long-stemmed roses to celebrate her Wollstonecraft Prize. I envision her dressed in that wonderful khaki green flowing suit, beautifully radiant in her "dress-me-up-professional" garb so unlike the daily jeans. And I feel the warmth of her hug the last time we met at the Heath Anthology party at the Chicago MLA. She wrote me shortly thereafter with a characteristic staccato exuberance:

> I'm sorry we were interrupted . . . at the Heath Anthology celebration. I felt we were just beginning to catch up! . . . I finally have a study of my own, after all those yrs. of bedroom-study combos, and I've already outgrown it. I spent 6 hrs. w/Forché the day after the Anthology celebration. Superb interview. I wish though that you & I could have snuck out after Carolyn's reading (the 2 men were disappointing to me, & not just because they were men) and continued our chat. Linda Wagner-Martin thinks I should do a bk on Forché & thinks I could get an advance contract. Forché thinks I oughta do it, would open her files to me, cooperate completely. Exciting, no? I want to be three people. (January 10, 1990)

Scribbled on the envelope, "No request for letter of rec. enclosed!"

But I can sense Constance nudging me impatiently to get on with it, to move beyond the memories, the telling of her story, to the creation of a future in which her voice will continue to speak to us and through us. At her farewell party in 1988 when she went to Binghamton, I gave her an old-fashioned iron, so that Tillie's words, "I stand here ironing," would be signified by a material object transported across the United States, this time from the west to the east. We put on her cake "May women's voices speak to you always." In her final letter to me in January 1996, she expressed a longing to come back to the family of scholars, friends, and relatives in Southern California. She wrote, "Keep your ears open for any opening in the L.A. area. I'd love to come home." Los Angeles and UCLA are the home where Constance came into her own as a scholar, but as a human being, she came into our lives as an already wise woman who cared about political issues, about feminist activism, who fought tooth and nail for socialist and liberal causes, and who made that passion for working-class peoples and feminist writers into a truly lived life. An author unknown to me has written, and I have gendered, the following:

> *There is a destiny that makes us all sisters*
> *And no one goes her way alone.*
> *All that we send into the lives of others*
> *Comes back into our own.*

Constance gave gifts to all of us—beauty, vibrancy, spunk, passion, courage, a love of teaching, and a fierce love of Stephen and Ana, her sisters, and her mother. I hope that I can, that we can, continue, in silent and voiced acts of memorial, to send into the lives of others what Constance Coiner brought into our own.

Afterword

Tillie Olsen dedicates "Tell Me a Riddle" to Seevya Dinkin and Genya Gorelick, two activist immigrant women of Olsen's parents' generation. Genya Gorelick was an orator in the 1905 revolution.

> *Two of that generation*
> *Seevya and Genya*
> *infinite, dauntless, incorruptible*

For Stephen Duarte for whom Constance Coiner and Ana Duarte-Coiner were, like activist women of the 1930s, 1960s, and 1990s, infinite, dauntless, and incorruptible.

For Virginia and Mary, I offer this feminist variant of the familiar hymn from Constance's childhood as a

> **Consolation from God, Nature, and Music—**
> **One Lapsed Lutheran Feminist to Another**
>
> *Why should I feel discouraged,*
> *Why should the shadows come,*
> *Why should my heart be lonely*
> *And long for heaven and home.*
> *When God is my portion,*
> *My constant Friend is She.*
> *Her eye is on the sparrow,*
> *And I know she watches over me.*
> *I sing because I am happy.*
> *I sing because I am free.*
> *Her eye is on the sparrow,*
> *And I know she watches over me.*

From Diana Hume George, professor of English and women's studies at Penn State University at Erie, Behrend College: For Constance and Ana's Memorial Service at Binghamton, New York, October 1996

"When we can't dream any longer, we die," said Emma Goldman. I don't know whether Constance and Ana are still dreaming their dreams in some form. But I do know that we are still dreaming Constance's own dreams, collectively, in solidarity, when we act in faithful concord with her principles, when we try to work toward the reality of these dreams of equity, justice, and awakening to which she dedicated her life on earth. In the only form of immortality I know, the only form Constance herself knew, we keep her and Ana with us when we dream, when we act, when we love.

In September 1996, I sent to the University of Illinois Press the final manuscript of Constance's second book, known in manuscript form as "Silent Parenting in the Academy," to be published as *The Family Track: Keeping Your Faculties While You Mentor, Nurture, Teach, and Serve* (due out in mid-1998). This work was at the core of what mattered to her—working-class, feminist, and family-centered concerns—and preparing it for publication has been my sole object since July 17. I am normally no more than a godless activist, but I can tell you that Constance Coiner's passionate presence has worked on her book with me, refusing to budge until it is done. I cannot explain just what I mean—she's not here with wings on; I have not gone entirely around the bend yet—but her presence is more vivid in our mutual work now than it has ever been. This should surprise no one who knew her. Could anyone think she would leave it entirely to another person? After another year of editing and production, there will be this book to celebrate her life again and again, which many of us will do until we follow her out of here.

Constance sent out to all of us the light of unanointed blaze that Emily Dickinson described in herself and other like souls. Constance's was more often at white heat than any I've known. I was heated by her warmth, sometimes almost in awe of her intense purity, her clean vision. No one ever meant her name more than Constance did. Pure conviction drove her. Her commitment was unwavering. The energy that pulsed from her bones and her flesh often rendered her radiant, nearly magical in presence. Ana had this same energy in child-becoming-woman form. When I went to her home for our first workfest, Ana was eight. Constance and Ana were on the sidewalk dancing together. She was always ready to dance—and to work, to speak out, to challenge, to struggle, to make peace. And to teach. After she read something I wrote about my resonant love for a place, a geography, she said, "The only place I feel alive like that is not an absolute geography—it's in my teaching, in the classroom."

The night after their deaths, I followed the trajectory of an injured firefly falling through the dark yard. I scooped it up and urged its flight. It fell again, and it fell again. But then it flew away, blinking light. Coming into the house that night, I saw on the door a moth of amazing beauty, its gold deeper than that of a butterfly, more muted, the black border circled with blue. It vibrated on the glass a while, then flew away. When these two creatures left, I felt the beating of Constance's and Ana's own wings. All winged creatures flying into the dusk, free and alive, are these two women now for me, and this will always be so. I think of her and Ana, elated, holding hands, embarking on this adventure, beaming that warmth I have seen Constance share with Ana. There they will always be, her choice to be with her daughter clear against the backdrop of loved work, put finally aside. As Carolyn Forché put it, she will always be flying away free, to Paris with Ana.

To keep her fire in me, Constance left work for me to finish, this work that occupied her core. I think she left work for all of us to finish. We do that work by opposing privilege, especially when we reap its benefits. We keep her alive by challenging ourselves to act with integrity and to be of use every day, by speaking out for people in poverty, damaged women, children, working men. She was made of eloquent vigilance, and her heart beating in us can make us more honest every moment of whatever lives we have left.

From Liz Rosenberg, professor of creative writing, State University of New York at Binghamton: Remarks from the Gathering to Celebrate the Lives of Constance Coiner and Ana Duarte-Coiner, Binghamton, New York, October 5, 1996

Constance was one of my best friends, a colleague in the English department in every way. Her daughter Ana was dear to me both for Constance's sake and because of who and what she was at such a young age. She came into her own very early, and if what Constance told me is true, the first thing Ana did after being born was to knock the delivering doctor's glasses across the room. Both Constance and Ana were enthusiasts.

The poet John Keats described life as "the education of a soul." Like Constance and Ana, Keats had a short, intense life, so like them he must have been a brilliant student. I don't want to embarrass or aggravate Steve with any talk about what I believe to be their eternal and energetic aspects. I will, though, quote Einstein, and not the Bible, in saying that matter is energy and can be neither created nor destroyed.

What I want to talk about and celebrate today is the way in which Constance and Ana are teachers for the rest of us who are slower learners.

Steve told me that Ana had had only one or two nightmares during her lifetime. She greeted the day with optimism and joy. I wonder how many of us can say that? Jennifer Evans at Channel 12's *Action News for Kids,* said that one day they had to film a story in the snow. All the grown-ups were grumbling, but Ana was enthusiastic, eager to get out into it. How many of us loved the snow when we were children? That is an easy lesson to forget—but an important one, living as we do in the Southern Tier. Ana was the most beautiful girl I ever saw. Golden hair, with dark brown eyes—her mother's hair, her father's eyes. Her eyes had a depth of sadness to them, what the Portuguese call *sow-dadge*—a longing or mournfulness beyond words. They also had a shine of pure joy. I saw that shine when Ana would sit in her father's lap—they were such good friends—and once when she was checking a computer, looking up her mother's published works, with her eyes lighting up when she saw the size of the list. How many of us are so generous about the success of even those we love?

Constance maintained a child's generosity and enthusiasm all her life. I never knew anyone so quick to celebrate another person's accomplishments. She was modest about her own successes and secretive about her past life, or lives. Yet in nearly every other way she was wide open—in her outrage, love, enthusiasm, ambition, and affection. Justice, fairness, were so important to her. Don't mourn, organize! she used to say to me. It is very good advice.

When Constance won the Chancellor's Award for Excellence in Undergraduate Teaching, I had much help from David Bartine, who had nominated her the year before, and from Constance herself, that demon of good organization, but most of all from the dozens of students who wrote on her behalf.

Here are some quotations from these letters. "In the great novel *The Assistant* by Bernard Malamud, Ida asks her daughter, 'Who gets rich from reading?' To answer her question, I would say I get rich from reading. In Professor Coiner's class I got very very rich . . . because I saw myself in the literature we read and she helped me make the connection." Two students writing together describe her opening class: "Students fight for a seat in the hot, overcrowded room, as they await her arrival. Several arms waving petitions fan her as she bursts into the room. She gets down to business right away, in a style so dynamic that the students hang on her every word." Another student described her as "a master of time." Her syllabi were like detailed maps—watch out, there's going to be a lot of reading next week! Your midterm paper is coming up in two classes—Constance planned meticulously for other people's freedom. My favorite came from this student:

> I am a Latina born in the Dominican Republic. At home we have a saying for a determined person . . . "un platano toffe" (a tough green banana). The very first day at Professor Coiner's class I said to myself, "Now this is going to be un platano toffe" . . . in the classroom she is enthusiastic and "alive" to say the least. Many times when the clock hit 1:05 P.M., I wanted to stay. "Forget about lunch," I'd say to myself.

So many students wrote in their letters "Constance Coiner has changed my life" that my husband and I kidded about having a T-shirt made up with the slogan.

For my birthday once, Constance bought me a hand-crafted journal from The Goldsmith here in Binghamton, with an engraving of the moon on the cover. Inside she had copied down a few of her favorite quotations. One of them came to seem almost prophetic after the plane crash. It is from Marge Piercy: "Despair is the worst betrayal . . . to believe at last that the enemy will prevail. . . . There is finally a bone in the heart that does not break when we remember we are still part of each other, the muscle of hope that goes on in the dark." "My heart is breaking with hope," Constance once told me, quoting someone else. She was a human conduit for other voices. "Don't mourn, organize!"

Constance had detractors as well as friends. Not everyone likes a bolt of lightning, and it can strike hard what it illuminates, though I believe that Constance did not have one mean bone in her body, one ounce of bad will. I wish the same might be said of us all someday. I want us to be more like Constance and Ana, so beloved and full of love. I would like to end with a poem—not because I think it's very good, but because some things I can say only in poetry.

For Constance Coiner and Ana Duarte Coiner

"Walking, there is no path. You make the path in going."
                    —Antonio Machado, inscribed on his gravestone

Walking, there is no path.
You make the path
in going.
What an arc you've cut
across our summer sky,

my fiery friend. Oh for your anger now!
and just the smallest dose
would cure me. Rave against careless handlers
shoving baggage through the belly
of the plane, and
mouths that claim care
takes too long.
It never was too much work for you—
Your small tense hands, bony and quivering with passion,
the eyes burning and upside-down smile near tears.
"Nobody's perfect, so if you want to love
you're going to have to learn to forgive."
Now I will never know you entirely.
What spun your "merry-go-sorrow"
around and flung you, daughter in tow,
to land inches apart in fifty feet of water.
Nobody's hands are clean enough to greet you.
You wanted your daughter
to succeed, yourself
to shine in a just world.
Lean on the far side of the gate, Constance,
you blazed a shortcut through.
I am taking the long way around
to meet you.

From Lisa Orr, visiting assistant professor of English at Utica College of Syracuse University

Constance was my teacher at the State University of New York at Binghamton, in my first year of graduate school while I was wondering what I was doing there. I met her first at a pizza party: someone addressed me, and a voice said from behind me, "Oh, so you're Lisa Orr." I had just signed up for her class on multicultural women writers for the coming semester, and already she knew my name—knew, no doubt, all our names. And in naming me she claimed me; I became one of the legion of students who followed her with an almost religious enthusiasm. She would laugh if she could hear me say she had a cult following, but it is true. Leaning forward from her end of the table in her graduate seminar, Constance compelled all of us to engage texts, her, one another. As she pounded an essay and cried, "Here's where we could sit down and drink a beer with the author!" we felt, here's where the study of books can really make a difference, here's where the vital heart of literary studies resides.

She also promptly appointed herself my mentor, to my great good fortune, because Constance redefined mentoring, too, approaching it with her characteristic enthusiasm. She advised me on everything, from how to pick a dissertation committee to how to fit in childbearing around graduate school. I still have insanely long e-mails from her detailing exactly how to dress for the MLA convention. "If only someone had told me these things," she would say, searching her memory for difficulties she had faced, trying to smooth them all away for me. I soon learned that one had to be careful what one asked for from her, because she would do it, even if it drained every last drop of her energy. Constance's was the most unusual brand of ambition I have ever seen, for while she was ambitious for herself, she was equally ambitious for everyone she loved.

And as generous as she was in a professional mode, she was even more generous on the personal level. In fact, it is a mistake even to speak of the two separately: Constance merged them even as she worried she could not. Cramped under a looming deadline, she once wrote me, "I would like nothing better than to talk with you about all the stuff that was in your e-mail, right now, in person. I felt deprived that I couldn't respond immediately and lovingly. Shit, Lisa, I hate always deferring BEING HUMAN!" The truth, of course, is that she never gave up "being human"; more than anyone I know she was fluent in what she called "emotional literacy."

It wasn't until after her death that I realized part of why I felt so lost was that Constance had been my "academic Mom"—though I'm not sure how she would have felt about that, given her sharp awareness that women professors were too often expected to be the nurturing, self-sacrificing, all-giving ones in their departments. But she, who always spoke of foremothers, was one to so many of us, that for years now English departments across the country will be shaped by her. No doubt many of us found ourselves thinking the same selfish thought that kept going through my head in the days after her death: Constance, you can't be dead. I still need you. We all still need you.

From Janet Zandy, associate professor of language and literature at the Rochester Institute of Technology: Dedication of the Youngstown State University Working-Class Studies Conference, 1997

For the 1995 Youngstown conference on working-class lives and studies, Constance Coiner helped organize a roundtable session bringing together faculty, graduate students, and the audience for a conversation on "outing class in the classroom," a strategy for radical teaching and social transformation. Constance loved these opportunities for multiple voicings; they were natural expressions of her deeply democratic sensibility, her respect for all human voices, and her great capacity to listen and to speak. Constance had a wonderful time at Youngstown in 1995.

On July 17, 1996, Constance Coiner and her twelve-year-old daughter Ana died in the TWA plane crash that killed 230 people. It is impossible to measure or speak the depth of our loss. I say "our" loss because what I want to voice today is not the unspeakable private anguish of those who were closest to her and Ana but, rather, our collective loss. The public Constance Coiner was an extraordinary teacher, activist, editor, writer, and scholar—all roles inseparable from the private Constance who was a lifelong partner, friend, trusted colleague, mother, daughter, and sister.

Constance was a magnificent teacher because she created a space for students to engage—language, literature, politics, the world. She won the State University of New York Chancellor's Excellence in Teaching Award, and in letter after letter, students wrote about how her class changed their lives. She was happiest in the classroom, the one place where she could be most her self, fully expressive, away from the academic pressures to perform and produce. I grieve for the students who will not know her.

Constance Coiner was one of those rare humans who could hold in her consciousness both the macrocosm and the microcosm. I frequently marveled at the capaciousness of her political and historical sense and, simultaneously, her absolute attentiveness to the ordinary— a meal, a joke with a friend, her young daughter's drawings. The trip to Paris was a long overdue celebration for Constance and Ana. Ana's life was just beginning to bloom as she was recognized by her Binghamton community as one of the town's brightest students. Constance's book and long labor of love, *Better Red: The Writing and Resistance of Tillie Olsen and Meridel Le Sueur,* was published (and, happily, will be reprinted in paper by the University of Illinois Press). She was in the process of completing with her coeditor, Diana Hume George, what will surely be a groundbreaking book, entitled *The Family Track: Keeping Your Faculties While You Mentor, Nurture, Teach, and Serve,* and she had begun work on a book about the poet Carolyn Forché. These are only a few highlights of a very active professional life.

"Sorrow is tongueless," Tillie Olsen writes in *Yonnondio.* In *Better Red,* Constance Coiner examines that phrase, turns it over and over, and addresses "the condition of the potentially redeemed reader who, recognizing that 'sorrow is tongueless' meets Olsen's challenge to forge conditions in which all people can speak" (187). Every day Constance Coiner took up the challenge of forging conditions in which all people can speak. The terms *multivocality* and *heteroglossia* were not merely critical categories for her; she structured her life and work around these democratic aesthetic and political impulses.

Constance loved language, and she was an accomplished storyteller. She took her time, relished every detail, made the story fresh for even those jaded listeners who had heard it all before. Her stories entered her professional writing. In her essay "Silent Parenting in the Academy," she writes:

> When I completed my Ph.D. and went on the job market in 1987, the professor responsible for shepherding candidates through the job search advised me to replace the message on my answering machine that included Ana's cheery four-year-old voice. "And I wouldn't let her answer the phone 'til this shootin' match is over," he added ominously. With misgivings I complied with his instructions. But Ana, who was proud of her newly-acquired phone-answering skills, was not to be silenced. Unexpectedly, at eight one Saturday morning, the phone rang. Forgetting about the time difference between the east and west coasts, I relented and allowed her to answer, believing that only my mother would call at such an early hour. Ana put down the phone receiver and screeched, "Mommy, Mommy, it's the University of Transylvania!" In the seconds before I spoke to the chair of the University of Pennsylvania's search committee, I saw my fledgling career as a minefield.

Constance had tremendous personal and professional generosity. Her preface to *Better Red* may be the longest list of acknowledgments in academic publishing history. Constance thanks everyone, from her dissertation committee, to Stephanie Koviak, the feminist hero of the 1948 novel *The Great Midland* by Alexander Saxton (soon to be reprinted with commentary by Constance), to students who enrolled in her course "Multicultural Women Writers of the U.S.," to her sisters, mother, and nieces and nephews, to her child care providers. On that part of her life, she comments:

> When I was a graduate student and my daughter, Ana, was a newborn, I received a note from Tillie Olsen on one of those scraps of paper that are her trademark: "Thieve all the time you can for Ana" was all it said, but I hung on to that scrap of permission to love my child while working my way into a profession that is often incompatible with the needs of children and parents.

And in that same paragraph, Constance addresses her daughter directly: "Ana," she writes, "I'll send a message into your future in your own voice, with your own current favorite expression: 'You go, girl.'"

Thieve indeed. Every day I mourn the theft of the lives of Constance and Ana. Constance Coiner constructed what some of us can only imagine: a whole, beautiful life. All the parts fit and complemented one another: her scholarship, her teaching, her politics, her friendships, her parenting, her loving of kin and kind. I will never think of her in the distanced way that people speak of the dead. She was the most alive, joyful friend I have ever had.

In many memorials, Constance is described by those who love her as "white light," "magnetic," "white heat," "a thunderbolt," "radiant." All true. But her partner Steve Duarte reminds me to emphasize the struggle, not to anoint her. Constance valued the 1995 Youngstown conference so much because of its emphasis on laboring, on the process of production, on the struggle of the worker. As Steve says, she was wonderful and she was tormented, frequently worn down by the energy it takes to deal with the academy and all those moments away from Ana. It was, is, a struggle.

It seems impossible and wrong to write that bland, passive word *was* after Constance's name. I hate those "was's." Constance is.

This small tribute is not a mark of closure but a call to opening. Read Constance Coiner's own words. Keep her alive in the reading of her own writing. Use the example of her life to struggle for good work and justice, because it is her life, not her death, that attests to the possibility of a full humanity for us all.

Newsbriefs

CALL FOR PAPERS

Bottom Dog Press seeks personal essays for a collection, *Writing Work: Writers on Working-Class Writing*. The editors are looking for honest and reflective prose that connects with working-class culture and reveals its impact on the writer. Deadline: September 1, 1998. Contact: Bottom Dog Press, c/o Firelands College, One University Rd., Huron, OH 44839.

CALLS FOR SESSIONS

The Ph.D. program in history at the **Graduate School and University Center at the City University of New York** invites proposals for "Reproducing Women's History, Working Seminars Across the Generations," to be held in New York City on March 12–13, 1999. Established scholars are urged to apply in pairs with a graduate student or recent Ph.D. The focus will be on recent scholarship, with special interest in approaches that question accepted temporal and national historical divisions. Deadline: September 30, 1998. Contact: Ph.D. Program in History, City University of New York Graduate Center, 33 West 42nd Street, New York, NY 10036, Attn: Bonnie S. Anderson.

Southern Connecticut State University announces an upcoming women's studies conference on Women and Disabilities, October 2–3, 1998. Deadline: June 1, 1998. Contact: Vara Neverow, Women's Studies Program, Southern Connecticut State University, EN 271, New Haven, CT 06515-1355; phone: (203) 392-6133; fax: (203)392-6723; e-mail: womenstudies@scsu.ctstateu.edu;WWW:http://scsu.ctstateu.edu/~womenstudies/wmst.html.

PUBLICATIONS

The American Association of University Women Educational Foundation announces the publication of a research report, *Separated by Sex: A Critical Look at Single-Sex Education for Girls*. This report is the result of commissioned papers, a review of the literature and proceedings from the Foundation's national roundtable that assess the research on single-sex education in K–12 public education. Contact: AAUW Educational Foundation, 1111 Sixteenth Street NW, Washington, DC 20036; phone: (202) 728-7602; fax: (202) 872-1425; e-mail: foundation@mail.aauw.org; WWW: http://www.aauw.org.

The Center for Reproductive Law and Policy has recently published a report, *Mujeres del Mundo: Leyes y Políticas que Afectan sus Vidas Reproductivas-América Latina y el Caribe.* Contact: CRLP, 120 Wall Street, New York, NY 10005; phone: (212) 514-5534; fax: (212) 514-5538.

Drumadravy Books announces the publication of *Beloved Dissident Eve Smith,* a tribute to a remarkable British Columbia woman who was a political educator, peace activist, naturalist, self-educated ecologist, environmental columnist, and prolific writer. To order, phone (519) 523-4979 or fax (519) 523-9874.

FEMSPEC, an interdisciplinary journal dedicated to critical and creative works in the realms of science fiction, fantasy, magic realism, and other supernatural genres, is recruiting editors, readers, and manuscripts. The journal seeks those interested in speculating, theorizing, creating, and questioning gender across the boundaries. Contact: Batya Weinbaum, POB 69, East Montpelier, VT 05651-0069; phone: (802) 472-8527; e-mail: batyawein@aol.com.

The **Seminary of Judaic Studies** in Jerusalem announces the inauguration of an English-language journal *NASHIM: A Journal of Jewish Women's Studies and Gender Issues.* Contact: The Seminary of Judaic Studies, POB 8600, Jerusalem 91083, Israel.

The Agender Co-op announces the arrival of *sibyl,* a new magazine for women with an interest in gender politics and feminism. It will include news analysis from a woman's perspective, regular information on campaigns and organizations, coverage of women's arts and writing, interviews, and humorous features. Contact: Agender, Unit 19.4 Aberdeen Studios, 22-24 Highbury Grove, London N5 2EA.

Women's Environment and Development Organization announces the publication of *Mapping Progress: Assessing Government Implementation of the Beijing Platform for Action,* a global survey of successes and challenges in advancing commitments made at the Beijing women's conference.

Contact: WEDO, 355 Lexington Ave., 3rd Floor, New York, NY 10017-6603; phone: (212) 973-0325; fax: (212) 973-0335; e-mail: wedo@ igc.apc.org; WWW: http://www.wedo.org.

RESOURCES

The Center for Women's Global Leadership announces the *1998 Global Campaign for Women's Human Rights* web site. Users can participate in the postcard campaign, post their own activities, fill out a Women's Global Leadership Institute application, and link to other human rights sites. WWW: http://www.rci.rutgers.edu/~cwgl/humanrights/.

The New York City Commission on the Status of Women has recently published the fifth edition of *Women's Organizations: A New York City Directory*, a comprehensive, up-to-date, annotated listing of local and national women's groups. Single copies are available for $10, plus $2 for shipping and handling. Multiple and bulk discounts are available. To order, phone (212) 788-2738.

Each year through training, support services, and advocacy, **Nontraditional Employment for Women (NEW)** prepares hundreds of women for work in the construction trades and other blue-collar jobs and assists women seeking advancement in nontraditional occupations. Training includes math, fitness, safety, job readiness, and basic skills in carpentry, electrical, and plumbing. In addition to training and advocacy, NEW also provides technical assistance to employers and unions to create hostile-free work environments in order to improve the recruitment and retention of women. Contact: NEW, 243 West 20th Street, New York, NY 10011; tel: (212) 627-6252; fax: (212) 255-8021.

The Women and Human Rights Documentation Centre at University of the Western Cape in South Africa has published a bibliography *Legal Reform Relating to Violence Against Women*. Contact: Women and Human Rights Documentation Centre, Community Law Centre, University of the Western Cape, Private Bag X17, Bellville 7535, South Africa; phone: (021) 959-2950/1; fax: (021) 959-2411; telex: 526661.

The Women's Network on Health and the Environment announces the release of the documentary *Exposure: Environmental Links to Breast Cancer*, a film that explores the connections between environmental toxins and breast cancer. *Exposure* raises questions and awareness and also offers strategies for generating necessary social and political changes. Contact: Women's Network on Health and the Environment, 736 Bathurst Street, Toronto, ON M5S 2R4 Canada; phone: (416) 516-2600; fax: (416) 531-6214; e-mail: weed@web.apc.org.

NISC DISC has released ***Women's Resources International (1972–present),*** a new CD-ROM of more than 116,000 records drawn from a variety of essential women's studies databases. Coverage includes humanities, social sciences, health, law, grassroots feminism, and feminist organizations. Contact: NISC, Wyman Towers, 3100 St. Paul St., Baltimore, MD 21218; phone: (410) 243-0797; fax:(410) 243-0982; e-mail: sales@nisc.com.

Working Press, an independent company that publishes books by, for, and about working-class artists, announces a new web site dedicated to working-class studies. Read about publishing projects, browse the books, link to related sites, and even download selected chapters or full texts of pamphlets. Contact: Working Press, 24 Green Lane, Hanwell, London W7 2PB, United Kingdom; WWW:http://ourworld. compuserve.com/homepages/working_press.

SCHOLARSHIP

Spinsters Ink, a feminist publishing house, announces the establishment of the Spinsters Ink Young Feminist Scholarship program as part of the twentieth anniversary celebration of the founding of the press. Beginning in 1999, a $1,000 scholarship will be awarded each year to the student in her last year of high school who submits the best essay on feminism and what it means to her. Deadline: January 1, 1999. Contact: Claire Kirch, Spinsters Ink, 32 E. First St., #330, Duluth, MN 55802-2002; phone: (218) 727-3222; fax: (218) 727-3119; e-mail: claire@spinsters-ink.com.

Calls for Papers for Forthcoming Issues of *Women's Studies Quarterly*

Since 1972 *Women's Studies Quarterly* has been the leading journal on teaching in women's studies. Thematic issues feature vital material for specialists and generalists alike, including the most recent scholarship available in jargon-free language; classroom aids such as course syllabi; discussions of strategies for teaching; and up-to-date, complete bibliographies as well as hard-to-find or never-before-published documents and literary materials. The intersections of race and class with gender are of special concern, as are international perspectives.

Women's Studies and Activism: Theories and Practice, edited by Diane Lichtenstein and Colette Hyman

Women's Studies Quarterly is now seeking submissions for a special issue entitled *Women's Studies and Activism: Theories and Practice,* slated for publication in fall/winter 1999. The issue will focus on the relationship between feminist activism and academic women's studies, with an emphasis on how and what to teach undergraduates about this relationship. The purpose of the issue is twofold: first, to provide women's studies scholars and teachers with new theoretical perspectives on the interconnections between "theory" and "practice" and to reexamine that dichotomy itself; second, to assist women's studies teachers in integrating practical as well as philosophical questions regarding feminist social change work into women's studies courses. Toward these ends, the editors are seeking articles exploring the "practice"/"theory" nexus, discussions of classroom strategies from teachers who have attempted to make the connection between activism and academe, and statements from activists about how their work for social change benefited from their education in women's studies and/or how the field of women's studies could make itself more useful to direct social change activism. Issue editors are Colette Hyman, associate professor of history and former director of women's studies, Winona State University, and Diane Lichtenstein, professor of English and former co-chair of women's studies, Beloit College. Please submit by September 1, 1998, a disk and two hard copies of essays no longer than fifteen typed, double-spaced pages to Diane Lichtenstein, Department of English, Beloit College, 700 College Street, Beloit, WI 53511.

Women and the Environment, **edited by**
Diane Hope and Vandana Shiva
Women's Studies Quarterly is now inviting submissions for a special spring/summer 2000 issue on women and the environment. Articles, syllabi, pedagogical essays, bibliographies, biographies, fiction, poetry, and black-and-white art are welcome. Suggested areas of focus include, but are not limited to, feminist analysis of environmental issues; collective and individual work by women on environmental problems and solutions; reports of environmental issues with particular impact on women; biographical sketches; personal stories; conference and organizational reports; and relevant artwork. Manuscripts primarily focused on issues most pertinent to the United States should be sent to Professor Diane Hope, Rochester Institute of Technology, College of Liberal Arts, 92 Lomb Memorial Drive, Rochester, NY 14623. Manuscripts international in scope should be sent to Vandana Shiva, Director, Research Foundation for Science, Technology and Ecology, A 60 hauz khas, New Delhi, 110 016, India; fax 91-11-6856795 and 4626696. Deadline for submissions is November 30, 1998.

NONFICTION AND MEMOIR
FOR COURSE USE IN WORKING-CLASS STUDIES
available from The Feminist Press at The City University of New York

A Lifetime of Labor: The Autobiography of Alice H. Cook (1998).
$29.95 jacketed hard cover.

Las Mujeres: Conversations from a Hispanic Community (1980), Nan
Elsasser, Kyle MacKenzie, and Yvonne Tixier y Vigil. $12.95 paper.

The Maimie Papers: Letters from an Ex-Prostitute (1997), by Maimie
Pinzer. Edited by Ruth Rosen. $19.95 paper.

Ripening: Selected Work of Meridel Le Sueur (1990), fiction, journalism,
and autobiography by Meridel Le Sueur. Edited by Elaine Hedges.
$10.95 paper.

Salt of the Earth (1953), screenplay by Michael Wilson. Historical
analysis by Deborah S. Rosenfelt. $12.95 paper.

The Seasons: Death and Transfiguration (1993), a memoir by Jo
Sinclair. $35.00 cloth. $12.95 paper.

Streets: A Memoir of the Lower East Side (1995), by Bella Spewack.
$10.95 paper, $19.95 jacketed hardcover.

With These Hands: Women Working on the Land (1981), edited by Joan
M. Jensen. $9.95 paper.

Women Have Always Worked: A Historical Overview (1981), by Alice
Kessler-Harris. $12.95 paper.

Working-Class Studies (spring/summer 1995 issue of *Women's Studies
Quarterly*), edited by Janet Zandy.

To receive a free catalog of The Feminist Press's 150 titles, call or write The Feminist
Press at The City University of New York, Wingate Hall/City College, New York,
NY 10031; phone: (212) 650-8966; fax: (212) 650-8869. Feminist Press books are
available at bookstores, or can be ordered directly. Send check or money order (in
U.S. dollars drawn on a U.S. bank) payable to The Feminist Press. Please add $4.00
shipping and handling for the first book and $1.00 for each additional book. VISA,
Mastercard, and American Express are accepted for telephone orders. Prices subject
to change.

CONTEMPORARY AND HISTORICAL FICTION
FOR COURSE USE IN WORKING-CLASS STUDIES
available from The Feminist Press at The City University of New York

Call Home the Heart (1932), by Fielding Burke. $9.95 paper.

Confessions of Madame Psyche (1986), by Dorothy Bryant. $18.85 paper.

The Convert (1907), by Elizabeth Robins. $12.95 paper.

Daddy Was a Number Runner (1970), by Louise Meriwether. $10.95 paper.

Daughter of Earth (1929), by Agnes Smedley. $11.95 paper.

Daughter of the Hills: A Woman's Part in the Coal Miners' Struggle (1950), by Myra Page. $8.95 paper.

Ella Price's Journal (1972), by Dorothy Bryant. $14.95 paper, $35.00 cloth.

Folly (1982), by Maureen Brady. $12.95 paper, $35.00 cloth.

Life in the Iron Mills and Other Stories (1861), by Rebecca Harding Davis. $10.95 paper.

Margaret Howth (1862), by Rebecca Harding Davis. $11.95 paper, $35.00 cloth.

Miss Giardino (1978), by Dorothy Bryant. $11.95 paper, $32.00 cloth.

The Parish and the Hill (1948), by Mary Doyle Curran. $12.95 paper.

Paper Fish (1980), by Tina De Rosa. $9.95 paper.

Ripening: Selected Work of Meridel Le Sueur (1990), fiction, journalism, and autobiography by Meridel Le Sueur. Edited by Elaine Hedges. $10.95 paper.

The Silent Partner (1871), by Elizabeth Stuart Phelps. $12.95 paper.

This Child's Gonna Live (1969), by Sarah E. Wright. $10.95 paper.

Weeds (1923), by Edith Summers Kelley. $15.95 paper.

Winter's Edge (1985), by Valerie Miner $10.95 paper.

Women and Appletrees (1973), by Moa Martison. $11.95 paper.

Writing Red: An Anthology of American Women Writers: 1930-1940 (1987), edited by Charlotte Nekola and Paula Rabinowitz. $15.95 paper.

To receive a free catalog of The Feminist Press's 150 titles, call or write The Feminist Press at The City University of New York, Wingate Hall/City College, New York, NY 10031; phone: (212) 650-8966; fax: (212) 650-8869. Feminist Press books are available at bookstores, or can be ordered directly. Send check or money order (in U.S. dollars drawn on a U.S. bank) payable to The Feminist Press. Please add $4.00 shipping and handling for the first book and $1.00 for each additional book. VISA, Mastercard, and American Express are accepted for telephone orders. Prices subject to change.

BACK ISSUES STILL AVAILABLE! ORDER NOW!
Working-Class Studies
Edited by Janet Zandy
Women's Studies Quarterly 23, nos. 1 & 2 (spring/summer 1995)

Working-class history and literature are often ignored in traditional curricula, invisible in most texts, and unavailable to students and teachers. Janet Zandy joins together the voices--in poetry, narrative, and song--of working-class women throughout history, with critical essays to place working-class studies in perspective for teacher and student. Scholars in the field write about recovering autobiographies and oral histories, practicing working-class studies, and current and emerging texts and theories. Honored with an award from the Council of Editors of Learned Journals, and thoroughly interdisciplinary, this volume contains poetry, course syllabi and curriculum materials, fiction and memoir, a photo essay, and songs.

CONTENTS: * Editorial ** WORKING-CLASS VOICES * School Clothes AND Go See Jack London, *Wilma Elizabeth McDaniel* * Stories from a Working-Class Childhood, *Lisa Orr* * Proud to Work for the University, *Kristin Kovacic* * Ruth in August, *Barbara Horn* * Death Mask, *Joann Quinones* * The Pawnbroker's Window AND Praise the Waitresses, *Pat Wynne* ** RECOVERING WORKING-CLASS AUTOBIOGRAPHY AND ORAL HISTORY * We Did Change Some Attitudes: Maida Springer-Kemp and the International Ladies' Garment Workers Union, *Brigid O'Farrell and Joyce L. Kornbluh* *Autobiography and Reconstructing Subjectivity at the Bryn Mawr Summer School for Women Workers, 1921-1938, *Karyn L. Hollis* * *Working* Class Consciousness in Jo Sinclair's The Season's, *Florence Howe* *The Writing on the Wall, or Where Did That Dead Head Come From? *Cy-Thea Sand* * Autobiographies by American Working-Class Women: An Annotated Bibliography, *Cherly Cline* ** PRACTICING WORKING-CLASS STUDIES * Reclaiming Our Working-Class Identities: Teaching Working-Class Studies in a Blue-Collar Community (Course Syllabi), *Linda Strom* * A Wealth of Possibilities: Workers, Texts, and Reforming the English Department, *Laura Hapke* * A Community of Workers (photos and text), *Marilyn Anderson* * "Women Have Always Sewed": The Production of Clothing and the Work of Women, *Janet Zandy* * Sisters in the Flames, *Carol Tarlen* * rituals of spring (for the 78th anniversary of the shirtwaist factory fire), *Safiya Henderson-Holmes* ** WORKING-CLASS TEXTS AND THEORY *Readerly/Writerly Relations and Social Change: *The Maimie Papers* as Literature, *Carole Anne Taylor* *Between Theories and Anti-Theories: Moving Toward Marginal Women's Subjectivities, *Roxanne Rimstead* * "People Who Might Have Been You": Agency and the Damaged Self in Tillie Olsen's *Yonnondio, Lisa Orr* * Industrial Music: Contemporary American Working-Class Poetry and Modernism, *Julia Stein* * U.S. Working-Class Women's Fiction: Notes Toward an Overview, *Constance Coiner*

Back issues still available. 280 pages/1-555861-121-5/$18.00. TO ORDER: Call or write The Feminist Press at The City University of New York, Wingate Hall/City College, New York, NY 10031; phone: (212) 650-8966; fax: (212) 650-8869.

Subscribe to *Women's Studies Quarterly*

U.S. SUBSCRIBERS

Individuals: $30.00 for 1 year, $70.00 for 3 years.
Institutions: $40.00 for 1 year, $100.00 for 3 years.

SUBSCRIBERS OUTSIDE THE U.S.

Individuals: $40.00 for 1 year, $100.00 for 3 years.
Institutions: $50.00 for 1 year, $120.00 for 3 years.

Type of subscription $ _____.

Total enclosed $ _____.

All orders must be prepaid by checks or money orders
payable to The Feminist Press in U.S. dollars drawn on a
U.S. bank. VISA, Mastercard, and American Express are
also accepted for telephone orders.

Name _____

Institution _____

Address _____

_____

Phone (   ) _____

Mail to: *Women's Studies Quarterly*, The Feminist Press at The
City University of New York, Wingate Hall, City College/CUNY,
Convent Avenue at 138 Street, New York, NY 10031.
Tel. (212) 650-8966   Fax (212) 650-8869

 *The Cushwa Center for the Study of
American Catholicism
at the University of Notre Dame*

*Announces Dissertation Awards
in the History of Catholic Women
in Twentieth-Century America*

The Charles and Margaret Hall Cushwa Center for the Study of American Catholicism, with generous support from the Lilly Endowment, Inc., and the University of Notre Dame, announces a grant competition for scholars interested in exploring the history of American Catholic women in the twentieth century. These fellowships are part of an initiative in Catholicism in Twentieth-Century America.

This initiative seeks to support scholarship that integrates the experiences of Catholics more fully into the narratives of American history. The initiative will fund innovative and carefully conceived Ph.D. dissertations that explore the historical experiences and contributions of Catholic women, both lay and religious, in twentieth-century America.

Proposals might address themes such as: the history of Catholic women in American institutional, intellectual, cultural, and spiritual life; Catholic women in social movements; the evolution of vocational and professional life choices of Catholic women; changing public images of Catholic women; and changing attitudes and practices related to sexuality.

Ph.D. candidates whose dissertation proposals have been approved and whose research promises to advance the historical study of twentieth-century Catholic women in America are invited to apply. Dissertation fellowships carry a stipend of **$15,000** for the year 1999–2000. Applications must be received at the Cushwa Center by **February 1, 1999.** Awards will be announced by **April 15, 1999.**

**For further information please write:
Cushwa Center
1135 Flanner Hall, University of Notre Dame
Notre Dame, IN 46556-5611
E-mail: cushwa.1@nd.edu**

WISE
Women's International Studies Europe

Women's International Studies Europe (WISE) is a feminist studies association that promotes women's studies teaching, research, and publication in Europe. WISE aims to initiate and facilitate the exchange of students and staff and to defend the interests of women's studies in Europe. To this end, WISE publishes a newsletter, collects and disseminates information, advises members, organizes seminars, and develops and supports other initiatives related to women's studies.

For more information about Women's International Studies Europe, contact WISE.

WISE
Heidelberglaan 2
3584 CS Utrecht
The Netherlands
telephone: 31 30 2531881; fax: 31 10 2531619
e-mail: Wise.secretariate@FSW.RUU.NL
http://hgins.uia.ac.be/women/wise/index.html

AJWS   Asian Journal of Women's Studies

Asian Center for Women's Studies
Ewha Womans University Press

AJWS is an interdisciplinary journal, publishing articles with a feminist perspective pertaining to women's issues in Asia. The journal offers articles with a theoretical focus, country reports providing valuable information on specific subjects and countries, and booknotes containing information on recent publications on women in Asia.

For more information, contact *AJWS*, Asian Center for Women's Studies, Ewha Womans University, Seoul (120-750), Korea; telephone: 82 2 360 2150; fax: 82 2 360 2577; e-mail: acwsewha @nownuri.net.

Individual copies of the journal are available from The Feminist Press and from *AJWS*. For subscription information, please contact *AJWS*.